The
Foxfire
Book

The Foxfire Book

hog dressing; log cabin building; mountain crafts and foods; planting by the signs; snake lore, hunting tales, faith healing; moonshining; and other affairs of plain living

edited with an Introduction by
ELIOT WIGGINTON

Anchor Books
Anchor Press | Doubleday
Garden City, New York

Eliot Wigginton received a B.A. and an M.A. from Cornell University and an M.A. from Johns Hopkins University. He has taught English and journalism at the Rabun Gap-Nacoochee School, the home of *Foxfire,* since 1966, and has been faculty advisor of the magazine since its inception in 1967. He has published articles in the *National Geographic School Bulletin, Media and Methods,* and the *James Joyce Quarterly.*

Portions of this collection first appeared in
Foxfire magazine, Copyright © 1968, 1969 by
Brooks Eliot Wigginton, Copyright © 1969, 1970,
1971 by Southern Highlands Literary Fund, Inc.

30 29 28 27 26

This book is dedicated to the people of these mountains in the hope that, through it, some portion of their wisdom, ingenuity and individuality will remain long after them to touch us all.

ACKNOWLEDGMENTS

A project of this sort reaches out and involves so many people.

My father, for example. It was he who brought me to the mountains when I was a small boy. I never forgot. And it was Mary Hambidge, Margaret's honey cookies and cheese souffles, Dean's quiet strength and Claude's open friendship that brought me back.

To Mrs. Hambidge and the Jay Hambidge Art Foundation I am forever in debt for the most extraordinary kind of friendship and support. Not only has she been a constant source of inspiration, but she also, in a more practical sense, allowed me to build on the Foundation land the cabin in which I now live. If anything good has come of my work in Rabun County, she must share a large portion of the credit. She is the most remarkable woman I have ever met.

I am also indebted to my school's Principal, Mr. Morris Brown; its Dean, Mr. Donald Arbitter; and its President, Dr. Karl Anderson. They have given me a tremendous amount of freedom in working with the students here, they have trusted me, and they have often encouraged me. Their patience has been phenomenal.

Without the financial assistance of individuals like John Dyson, Mrs. Katharine Graham and George W. Woodruff; and organizations like the National Endowment for the Humanities, the Coordinating Council of Literary Magazines, the American Folklore Society, the Newport Folk Foundation and the Edward H. Robertson Foundation; and the generous, enthusiastic recognition given us by newspapers, magazines and groups too numerous to mention, we would never have lasted. Of that there is no doubt. This is as much their book as it is ours.

To our Board of Directors and our Advisory Board, my genuine gratitude. You had faith in us, and you encouraged us when we were too young to deserve your trust; but without it I would not have had a chance to thank you in this manner.

And to the hundreds who actually shouldered the load, I can only express my awe at what you've done and my joy at being fortunate enough to be a part of it. Suzy, Hydie, the kids—all of you—you were the roots of the tree. They're dug in deep, you guys. You've done so well.

BEW

CONTENTS

Acknowledgments 6

Introduction 9

"this is the way I was raised up" 15

Aunt Arie 17

Wood 31

Tools and Skills 38

Building a Log Cabin 53

Chimney Building 108

White Oak Splits 115

Making a Hamper out of White Oak Splits 119

Making a Basket out of White Oak Splits 123

An Old Chair Maker Shows How 128

Rope, Straw, and Feathers are to Sleep on 139

A Quilt is Something Human 142

Soapmaking 151

Cooking on a Fireplace, Dutch Oven, and Wood Stove 159

Daniel Manous 165

Mountain Recipes 167

Preserving Vegetables 174

Preserving Fruit 181

Churning Your Own Butter 185

Slaughtering Hogs 189

Curing and Smoking Hog 199

Recipes for Hog 202

Weather Signs 208

8   CONTENTS

Planting by the Signs   212
The Buzzard and the Dog   228
Home Remedies   230
Hunting   249
Dressing and Cooking Wild Animal Foods   264
Hunting Tales   274
Snake Lore   289
Moonshining as a Fine Art   301
Faith Healing   346
Hillard Green   369

Index of People   382

INTRODUCTION

The contents of this book need little introduction; they stand on their own as helpful instructions and enjoyable reading. But what is not immediately apparent is that the material here was collected and put together almost entirely by high school students. And that makes the book a little special—for me at least, since they were kids I was supposed to be teaching.

It was 1966, and I had just finished five years at Cornell. I had an A.B. in English and an M.A. in Teaching, and I thought I was a big deal—a force to be reckoned with. So I went to Georgia and took a job at the 240-pupil Rabun Gap-Nacoochee School where I taught ninth and tenth grade English, geography, and had about ten other side responsibilities. Rabun Gap is right in the Appalachians. God's country, as they say here, and I'll go along with that.

About six weeks later, I surveyed the wreckage. My lectern (that's a protective device a teacher cowers behind while giving a lecture nobody's listening to) was scorched from the time Tommy Green tried to set it on fire with his lighter—during class. Charles Henslee had already broken off the blade of his Barlow knife in the floorboards. Every desk was decorated with graffiti. My box of yellow chalk was gone, and so were the thumbtacks that had held up the chart of the Globe Theatre. The nine water pistols I had confiscated that very afternoon had been reconfiscated from under my nose.

And it was with a deep sigh that, as I launched one of several paper airplanes within easy reach, I began to ponder greener pastures. Either that or start all over.

The answer was obvious. If I were to finish out the year honorably, it would be necessary to reassert my authority. No teenagers were going to push me around. Besides, my course was too important. First offense would be an "X" in the grade book. Second, a paddling. Third, to the principal. Fourth, out of class for two weeks.

It frightens me to think how close I came to making another stupid mistake. First, I had bored them unmercifully. Now I was about to impose a welcome punishment. Two weeks out of that class would have been more pleasure than pain.

Those who cannot remember the past not only relive it; they tend to impose it, mistakes and all, on others. My own high school— monumentally boring texts and lectures, all forgotten; punishments and regulations and slights that only filled a reservoir of bitterness; and three blessed teachers who let me make things, helped me make them, and praised the results.

Luckily, it took only a few rewards to keep me going. How many students were denied even those few scraps of self-esteem from anyone other than their peers? And how many was I now denying?

I am not sure what the magic formula is or whether I have it pegged yet, but it involves a chemistry that allows us to believe we may have worth after all. Someone says, "You've done well," and we hunger to make that happen again and again. Too often we, as teachers, slip, and that first flush of success our students get comes after they've survived a night of drinking Colt 45, stuck up the local gas station, or taken two tabs of acid and made it out the other side alive.

We could catch some of those if we would.

The next day I walked into class and said, "How would you like to throw away the text and start a magazine?" And that's how *Foxfire* began.

From the beginning, the idea was to involve everyone. (It hasn't always worked, but we try.) We decided to print one issue put together by all of us as a class and during class time. If that issue did what I hoped it would do for my ailing classes, we might try to make it a regular thing. But for the time being, one issue only.

The contents? There were lots of possibilities. Many older people in this area, for example, still plant today by the signs of the zodiac and the stages of the moon. I had heard them mention it, but I didn't know what it meant. Rather than interrupt a conversation to find out, I figured I'd get my students to tell me. They'd probably know since it was mostly their parents and grandparents who were doing it. But my kids didn't really know what it was either, and soon they were as curious as I was. Why not find out and turn the information into an article?

So they went home and talked—really talked—to their own relatives, some of them for the first time. From those conversations came superstitions, old home remedies, weather signs, a story about a hog hunt, a taped interview with the retired sheriff about the time the local bank was robbed—and directions for planting by the signs. It was looking good.

Another possibility was poetry. Many of my students hated the stuff. I suspect one of the reasons was that they were forced to read pages of sentimental greeting card verse before they ever got to high school. In any case, working with poetry from an editor's point of view might be one way to overcome an already deeply rooted bias, and they were willing to try. So we added poetry too. Some was from our school (and some was from notably bad students in an effort to give them a boost they were hungry for). Some of it was from students in other schools in the state. And some was even from practicing poets. As we said in the first issue, "We hoped that they would remember their own beginnings and their own battles to be recognized and not be too proud to provide us with examples to follow—pieces we could aspire to in our own work."

The name? Each student submitted three choices. Duplications were eliminated, a master list was mimeographed and passed out, the obviously unworkable ones were dropped, and the kids voted from among those left. They chose "foxfire," a tiny organism that glows in the dark and is frequently seen in the shaded coves of these mountains.

And money? The school could provide no support at all. Any financial obligations would be my problem—not theirs. Looking back, I can see what a blessing in disguise that was. It meant the magazine had to sell, and that literally forced us to emphasize folklore rather than poetry, for magazines devoted to verse almost never survive for very long on the market. It also meant the kids had to find the money for that first issue themselves, and that made them more determined to see the magazine go than anything I could have said.

And so they hit the streets after school. Any donor, no matter how small his gift, would be listed in the issue, and he would receive a free copy signed by all the kids.

They collected four hundred fifty dollars. The local printer said that was enough to print six hundred copies photo-offset. So we printed six hundred copies, sold out in a week, and printed six hundred more.

It sounds simple doesn't it? I can promise there were times we almost chucked the whole thing and went back to *Silas Marner*. In our total ignorance we made some colossal blunders. We went broke a couple of times, for one. People like John Dyson and groups like the Coordinating Council of Literary Magazines came along and pulled us out of the mud, brushed us off, and wound us up again.

And each time we flopped, we got up a little stronger. Now, in Rabun Gap, there exists a magazine that has subscribers in all fifty states and a dozen foreign countries. It has been written about in magazines like *Saturday Review, New Republic, National Geographic School Bulletin, Scholastic Scope,* and *Whole Earth Catalogue.* It has received two grants from the National Endowment for the Humanities, one of them for $10,000. But most important, it is run by high school students—students who are going on to college knowing that they can be forces for constructive change; knowing that they can *act* responsibly and effectively rather than being always *acted upon.*

Looking beyond Rabun Gap and *Foxfire,* I can't get over the feeling that similar projects could be duplicated successfully in many other areas of the country, and to the genuine benefit of almost everyone involved.

Daily our grandparents are moving out of our lives, taking with them, irreparably, the kind of information contained in this book. They are taking it, not because they want to, but because they think we don't care. And it isn't happening just in Appalachia. I think, for example, of numerous Indian reservations, Black cultures near the southern coasts, Ozark mountain communities, and a hundred others.

The big problem, of course, is that since these grandparents were primarily an oral civilization, information being passed through the generations by word of mouth and demonstration, little of it is written down. When they're gone, the magnificent hunting tales, the ghost stories that kept a thousand children sleepless, the intricate tricks of self-sufficiency acquired through years of trial and error, the eloquent and haunting stories of suffering and sharing and building and healing and planting and harvesting—all these go with them, and what a loss.

If this information is to be saved at all, for whatever reason, it must be saved now; and the logical researchers are the grand-children, not university researchers from the outside. In the process, these grandchildren (and we) gain an invaluable, unique knowledge about their own roots, heritage, and culture. Suddenly they discover their families—previously people to be ignored in the face of the seventies—as pre-television, pre-automobile, pre-flight individuals who endured and survived the incredible task of total self-sufficiency, and came out of it all with a perspective on ourselves as a country that we are not likely to see again. They have something to tell us about self-reliance, human interdependence, and the human spirit that we would do well to listen to.

Is the subject, English, ignored in the process? Hardly. In fact, the opposite is true. English, in its simplest definition, is com-munication—reaching out and touching people with words, sounds, and visual images. We are in the business of improving students' prowess in these areas. In their work with photography (which must tell the story with as much impact and clarity as the words), text (which must be grammatically correct except in the use of pure dialect from tapes that they transcribe), lay-out, make-up, corre-spondence, art and cover design, and selection of manuscripts from outside poets and writers—to say nothing of related skills such as fund raising, typing, retailing, advertising, and speaking at confer-ences and public meetings—they learn more about English than from any other curriculum I could devise. Moreover, this curriculum has built-in motivations and immediate and tangible rewards.

The project also has benefits for the community at large. The collection of artifacts, tapes, and photographs is a valuable addition to any community museum. Furthermore, many still culturally dis-tinctive areas, cut off from the main thrust of our country, are also economically and educationally deprived. Articles about local crafts-men and craft cooperatives, to give only one small example, can result in a welcome flow of income from a population grown weary of a plastic world. And the education the students can acquire in the process can be a welcome supplement to their ordinary routine.

And the whole thing doesn't cost that much. In pure business terms, you can get a staggering return from a relatively small investment.

The kid who scorched my lecturn had been trying to tell me something. He and his classmates, through their boredom and restlessness, were sending out distress signals—signals that I came perilously close to ignoring.

It's the same old story. The answer to student boredom and restlessness (manifested in everything from paper airplanes to dope) maybe—just maybe—is not stricter penalties, innumerable suspensions, and bathroom monitors. How many schools (mine included) have dealt with those students that still have fire and spirit, *not* by channeling that fire in constructive, creative directions, but by pouring water on the very flames that could make them great? And it's not *necessarily* that the rules are wrong. It's the arrogant way we tend to enforce them. Until we can *inspire* rather than babysit, we're in big trouble. Don't believe me. Just watch and see what happens. We think drugs and turnover rates and dropouts are a problem now. We haven't seen anything yet.

Foxfire obviously isn't the whole answer. But maybe it's a tiny part of it. If this book is worth anything at all, it's because every piece of it was put together and handled and squeezed and shaped and touched by teenagers.

And it's been a long time since I found a paper airplane under my desk.

                                                                    BEW

"this is the way I was raised up"

by Mrs. Marvin Watts

The following article was given to us by its author, Mrs. Watts, during a recent visit to her home. It was painstakingly written out in pencil on notebook paper that had been folded and refolded many times. It is presented here exactly as it was given to us.—*Editor*

my dadie raised the stuff we lived one   he groed the corn to make our bread   he groed they cane to make our syrup allso groed they Beans and Peas to make the soup beans out of and dried leather Britches beans and dried fruit enough to last all winter   he Killed enough meat to last all winter

he Killed a beaf and a Sheep and two or three hogs for the winter   he diden have mutch money for anything   we just had our biskets for sunday morning and when mother ran out of coffie she parched chustnuts and ground them one her coffie mill to make coffie out of   and when it rained and the mills coulden grind our bread we ate potatoes for bread   my dad usto make our shoes   I can remember waring them   my mother usto weaved woal cloth to make blankets and cloths out of   I have worn woal dresses and my dad has worn home made Britches out of woven woal to   my mother also knit our Stockings and socks to   I have hope my dad Shear Sheep a lot of times to get that wool my mother would wash it and Spen it make it into thread and then weave it one

her loom to make her blankets and cloth out of   we usto have corn
Shukings to get our corn all shucked

we had our crib full   that lasted till the next fall   every body
in the neighborhood come and my mother cooked a big dinner
for the crowd   seames as every body was happie to   I rember when
my mother had to cook one the fire place   she cooked her dried
fruit and every thing one the fire place   it sure was good back in
them dayes to   I usto help my brothers Saw wood to make fires out
of to keep warm   we lived in a log house   it was pretty hard to
keep warm by an open fire place but we never was Sick back
then   we played out the bigest Snow ever com   we had a Spring
to cary our watter from and my dad had to take his Shovel and
ditch out a way through the Snow for us to get to the Spring   the
snow was waist deep

we usto make our play houses out in the woods   make our
rag dolls to play with   my brothers Sawed pine wagon wheels and
made there wagons to play with   I have sent to the mountains
and hope my dad and brothers Snake out tan bark to get a little
money to buy things with   One Xmas Santa Clause gave us three
or four sticks of candie and a ornge   he put it in our Stocking
and we was as pleased as if he had give us a box full of candy
we lived one a hill out of site of the road and we was toaled
the was a car coming through that day   it was a teamotel ford   tom
mitchel was driving it and we sit one the hill all day to get to
see it   we haden never saw a car   that was our firston

AUNT ARIE

Far back in the neighboring mountains, alone in a log cabin with no running water and only a single fireplace for heat, lives an elderly lady. She draws her water from a well; she raises her own vegetables in the spring. Even though her husband died several years ago, and one side of her body was later paralyzed due to a stroke, Aunt Arie refuses to leave. With her husband's clothes still hanging inside, washed and ready to wear, her home has become a sacred place over which she alone must now keep watch.

Her occasional visitors are also sacred, as we were shown when she said, on our arrival, that she had wanted to go somewhere but had stayed at home simply because she felt like someone was coming. And she showed us by her warmth that she really meant we were welcome in her home, though we had met her only moments before.

Talking to her was like talking to one's own grandmother. She told us stories of her past, spiced now and then with local gossip, and she also gave some advice in her reflections about living in today's world.

It is somehow reassuring to know that even now, in our time, there are Aunt Aries left from an age which has so much to teach us.

MIKE COOK

PLATE 1

PLATE 2

PLATE 3

PLATE 4

It wasn't until I had worked on *Foxfire* for five months that an inexplicable void between myself and the old people of our region disappeared. This void was mysterious, but it still existed. Maybe it was instilled hostilities toward older generations. Maybe it was the fact that I just couldn't see their importance or the relevance of what they had to say to the way I live today.

Then I met Aunt Arie. It was a cold day, and I can remember the jeep traveling far back into a remote area. I was apprehensive because I didn't know what to expect. Her log cabin was a time machine taking me back to the eighteen eighties. Everything she had—from the stern-looking pictures of her grandparents to the fireplace that was her only source of heat—made me stop and look deeply for the first time.

For the most part she is self-sufficient. She grows a huge garden, and her only source of water is a well outside her door. She does have electricity, but she uses it little. Her days are filled with preserving food, reading the Bible and a daily newspaper, and talking to friends who come to visit.

The friendly fireplace, the hot wood stove, and the food she prepared for us one night made Aunt Arie a person I cannot forget. She put on no front, condemned no one, but still said what she thought. As we talked, she told me how she used to live, but without feeling sorry for herself and without saying how many miles she walked to school each day. She was proud of what she had done and what she had accomplished, but there was no need in her mind to try to make me feel that I should be in awe of what she said.

PAUL GILLESPIE

Aunt Arie's conversation was so interesting that, rather than summarize what she told us, we have let her speak for herself. As the tape recording begins, we have just walked in on her as she is trying to remove the eyes from a fresh hog's head just given to her by a neighbor. Unable to do it herself, she asks for our help.

Now see if you can take your fingers and pull that eyeball up and cut it. Now I can, if I had strength.

What are you going to make with all this?

Souse meat. Boy, that's the best stuff I ever eat. I love it better'n sausage.

How do you make that?

Take this now; I'll soak this now, and soak all th' blood out of it until in th' mornin' it's just as white. Then I'll take an' grind it on that sausage grinder an' take th' juice that this is cooked in, part of it, and put some sage'n'black pepper'n'red pepper and stir-r-r it all up until it's so good'n'fine as it can be, and then put it in them cannin' jars'n'seal it. Then open it in th' winter. I love it better'n anything in th' world. Why, lot'a people eats it cold.

Let me see one more time. I might can do it. I don't know now. I don't believe I can on account'a this hand. Break m'knife. If I's stout enough I could pull it out (*struggling*) but I ain't. I don't know how t'get it out. I know yore hand's stouter'n mine. I never done 'at in my life. That knife's been t'breakfast I think. It's dull as a froe. Doin' any good?

Doesn't this bother you—pulling eyes out of things like this?

I don't care fer't bit more'n spit'n'th' fire. Ah, I've just done anything'n'ever'thing in my life 'til I don't care fer nothin' 'at way. I don't. Nothin' just don't never bother me, what I mean, make me sick. They lot'a people can't when th' blood comes s'bad'n's'bad'-n's'bad—they run off'n leave it. They can't stand it. I don't pay it a bit'a'tention in th' world.

What will you do with the eye?

Throw it away. You know, I went t'a place up on Coweeta one day—th' schoolhouse up there—an' they had hog's head cooked, an' they wanted me t'eat some of it. An' I eat some'a that hog's head when that eye'd been cooked in it. I didn't know it. An' atter I eat it, I wouldn't eat—why, you couldn'a hired me t'eat that with th' eye in't. No! I wouldn't eat a bite a'that. But I eat it an' didn't know it!

Now he's havin' a hard time with that, ain't he? Well, 'at's hateful, ain't it? I wish I had somethin'—one thing, that knife's too dull. An' I don't think I got ary'nother'n's any sharper. I've got a good notion t'go in ther'n get that hand saw'n let'cha saw that in two right through here. Then you'd get 'at out! If it takes y's'long t'get that out as't do that other'n, we'll be worried t'death. We could try that saw. You reckon that'd get't out any better? Might ruin th' hand saw. I don't know whether bones—aw, I don't reckon bones'd hurt a hand saw any worse'n wood. (*She goes to get the saw.*) I wish y'did have somethin' sharp t'get't out. That saw ain't been used in s'long I don't know. Let me reach my fingers down in there'n see if I can pull it out. Wish I could get this knife down in there. Well, I can't cut nothin'. It's s'near out now y'hate t'saw't in two, don'cha? I don't want t'cut that eye if I can help it 'cause th' black stuff'll run all over ever'thing. Give't good pull see if y'can pull it out a little further. Oh, my goodness alive! (*Laughing.*) I wish I *was* stout like I use t'be. I been awful little all my life. My hands never has been nothin', but boys they's done lots'a hard work. I wish I could . . . well, they ain't no use in wishin' such as 'at, call back twenty-five years ago. That's silly. I think I honestly lived an'done th' best I could; and then wish y'could go back over your life again. I think that's silly in a way. There's not a thing in this world—in my life—that I'm ashamed t'meet nobody with. Yall remember that, children. Don't never do a thing in this world that you don't want your poppy and mommy t'know. And then, when th' last roll's called, you'll be ready t'go where you're gonna spend eternity out yonder. Remember that. I'd be glad t'meet ever'one of you some of these days. 'Cause that's where I'm a'headin' for. Some of these days I'll have a road t'walk on 'stead'a walkin' in th' mud.

Ain't we never gonna get it?

Yep. I got it.

Well, I never knew you could get it. Now you let me have't an' I'm 'one' take it'n throw it away. Now what about—they's another'n here just th' same way.

(*She takes the first eye to the back door and throws it out. It sails through the air, lands on a nearby tin roof, rolls off and hangs bobbing on the clothesline. All of us are laughing so hard we can hardly see to work on the second eye. Finally, we start again.*)

What was in this hole here?

His ears. Lot'a people eats 'em. I wouldn't eat one fer nothin'. Y'd have t'clean 'at old hair off 'n scrape it all off good. It's good'n clean's any of it but I don't want none of it.

I ain't never see'd so much meat left on nothin' in my life. I want you'n's t'look'a there. Did you ever see as much meat left on a hog's jaw in yore life? Oh-h-h. Don't look like he'd want'a give such as 'at away. An' they wouldn't have a cent fer't. No sir. They gi'me one last year too. They good neighbors—law, what good neighbors'ey are.

Take all th' hairs off. Gags me when I get a hair in my mouth. Oh, I just gag an' keep on'n'on. Ulysses'd laugh at me. He'd just die laughin' at me; an' I'd get up'n go out on th' porch'n not eat nary another bite. I don't know why I do it, but I do do it.

Lord, how I do love t'fix somethin' t'eat. Ye-e-e-s. 'At's what we live on, ain't't? Yes sir. You'll always remember what'cha done today when y'come back, won't'cha?

How did you preserve meat? Smoke it?

I don't want no old smoked meat. You might, but I don't. You see 'at little house right out there? Well, 'at's a smoke house. Well now, we'd kill high as four big hogs at one time; take'n cut it all up like this is. And we always salted ours th' day that we cut it up. Some people wait's t'th' next day, but I don't like that. Take 'n spread it all out along a bench—Ulysses made benches in there —an' spread it all out an' take salt'n'black pepper—not *too* much black pepper—and mix it all up in a pan, we always did; an' lay it out there 'til it got cured. Then, see, that black pepper keeps th' flies off of it. An' that's preserved then; that salt preserves it.

If your flies comes—if they smell fresh meat they'll come an' then they'll blow it, you know; they lay eggs there'n'that'll make worms —well now, you can hear'em when they come. We've got an old oven—looks like a large iron frying pan with legs and a lid—we used't'bake bread in. You put coals down in it an'take red pepper and put down in them coals'n set't afire an'set it down under th' meat an'run th' flies off. Th' oven's iron, y'know, an'it won't burn th' floor. I don't know where my oven is. I's studyin' about it th' other day.

Used t'make our own lard an'put't up in four gallon jars too. I always saved th' gut fat—come off th' guts inside a'th' hog. Commence at one end of 'im an'strip it off. You have't'be awful careful. You have t'know how t'do things.

I'm worried about ruining this saw.

Aw, it won't hurt it. If't does, let it holler. It's spent its days. Don't you hit th' eyeball if y'can he'p it. That old black stuff'll just run out all over y'. I don't wan't'see't. It ain't a bit nasty in th' world. I just don't wan't'see't.

At's about's hard's th' other way, ain't it? I never did try t'take out nary'n before. What about me eighty-four years old 'n'helped with th' cookin'n'ever'thing all my life . . . but see, at my house they was four boys an' they always done all such as 'at. An' momma wouldn't let me cut a stick a'wood. No sir. She'd hear that axe hit one lick'r two licks at th' wood pile. "Lay that axe down!" An'I knowed t'do it. She'd whup me all over.

(*We give up with the saw and try the knife again.*)

I wish I did have a good sharp knife. Used t'have a good grind rock put up there on th' crib shed, an'Ulysses'd hold th' knives an' I'd turn th' grind rock; but I got no way t'do that 'n'more. I hope you boys never has't'live by you'n'self. In one way hit's a joy, and in another way hit's lonesome; uneasy many times—nobody t'he'p y'. Don't make no difference how bad sick y'get—nobody t'hand y'a dose a'medicine, ner t'do a thing in th' world. Boys,

hit's not s'good. I c'n tell y'that now. I got sort'a scared here last week. I 'bout give out of a bite of anything t'eat. See, all th' meat'n stuff's in th' cellar except th' dried beans. Well, you can't eat dried beans in a minute. Y'have t'have time t'cook 'em. Well I couldn't get th' cellar door open. It come a freezin' spell an' that door swelled up. Well I tried ever'day t'open that door, an' I got a rock an' I tried t'rock it down 'til I could open it. Even had Irish 'taters in there and couldn't get Irish 'tater't'eat. I's sorta scared I tell you. You can't get nary hand on nary thing t'eat, cook. I can cook but couldn't get m'hands on't *to* cook. So I said, "Well, I reckon next thing best t'do's t'boil a big kettle a'water . . ."

First thing I done when I went in th' kitchen this mornin's t'go see if my door'd open so I have somethin' t'cook fer dinner, an' it opened just as pretty as it could be. Lord, I rejoiced! I did. I rejoiced an' run in there an' got me a can a'beans an' put on t'cook.

(*Finally we get the second eye out.*) Well! Done a little better'n th' other'n, didn't it? Well we *did* get that'n' right. Now that's all I want you t'do. That's a whole lot, but I just couldn't do that.

How will you get the other hairs off?

I'll put another fire in th' stove an' I'll either cut'em off or singe'em off or scald'em off. See, I've done got m'water on. Now that's all I'm goin' t'do with that 'til I get that an' wash it good'n clean; an' in th' mornin' it'll be just as white. Then I'll put it in a little cooker, I call it, and then all that meat'll come off'a them jaw bones. When y'take'n'boil these jowls—these jaw bones—an' take all th' meat off of'em an' get th' marrow out an' put sauce over't, it's just as good as it can be.

(*She goes to the door to throw the second eye out.*)

I trot m'self t'death. Ulysses used t'holler t' me about trottin' s'much. Now if I live, an' you'ns lives, an' you'ns comes t'eat with me any time this winter, I'll open a can a'souse. Oh, hit's good, souse is; that is if it's cleaned good and fixed good. I love 'at. An' you love th' tongue of a hog? Boys, I do if y'peel 'em off good. I don't never grind it up. I just put't in with th' head'n cook't all t'gether—th'tongue's good'n tender then—an'then peel it off; peel that old—aw, whatever't is; 'tain't no skin an'tain't got no hair on't you know th' tongue ain't.

An' I love th' feet. Do you love th' hog's foot? Law, how good they are. But hit takes awful'ot t'clean'em 'til they fit t'eat. Well, thank you'ns. An' I'll return th' compliment someday—you can't never tell!

(We draw a bucket of water from the well and begin to wash our hands.) Boys, I had a good Thanksgiving dinner all by m'self. I cooked a big chicken. I thought somebody'd come fer dinner but they never. I just eat chicken. I had beans'n stuff cooked, but I never eat nary bite'a nary thing more'n chicken. I love chicken. I'm silly about chicken.

If I had plenty a'money, I'd put me in a short sink right here so I wouldn't have t'trot outdoors ever'time t'pour th' water out; but I guess I got just about what I'll have when I'm took away from here. Look like th' porch out there's gonna have t'be fixed; an' they want me t'sell th' place *so* bad. I've already been offered lots fer't an' I wouldn't take it. This land goes over 'cross that mountain an' plumb on down on th' other side, an' th' gover'ment [government land] comes up there, an' they want that. I say I don't want'a sell it, an' they just looked up at me s'funny. Said, "What would I do with all that money?" You know, I don't care nothin' about money much.

My feet's gettin' sorta cold! *(We move to the living room where a fire is burning.)*

I was born an' raised on Hick'ry Knoll 'til I was eight years old. It'uz a hard livin'. I don't know how Poppy made it. Mommy never see'd a well day in her life. She was born with somethin' th' matter with her head—one side'a her head run from th' time she was born 'til she died. But I can tell y'one thing. In your life, don't never care a cent in this world t'wait on your mother, whether she's sick or not sick. When she's gone, you'll be glad y'did. Yes you will. 'Cause I've not got a thing in this world t'regret. I waited on my mother day and night—what I mean *day* and *night*. Many a night I been up waitin' on my mother when ever' body else was in th' bed asleep. I rejoice over that. God'll repay you for all that. God'll certainly bless y'fer it.

Poppy had a awful hard time, an' his daddy died a way 'fore he was born so he had a hard time t'begin with. Well, atter he's married he had a worse time *I'll* say, with all 'at sickness'n'ever'thing on 'im. Mommy did love wheat bread, an' he worked for a peck a'corn a day so he could get Mommy bread t'eat. Why, he'uz as good t'Mommy as a baby. Now Ulysses didn't believe this, an' I didn't care whether he did'r not—you know, if I tell anybody anything an' they believe it, it's all right; an' if they don't believe it, I don't care whether they do'r not—I never heard Poppy give Mommy a ill word in my life. Now we had some hogs, and one of our hogs got in a neighbor's corn patch an' eat some of his corn. And he come after Poppy an'told him t'come get his hog, an' he charged Poppy two dollers fer what it eat. Poppy's s'mad he didn't know what t'do. That'uz th' maddest I've ever seed Poppy in my life. An' Mommy—he called her Dink, that was her nickname—she said somethin' t'Poppy. "Now," he says, "Dink, don't you say a *word to* me while I'm mad." An' that was ever'thing's ever said about that. She hushed, of course. An' he never said nary another word. That was th' illest word I ever heered Poppy tell Mommy in my life.

It's a whole lot easier today. I've hoed corn many a day fer a quarter. *Many* a day. An' we used t'pick huckleberries, me'n m'brother did, an' swap two gallons a'huckleberries fer one gallon a'syrup. Had t'do somethin' t'make a livin'. But we always had plenty t'eat. We always had plenty a'what we had. We didn't have no great stuff that cost a lot. We never did buy that. Well, we just didn't have nothin't'pay fer't, an' we always tried t'pay as we went. You know, if y'get goin' in debt, next thing y'know you can't pay it t'save yore life. I'm scared t'death a debts. I owe fer this road now, an' it worries me t'death. Used t'be I didn't have enough money t'mail a letter with. An' you know how much candy I bought in my life 'fore I's married? I bought one nickel's worth a'candy in my life. I just didn't have nothin' t'buy *with*. Poppy hired a girl t'stay with Mommy 'til I got big enough t'do th' work, an' y'know how much he'd have t'pay? Seventy-five cents a week. They'd work all week fer seventy-five cents.

An' picked blackberries'n'strawberries. Always had somethin' t'eat. Pickled beans'n' ever'thin'. Why, we've pickled beans in a twenty gallon barrel; but I ain't got any this year. Groundhogs eat m'beans up an' I never had nary one t'pick. I had two bushel baskets full'a cans, an' I took 'em out there an' poured'em in th' groundhog's hole an' took a stick an' beat'em in. An' you know, that groundhog left an' never did come back. Couldn't bear them rattlin' things. Just couldn't stand'em (*laughing*).

An' we've raised high as seventy-five bushel a'Irish 'taters over'n'at field over there. Did'ja ever put up any sweet 'taters? Well, I'm gonna tell y'how. Law, I'uz s'glad t'know how I didn't know what t'do. Dig yer sweet 'taters an' sun'em 'til they gets just th' least bit swiveled, I call it; an' put 'em in pasteboard boxes an' cover'em up. They ain't nary one a'mine rotted yet. We kep'em in th' tater house. One day that 'tater house fell down—fell out, side of it did up there. I went t'get'taters an' they's th' biggest light in th' house, an' I said, "What in th' world's th' matter with th' tater house?" Here they was, th' side of it fell out.

Y'ever eat any lye hominy? Boys, 'at's th' best stuff ever you eat in yore life. It sure is. Boys, I've made many a pot full. And soap, law, I've made many a pot'a soap too. Had th' ash hopper, oak ashes. And bottomed chairs—I guess I bottomed 'bout ever'one a'these. He'ped to do it. I can't make th' splits. I bottom 'em with white oak splits. Some people bottoms 'em with bark, but I never did. Bark does easy t'what th' wood does. Course it don't last like wood. Tain't good like wood. (*We asked her to tell us more about the bark method.*) Use young poplar bark in th' spring a'th' year when th' sap rises; y'can't make it no other time. Only cut little poles certain lengths an' then peel 'em an' use that while it's green. If y'wait 'til it gets all dried up, it'll break all t'pieces. An' always join th' ends under th' bottom. Never do jine 'em on th' top a'th' chairs. On th' bottom so they won't bother nothin'.

An' I've made baskets. I've made lots'a baskets. I love t'fool wi'my hands. I just love t'fool with 'em. I made 'em with white oak splits, an' I've made some with willers. Willer baskets is hard 'cause y'have t'go off t'th' branch, an' we ain't got no willers grows on this place like a heap a'people has. Get'cha little willers, well, long as they grow. Ain't none of 'em big as yer finger. An' y'have t'have a big pot a'water by th' fire an' keep them willers soft in that. Didn't, they'd break all t'pieces. Put 'em in hot water an' th' bark just peels off like ever'thing. Gather 'em when th' sap first rises on 'em pretty good, an y'can skin 'em pretty well without scaldin 'em; but if y'don't, y'have t'scald 'em. I'd rather scald 'em. They last longer I always think.

An' I've made foot mats out'a corn shucks—t'wipe yer feet on. That's easy, an' that's th' prettiest work! They make th' best foot mats. I ain't made none since m'hand's paralyzed. I reckon God just didn't intend fer me t'work my hand!

Used t'raise corn pones too. You ever eat any corn pones were raised? It's made out'a corn meal. Now hits another hard job, an' I love it better'n a cat loves sweet milk, I shore do. But I ain't raised none in a long time. Poppy always had me t'raise him a corn pone t'go t'Nantahaly. See, Poppy raised stock an' turned on Nantahaly range. Whenever th' time come, "I'm' a goin' t'Nantahaly a certain day an' you raise me some corn pones," well, 'at's what I done. I had a big oven a'purpose t'bake 'em in. Have t'cook 'em on th' fireplace. An' Lester Mann, he found out I could do that, an' they's' good; why he a-a-a-always, when he started t'th' mountains, he always come an'

I raised him a corn pone. Hit'd be five inches thick. An' you take that corn pone an' slice it an' lay it in grease an' fry it in a pan in th' mountains, an' that was hot bread, y'see? An' law, they thought that'uz th' greatest thing in th' world. I've raised many a one that's went t'Nantahaly.

I'll tell'y', be a neighbor and you'll have neighbors. Now I've tried that by experience. I do try t'be good t'ever'body, and I try t'treat ever'body just as I'd have them treat me. I don't care th' goodness you do, you'll always get repaid for it. Double. Fourfold. You children remember that. Th' more you do for people, th' more they'll do for you. Always remember, t'have a friend, be one.

Doesn't being here alone bother you sometimes?

Well, it's mighty lonesome. When it comes storms an' things like that, it's not s'good. And still I don't mind it a bit in th' world. Ain't only one thing I'm afraid of, an' that's snakes. When 'at big'n come in that big pile here awhile back, hit scared th' life out'a me just about. I like t'never got over it. But I ain't like this pore old woman lives over here. She's afraid of a bear an' carries a'axe with her ever'time she comes over here. Tickles me. A little old hand axe. I said, "What you goin' do wi'that?" She said, "Kill a bear." I've lived here eighty years an' never see'd a bear in my life. An' I'll tell you th' truth, I'm not bothered with one single thing in this world here. That groundhog's only thing in this world that bothers me. An th' fox. They won't let me have a chicken. I had twenty hens an' two roosters, an' they catched th' last one of 'em. I wanted t'get s'more, an' Ulysses said they wadn't no use.

We made a good life here, but we put in lots'a'time. Many an' many a night I've been workin' when two o'clock come in th' mornin'—cardin'n'spinnin'n'sewin'. They want me t'sell an' move away from here, but I won't do it. It's just home—'at's all. I spent my happiest days here.

WOOD

The fact that an area's natural resources are the most vital factor in determining the way of life of a self-sufficient people may seem too obvious to need mention. However, the role that wood played in the settling of the Southern Appalachians cannot be overemphasized. Whereas wood is now often a luxury, it was an absolute necessity here for centuries. It provided shelter for people and animals, fire for warmth and cooking, material for wagons, tools, furniture, household utensils, toys, decorative objects, and a thousand other things. The trees themselves provided fruit, nuts, syrup, and the ingredients for many home remedies, and even gave clues as to what the weather would be in the coming months. The lives of the mountain people would necessarily have been drastically altered without this versatile, readily available resource.

The wood itself was used either green or seasoned, depending not so much on what kind of wood it was as on what it was to be used for. Pieces that had to fit tight and stay tight—the handles of tools, for example—had to be seasoned or else the wood would shrink and pull away as it dried. Items such as pegs, wheel spokes, fine furniture, buckets, and barrels had to be made of seasoned wood or they'd fall apart. For rafters, fence posts and rails, shingles, rough furniture, and so on, the parts did not have to fit so tightly together to remain serviceable, so they could be constructed of green stock.

There are several ways to cure wood. The method chosen depended on the size of the pieces and how quickly they were needed. Very small pieces which would fit into a pot were boiled. "Sometimes we boiled them all day and overnight, and they was cured good," says Harry Brown. The water would draw the sap out, and when the water itself evaporated, the wood would be ready to use. People also dried smaller pieces by the fire overnight, being careful that they didn't get too hot and warp or burn. They would often use this method to season tool handles, drying only the end that fit into the head of the tool.

Another way to cure lumber is to use a dry kiln. A large rack would be built three to four feet off the ground and covered with a roof—and sometimes walls—to keep out the rain. The lumber would be stacked crosswise on the rack for maximum air circulation, and under the lumber several small fires would be built. A similar way, according to Harry Brown, was to "make a little rack and stack your lumber up around it just like a tepee. Y'leave a space at th' bottom so's y'can get in, and build little fires under that. Sometimes people'd dry'em that way a week." In both methods the fires had to be tended constantly to make sure they didn't go out or get so large they'd warp or set the lumber on fire.

The simplest method of all was to stack the lumber crosswise and just leave it alone until it was needed. Small straight pieces such as tool handles and parts for furniture could be bundled together so they wouldn't warp, and set in a dry place. The problem was that it could take months for the wood to be properly cured, but for many, that made little difference.

"Back whenever they was puttin' up buildings," says Millard Buchanan, "they didn't cure nothin' only just what they could. See, they got t'cuttin' and fixin' t'put up a buildin', and it'd maybe take'em six or eight months t'get it hewed out, and sometimes they'd just pile it up. And then they'd go t'work on th' buildin' and cut it and lay it down. By th' time they got it done, th' wood had either cured a'layin' about or while they was buildin' with it. Why, it'd have all th' sun and air on it and it'd be dry. They didn't pay no 'tention to th' cracks bein' there nohow."

The woods themselves, and some of their uses:

CHESTNUT

Wild chestnut was very plentiful in the mountains before the blight killed it all. It grew very straight, sometimes to four or five feet in diameter, was fairly soft and light, easily split and worked,

PLATE 6 A split rail fence in the reconstructed pioneer settlement at the Cherokee, North Carolina, entrance to the Smokies. The "V"-shaped opening eliminates the need for a gate that opens and shuts.

and lasted forever. In fact, the stumps of huge chestnuts cut fifty years ago still dot the mountain slopes. It was the favorite wood of the old-timers, and it was used for almost everything.

Green chestnut was split into fence rails, puncheon floors, wide planking for doors and inside wall boards, and lathing to cover the cracks between wall longs. Larger pieces were used for the wall logs themselves, sleepers and sills, and plates. Slender poles made good rafters and joists. As the wood didn't rot easily if kept wet, it was also good for floating bridges and as framing for the rock in underground drainage ditches. The bark peeled intact from half a slender pole made a suitable pipe for running water from a spring.

Seasoned chestnut was used for caskets, all kinds of furniture, animal calls, dough boards, and kitchen utensils, and sometimes for double ox yokes.

HICKORY

Hickory is a hard wood with a slightly wavy grain that is quite difficult to work. Even so, it was desirable as it is heavy, fairly flexible, and very durable.

Green hickory makes the best fires according to all the people we spoke to. It takes some time to get started, but it gives the

most heat, burns the longest, and makes the best coals. It was used
for warmth, cooking, and smoking meat. The leftover ashes were
saved to make the lye used in homemade soap. Saplings were used
in stick and mud chimneys, larger logs were worked into wagon
beds and rough furniture, and withes served as rope for hanging meat
in the smokehouse. Withes were also strung between rafters for hanging dried fruits and vegetables. Sometimes the bark was split off
green and used for bottoming chairs, and often it was chewed like
gum.

Hickory had to be seasoned for tool handles and wagon pillars,
tongues, axles, spokes, and wheel hubs. It was the best material for
wagon parts as it is flexible and will take a great deal of strain
before breaking.

OAK

Oak is a very hard wood that has many of the same uses as
hickory but is far more easily worked. Unseasoned oak 'of any
variety makes hot, long-lasting fires and good coals that don't "pop"
so much as hickory. "Green oak is hard t'get started," says Esco
Pitts, "but after you've got a fire out'a that going, now you've got
something that'll last y'."

Unseasoned white oak was made into splits for baskets and chair
bottoms; and water, spanish, and red oak were all favorites for
boards to cover roofs. Oak was also used green for simple furniture,
wagon beds, and split rails for fences.

White oak saplings were used for making mauls, as shown in
plate 11 in the next chapter. Uncut saplings often served as springs
to power hand lathes and to spring the triggers on animal traps.

Oak was seasoned for wheel spokes, hubs, and felons (the wheel
rims). Split, it was used for flooring, furniture, spinning wheels,
and plow frames. Esco Pitts says, "The finest spinning wheels I ever
seen was made of oak, only hits hard t'work sometimes." White oak
made the best barrels, tubs, and buckets according to every one of
our contacts. For storing whiskey, the insides of the barrels were
charred to help age and improve the whiskey's flavor.

LOCUST

Locust is one of the hardest woods, difficult to work, but useful
nevertheless. It doesn't draw up a great deal, resists termites, and it
rarely rots when placed in water or underground. Sap locust is the
name given the younger trees, which grow fairly quickly to eight or
ten inches in diameter. The adult locust grows more slowly and is

much harder than the saplings. Called yellow locust, it was preferred over the younger trees, but it's getting scarce now. "They used t'be a whole lot'a that ol'yella' locust around these parts," says Millard Buchanan. "That's what th' old-timers liked best. Oh, hit'd last and just keep a'lastin'. Forever I guess. But they ain't too much around now. Hit's all been used up."

Green locust was often handy for foundation blocks. It also made fine floor sleepers, fence posts, stakes, railroad ties, and floating bridges. Seasoned, it was made into pegs, dowels, and wagon pillars and axles.

POPLAR

Poplar is light and grows very straight and fast with the limbs beginning far above the ground. It is termed white or yellow depending on the age and color. The younger, white poplar is fairly hard, and the older, yellow poplar is soft and easily worked. "Yellow poplar is aged, ripened trees that stood there for centuries and turned yellow. White poplar is th' same kind'a tree, but it don't get old enough in this day and time," says Millard Buchanan.

Green poplar was very good for cabin logs, rafters, joists, and weatherboard. Seasoned, it was used for furniture, paneling, caskets, dough boards, and dugout dough trays. It was also a favorite for ox yokes, being light, strong, and easily worked.

PINE

Pine is one of the softer woods. It grows straight, and is both durable and easily worked with hand tools.

Unseasoned, the large trees were used for cabin logs and occasionally even cut for foundation blocks. They were split to make paneling and flooring, and the slender poles were sometimes used for rafters and joists.

Seasoned pine is still easily worked, so it was used for doors and window and door frames that required careful fitting. It also made good furniture. The resin was widely used in homemade salves and remedies.

Pieces of fat pine were perfect for starting fires, and pine knots were prized for torches in night hunts.

WALNUT

Walnut is a hard wood that splits fairly easily and works well. We got the impression that it was used as much for its aesthetic qualities as its practicality. Lawton Brooks says, "It's a real pretty

PLATE 7   Bill Lamb with the ox yoke he used to use. The yoke was made by Mac Hopper, one of the finest yoke makers in the county until his death some years ago.

wood; got nice color and grain, but people just didn't seem t'use it as much as say oak or hick'ry."

Unseasoned, it was sometimes used split for fence rails and paneling. Seasoned, it had more uses—fine furniture primarily.

MAPLE

Maple is a hard wood with light color and wavy grain. The grain makes it good for carving, and when seasoned, it turns so well on a hand lathe that it was popular for furniture. It was also used seasoned for spoons, butter molds, gunstocks, drawer knobs, auger handles, and box planes. It can be worked and sanded very thin without splitting, and so it was perfect for making fiddles and guitars.

CHERRY

Wild red cherry is fairly hard, has a deep rich color and a slightly wavy grain. Seasoned, it was used primarily for furniture. The bark was a popular ingredient for cough medicines.

ASH

White ash is a very hard wood without much flexibility, and it has a fine, straight grain. Seasoned, it was made into rolling pins and handles for tools such as hoes and shovels that didn't require a lot of spring.

BLACK GUM

Black gum trees grow quite large, and the older ones are often hollow inside. For this reason, it was about the only tree used for bee gums. Toothbrushes were made from its twigs.

Slices of the trunk five or six inches thick could be used for solid wagon wheels. A hole would be bored in the center for the axle, and the unusual crosswise grain would keep them from cracking and splitting apart.

OTHERS

Other varieties had few uses, but they were often distinguished for at least one important function. Black birch, for example, was used seasoned for fiddles and guitars because of its curly grain. Sassafras was sometimes used seasoned for wheel hubs and ox yokes. Sourwood made fine canes and sled runners. Dogwood is so hard when cured that it was perfect for gluts and shuttles. Moth-resistant chests were fashioned out of cedar.

And for all of these woods, there are doubtless uses that we have not come across yet. The important thing, of course, is that each has its own distinctive characteristics, and few mountain men were ever without a working knowledge of these characteristics and how best to use them. Their survival too often depended on it.

TOOLS AND SKILLS

To the forests in which they settled, our ancestors brought little more than a few tools and a great deal of ingenuity. They had to find ways to convert wood into most of what they needed for survival, and the resulting reverence for and skill with wood was boundless and profound.

Many of the tools used for working wood were themselves made out of wood—as were the handles for most of the others—and they are easily reproduced today. A mallet, for example, was simply a two-foot section out of the limb of a hardwood tree like oak or hickory. While green, two-thirds of the limb was hewn into a handle (*Plate 8*) and then smoothed (*Plate 9*). It was then set up to cure so that it would not split while being used later.

A maul could be made in almost the same way, but on a larger scale (*Plate 10*). The early builders simply found a white oak sapling with a knob deformity in the trunk. Cutting the trunk just below the knob and as far above it as the length they wanted the handle (*Plate 11*), they hewed the handle out of the cut section of the trunk using the knob as the head of the tool.

Wooden wedges, or "gluts," were hewn out of eighteen-inch long, four to six-inch thick sections of hardwood limbs (*Plate 12*).

And a shaving horse could be quickly constructed out of old pieces. The one in Plate 13, for example, needs only one main brace (*6′×6″×2″*), two short legs (*11″×1½″×¾″*), two long legs ($2' \times 1\frac{1}{2}'' \times \frac{3}{4}''$), one arm ($26'' \times 1\frac{1}{2}'' \times 2''$), one block ($5'' \times 3\frac{1}{2}'' \times 3''$), and a foot pedal ($16'' \times 3\frac{3}{4}'' \times \frac{3}{4}''$).

Just as important as the tools themselves was knowing how to use them. Let's assume for the moment that you intend to build your own log cabin the old way. Here are some of the skills you will need to master, along with the tools required.

PLATE 8 Zero Webb shapes the handle for a hickory mallet.

PLATE 9 Lon Reid smooths the handle.

PLATE 10 A poleaxe and a maul leaning against a two-foot section of oak that is being split into shingles or "boards."

PLATE 11

PLATE 12

PLATE 13
A shaving horse.

HEWING

The tools needed are a broadaxe, a foot adze, a "falling" or pole axe, and a chalk box.

Hewing is the skill needed in order to make support beams and wall logs. By hewing, the rounded sides of a log are made flat.

The method is not difficult. Set the log to be hewn on blocks. Place wedges under the ends to keep it from rolling.

Now mark guidelines on the top surface so that the hewing will be done in a straight line. The lines were made with the equivalent of today's chalk box and string. A small box contained either fire coals (crushed charcoal) or a mixture of pokeberry juice and lime. The string, coiled in the box, was pulled out the length of the log, laid on the log where the hewing was to be done, stretched tight, and then "twanged" or "flipped," leaving a straight, clearly visible line. Then the string was rewound into the box to take on another coating of charcoal or juice, readying it for the next line.

Make as many lines on the log as there are sides to be hewn (*Plate 14*).

To hew, first "score" the log at two to three-inch intervals with the falling axe. Then, using the broadaxe as shown in Plate 15, slice off the chips. This axe has a curved handle to keep you from

PLATE 15 Bill Lamb shows how to use a broadaxe. The vertical marks on the log were left by the scoring process.

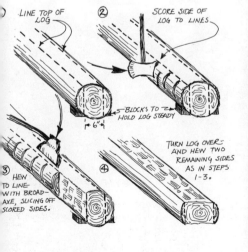

PLATE 14

skinning your knuckles against the side of the log as you hew (*Plate 16*).

If the log is to be hewn on all four sides, hew off two parallel sides first; then roll the log over onto one of the flat sides and repeat the process.

An alternative is to use the foot adze (*Plate 17*).

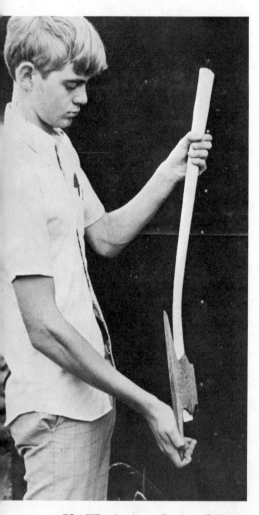

PLATE 16 As Paul Gillespie shows, a broadaxe has a curved handle to prevent the user's skinning his knuckles as he works.

PLATE 17 The proper stance to use when working with a foot adze is demonstrated by Bill Lamb. The handle of the adze has a double curve for ease in working.

NOTCHING AND JOINTING

The tools needed are a falling axe, a mallet, a chisel, a hand-saw, a double-bladed axe, a square, and a ruler.

To cut lap joints, mortises, and so on, early builders in this area marked off the joint to be cut using a square and ruler. They then made the necessary cut(s) against the grain with a handsaw, and going with the grain, split out the remainder with a chisel and mallet (*Plate 18*).

The process of cutting corner notches for a cabin is fully described in the following chapter.

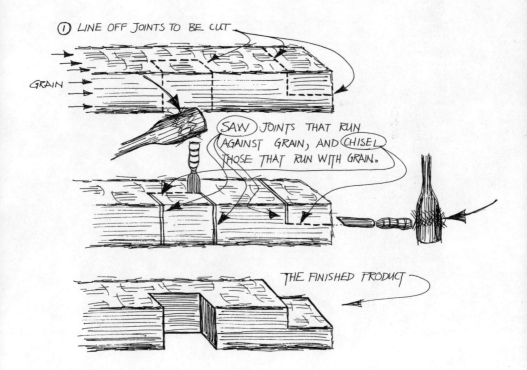

① LINE OFF JOINTS TO BE CUT

GRAIN

SAW JOINTS THAT RUN AGAINST GRAIN, AND CHISEL THOSE THAT RUN WITH GRAIN.

THE FINISHED PRODUCT

PLATE 18

PLATE 19   The two wooden wedges already driven into this huge trunk have begun to split it in half.

SPLITTING AND RIVING

The tools needed are a poleaxe, a go-devil, large wooden wedges, a maul, a froe, and a mallet.

If a large enough tree was found, a skilled builder could get more than one wall log out of the same trunk. Hillard Green told us of a house near Bryson City, North Carolina, for which such large poplar logs were used that the owner needed only four logs to complete his walls.

The log in Plate 19 is four feet in diameter. Locust wedges have begun the splitting process. With a maul, they are driven deeper and deeper into the trunk until it splits in half. Plate 20 shows how several wall logs and beams can be obtained from such a wide trunk.

Logs can also be cut into two- four- or six-foot lengths to be split with a froe and mallet into rough boards for flooring, paneling, lathing, or shingles ("boards").

For shingles to cover the roof or gables, the trunk is cut into two-foot lengths. Then it is split up into "bolts," and the bolts are "rived" into one-half inch thick slices, as shown in the following plates.

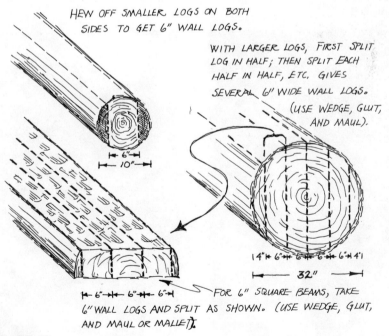

HEW OFF SMALLER LOGS ON BOTH SIDES TO GET 6" WALL LOGS.

WITH LARGER LOGS, FIRST SPLIT LOG IN HALF; THEN SPLIT EACH HALF IN HALF, ETC. GIVES SEVERAL 6" WIDE WALL LOGS.
(USE WEDGE, GLUT, AND MAUL).

6"
10"

14" 6" 6" 6" 6" 4'
32"

6" 6" 6"

FOR 6" SQUARE BEAMS, TAKE 6" WALL LOGS AND SPLIT AS SHOWN. (USE WEDGE, GLUT, AND MAUL OR MALLET).

PLATE 20

PLATE 21 The board-making process begins with a section of oak trunk. Working on one-half at a time, and with a go-devil and steel wedge, Bill Lamb first halves the trunk, and then splits that half into four equal pieces.

PLATE 22 Next, working on one section at a time, the heart is split out, and . . .

PLATE 23 . . . the remainder is split into four equal pieces.

PLATE 24 One section completed, Bill moves on to the next, and . . .

PLATE 25 . . . so on until the job is done.

PLATE 26 Now Bill takes one of the board "bolts" he has just split and . . .

PLATE 27 . . . "barks" it, or removes the bark and outer layers of fiber.

PLATE 28 The bolt now goes to the board "brake" to be converted into shingles. The brake, in this case, is the narrow "Y" crotch of a black gum tree cut about six feet long. The single end is propped up, and two stout poles are crossed in the double end. No nails or other braces are needed, for these poles wedge firmly enough to hold the end up. As one man said, "They work contrary to each other."

The top surface of the brake should be level. Then a block is placed underneath on which the bolt being split is rested.

PLATE 29 The bolt standing on end between the two arms of the brake, Bill places his froe against the bolt's end and . . .

PLATE 30 . . . strikes it sharply several times with the mallet thus driving the froe's blade into the bolt.

PLATE 31 Now, using the board brake as leverage and a brace, the shingle is pried off. The tendency is for the crack to move steadily toward the top of the bolt (or "run out"), thus making your shingles narrower at one end than at the other. To prevent this, the moment Bill sees the crack running out, he turns the whole bolt over, leaving the froe in place, and continues prying from this position. Pushing down hard on the bottom half of the bolt will cause the crack to come back toward the middle also. Let up, and again it moves to the top. If, when the bolt has been halved, the shingles are still too thick, each can be halved again using the same process.

PLATE 32 Bill prefers removing the sap from the finished shingle since the sap is softer and rots quickly when exposed to the weather. Some place the sap edges together on the roof and cover them with a third shingle for protection.

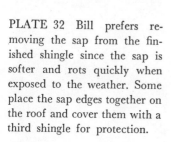

PLATE 33   The finished board is thrown aside to be stacked later. Often it took nearly five thousand of these boards to cover a large barn of about forty feet in length. A good board maker, however, could rive over a thousand boards a day if he kept at it steadily and didn't have to "bolt them up." If the boards have a slight twist, they can be "bumped," or the high places shaved off with an axe. Bill is making the boards in this photograph for Roy Thompson who is building a log cabin. (See next chapter.)

PLATE 34   Bill shows how the boards can be mounted on a roof.

DRILLING HOLES

The only tool needed is an auger, or gimlet.

Holes were made with an auger (*Plate 35*). Pegs to fill the holes were cut from one-inch wide locust boards as shown in Plate 36.

DRESSING

The tools needed are a drawing knife and a shaving horse.

Surfaces of boards and beams could be smoothed, or dressed, with a drawing knife (*Plate 37*). The beam, if long and heavy, could be dressed while on the ground or on blocks. Shorter boards were clamped in a shaving horse for smoothing (*Plate 38*).

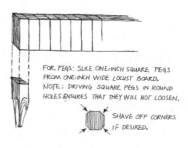

FOR PEGS: SLICE ONE-INCH SQUARE PEGS FROM ONE-INCH WIDE LOCUST BOARD.
NOTE: DRIVING SQUARE PEGS IN ROUND HOLES ENSURES THAT THEY WILL NOT LOOSEN.

SHAVE OFF CORNERS IF DESIRED.

PLATE 36

PLATE 35   Bill Lamb, with an auger, shows how one can get a "double lick" by crossing the hands thus allowing one complete revolution of the tool.

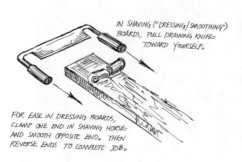

IN SHAVING ("DRESSING/SMOOTHING") BOARDS, PULL DRAWING KNIFE TOWARD YOURSELF.

FOR EASE IN DRESSING BOARDS, CLAMP ONE END IN SHAVING HORSE AND SMOOTH OPPOSITE END. THEN REVERSE ENDS TO COMPLETE JOB.

PLATE 37

PLATE 38   Bill Lamb dressing a shingle with his shaving horse and drawing knife. As his foot pushes forward on the pedal, the block clamps the shingle in place.

BUILDING A LOG CABIN

T he log cabin was once the only form of building in this area. With modern innovations and a general trend toward an easier life in the present century, the fine art of building a genuine log cabin is all but lost. True, many put up inexpensive imitations as tourist attractions and curiosities, but firsthand knowledge of the authentic, handcrafted cabin rests in the heads of four or five old-timers who have long since stopped that sort of work. The only way to preserve this art is to gather information from the men who know it best. We have presented it in the form of a set of instructions, as it was given to us.

Gathering the information was a long but enjoyable process. It took almost an entire summer tracking down leads, interviewing those leads, measuring and photographing over one hundred log structures, braving rains and wet sleeping bags, and suffering through one hundred degree afternoons. It was a search that carried us far into South Carolina to watch a two hundred-year-old building being painstakingly reconstructed, to the Great Smoky Mountains of North Carolina to study a reconstructed pioneer farmstead, and to the top of a mountain where Roy Thompson is actually building a cabin by hand.

As our stacks of information grew, so did our realization that it would be absolutely impossible to provide a set of blueprints for every cabin we saw—there are almost as many ways to build a cabin as

PLATE 39   This building near Highlands, North Carolina, shows why one might still take the time to build a log cabin.

PLATE 40   Before our contacts could show us how to cut notches, they first had to have the logs. Here, Mike Cook and Paul Gillespie saw up a poplar for use by Hillard Green and Harley Thomas.

there are people who have built one. Thus we have chosen to present here pages of skills and styles to which you must bring your own needs and desires, and from which you must extract information according to your requirements. Few measurements are included, as every man will want a cabin of a different size. While a cabin twenty-six feet long and sixteen feet wide may do well for a single man, it will hardly suit a family. Placement and sizes of windows and doors will depend on how you choose to arrange your rooms, and so forth.

The instructions are divided into nine sections, each dealing with a different part of the building. The first, for example, discusses the foundations and sills; the last, chinking and paneling. Each of these nine sections is further subdivided into three categories: *A, B,* and *C. A,* in each case, is devoted to the building of a crafted cabin—a cabin of genuine beauty and distinction. It requires the use of the original tools. *B* is devoted to a cabin that is far less complicated, and no work of art, but absolutely functional. For this type you may use power tools, sawmill lumber, and so on. *C* contains all the other variations we have found, some of which you may wish to substitute for the recommendations we have made in *A* or *B*. The final cabin, rather than being a carbon copy of one now in existence, will be the product of your own taste.

To those who would look on such a project as a farce, or a chore not worth the time, we have little to say. We speak instead to the individual who feels some loss in the realization that this age of miracles, miraculous though it is, has robbed us of the need to use our hands. We speak to the individual who feels that some-day, somewhere, the use of the instructions contained in these pages will be a source of tremendous satisfaction. And we speak, in a sense, to the child in man—that free spirit still building tree houses in the woods.

To the enthusiastic, all-things-are-possible child spirit, and to the man who longs for the peace that independence and skilled self-sufficiency brings, we address ourselves in this chapter. And we wish him well. He's one of us.

FOUNDATION ● SILLS

A   Build a solid rock foundation running the length and width of your projected house. We have been told that the foundation should be at least 18″ high as there is a prevalent belief that termites will climb no higher than 18″. The ends of the foundation may be built up about 4″ higher than the sides (*Plate 41*).

PLATE 41   A solid rock foundation, the ends of which have been built up, on the apple house in the reconstructed pioneer settlement at the Cherokee, North Carolina, entrance to the Great Smoky Mountain National Park.

Choose two logs for the sills (beams that rest directly on the foundation and on which the floor beams or "sleepers" are laid). The sills almost invariably run along the two longest walls of the building. Using a broadaxe, hew both sills down on all four sides until they measure square. If your house is over twenty feet wide, you may also wish to use a middle sill. Directions for this variation are covered at *C*9.

Put the two sills in place atop the two sides of the foundation. They need not be pinned down in any way (*Plate 42*).

B   Build a foundation of concrete blocks running the length and width of your projected house. Again, we suggest that it be at least 18″ above ground level (*Plate 43*).

PLATE 42

FOUNDATION MAY BE BUILT UP AT END ALMOST FLUSH WITH TOP OF
SILLS SO THAT FIRST END LOG WILL FIT MORE SNUGLY AS AT
THIS END — OR LEFT OPEN AS AT OPPOSITE END.

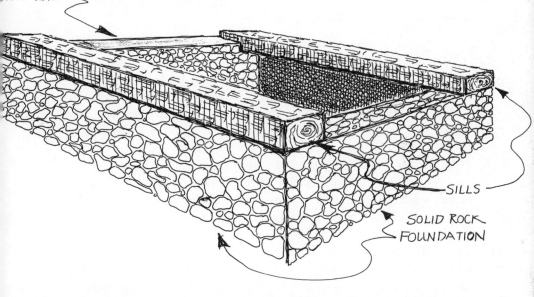

SILLS

SOLID ROCK
FOUNDATION

PLATE 43   A concrete block foundation built by Roy Thompson for his log
cabin on Commissioner Creek. The logs for the cabin lie in the foreground.

Choose two logs for the sills. Using a broadaxe or adze, hew the top and bottom of each log flat leaving the sides of each round. When finished, both logs should be the same thickness (6"–8" is recommended). If they are not the same thickness, the floor beams will be slanted when set into place. Again, a middle sill may be used if desired. (*See Section C.*)

Set the sills in place atop the two long sides of the foundation. They need not be pinned down.

C   1. An extremely common variation consists of a series of rock pillars spaced at regular intervals down the four sides. These pillars, rarely closer than six feet together, may either be carefully constructed so as to have squared off corners, or they may simply be several large rocks placed one atop the other (*Plates 44, 86*). We have also seen buildings that have only one large rock under each corner.

2. Concrete block columns can be substituted for the above.

3. Another variation is found in locust or oak poles, one end of which rests on a flat rock with the other under the sill (*Plate 45*). These poles should be spaced regularly around the perimeter of the cabin.

4. Sills may be hewed off only on the top surface, leaving the rest of the log round. In this variation, notches are cut into the underside of the log to accommodate the rock pillars that support it. These notches keep the sill from rolling or "kicking out" (*Plate 46*).

5. Sometimes the sill is left completely round. Locust poles with concave ends (as shown in an earlier diagram) support it from the bottom, and the ends of the sleepers are "round notched" to fit over the sill's rounded top surface.

6. Occasionally the ends of the sills are notched on top to hold the first two end logs. The logs shown in Plate 47 have been hewn off square. They also can be rounded, or flat on the top surface, etc. This notch can be executed with handsaw, chisel, and mallet.

7. A quarter-notch is a more elaborate variation, shown in Plates 48 and 49. Here, the inside top quarter of the squared sill is hewed out to fit both the first end log (in this case running across the front under the door) and the sleepers.

8. In rare cases, one-inch deep notches are cut in the top of the sill to hold the ends of each sleeper in place. If the sleeper ends have been left round, round notches are cut into the sill to hold them.

9. If the cabin is exceptionally wide, a middle sill (one running parallel to the other two and halfway between them) may be de-

PLATE 44 A foundation pillar made of rocks placed atop each other.

PLATE 45

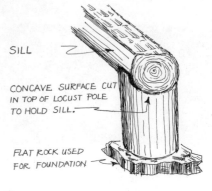

SILL

CONCAVE SURFACE CUT IN TOP OF LOCUST POLE TO HOLD SILL.

FLAT ROCK USED FOR FOUNDATION

PLATE 46

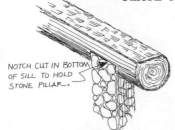

NOTCH CUT IN BOTTOM OF SILL TO HOLD STONE PILLAR.

PLATE 47

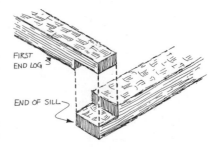

FIRST END LOG

END OF SILL

PLATE 48 In this building, part of the pioneer settlement, the sill is quarter-notched (arrow and Plate 49).

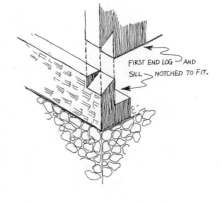

FIRST END LOG AND SILL NOTCHED TO FIT.

PLATE 49

PLATE 50　This middle sill (arrow) is supported by two rocks.

PLATE 51　This middle sill (arrow and Plate 52) in Thompson's cabin is lap-jointed and block-supported.

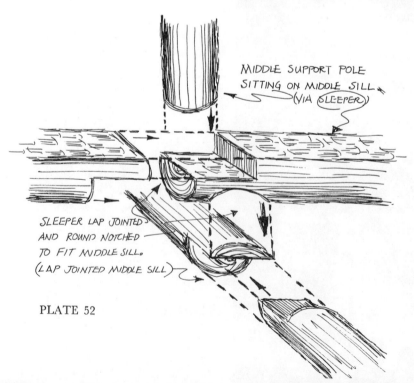

MIDDLE SUPPORT POLE
SITTING ON MIDDLE SILL
(VIA SLEEPER)

SLEEPER LAP JOINTED
AND ROUND NOTCHED
TO FIT MIDDLE SILL.
(LAP JOINTED MIDDLE SILL)

PLATE 52

sired to keep the floor from sagging. The supports set beneath this sill may be either rock columns or poles (*Plate 50*). Usually this sill is shaped to match the other two. If you built the end foundations several inches higher than the sides, as recommended, remove enough rocks to allow the ends of the middle sill to fit down into the foundation. The top surfaces of all three sills must be level with each other.

We saw one cabin where the middle sill was in two pieces. A lap joint was used (*Plates 51, 52*) to fit the two ends together, and a concrete block column was set beneath the lap joint as support.

SLEEPERS ● FLOOR

A   The sleepers are the floor beams of the cabin. They usually run the width of the building, their ends resting on the sills.

The number of sleepers needed depends on the length of the building. For *A*, subtract one foot from the total length to allow for a six-inch overhang on each sill end. If the result is a number divisible by four, we recommend setting the sleepers on four-foot centers (i.e., the distance from the center of one sleeper to the center of the next should be four feet as in *Plate 53*). The maximum distance between their centers should be six feet. If it is more, the floorboards may sag.

Choose the necessary number of logs, cut them six inches shorter than the width of the house, and with the broadaxe or adze, hew them off on all four sides until they are between four and six inches square. Again, you may choose the thickness you wish, but make sure that all the sleepers are the same thickness after hewing. Otherwise the floor may not sit level.

Next set the sleepers on the sills, spacing them the correct distance apart. There should be three inches left between each of their ends and the outside edges of the sills. With a pencil, outline the sleepers' ends on the sills. Move the sleepers aside and cut a lap joint half the thickness of each sleeper into the bottom of each sleeper and the top of the sill. Set the sleepers into place. The tops of each should be flush with the tops of the sills.

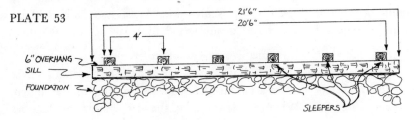

PLATE 53

21'6"
20'6"
4'
6" OVERHANG
SILL
FOUNDATION
SLEEPERS

With the auger, bore one hole through the center of each lap joint and well into the sill below. Cut the necessary number of locust pegs. They should be roughly square to make them bind against the sides of the hole, and the same thickness as the diameter of the holes. Thus, if the holes you drill are one inch in diameter, cut one-inch pegs. With an axe or knife, taper one end of each peg. Then drive the pegs, tapered ends first, into the holes with a mallet (*Plate 54*). Trim off any excess with a handsaw or knife.

With a crosscut saw, cut a large (at least two feet in diameter), straight-grained oak into lengths that match the distance between the centers of the sleepers. If the sleepers are set on four-foot centers, for example, cut the oak trunk into four-foot lengths.

Using the axe, locust wedges, and maul, split the trunk into quarters and then halve each quarter. Remove the heart and the bark. Then, using a froe, mallet, and board brake, and the same process used for making shingles ("boards") for the roof, split out two-inch thick puncheons, or floorboards. Remove the "sap" (the soft, new wood closest to the bark) if you wish. Cut lap joints in the ends of each to fit the sleepers (*Plate 55*).

Set the puncheons in place, and level the top surfaces. This can be done by either lifting the puncheon and cutting a deeper lap joint, or by hewing the top surface of the puncheon itself with an adze. Puncheons may be dressed further with a drawing knife.

B   Using the same method described in *A*, but allowing ten inches at either sill end (thus subtracting twenty inches from the total length of the building and figuring from there), determine the number of sleepers you will need. Cut that number of sleepers to the exact width of the house, and hew off the top surface of each with an adze or broadaxe. Leave the rest of the log round.

Cut a lap joint into the ends of each so that the ends of each sleeper are flush with the outside edges of the hewed portion of the sills. Set each in place atop the sills (*Plates 56, 57*).

Hew off high places with the adze, and then nail on a subfloor of sawmill planks. The top floor should not be put down until the roof is up. The planks for the subfloor may be used as long as you wish, spanning several sleepers at the same time. Their lengths should be such, however, that each end is supported by a sleeper at all times.

C   1. Sleepers are sometimes set on two-foot centers.

2. If the tops of the sills have been left round, a round notch is usually cut in the end of each sleeper so it will fit the sill's rounded surface (*Plate 58*). When this is the case, the sleepers are cut long so

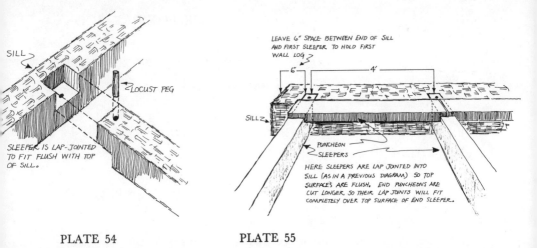

SILL

LOCUST PEG

SLEEPER IS LAP-JOINTED TO FIT FLUSH WITH TOP OF SILL.

LEAVE 6" SPACE BETWEEN END OF SILL AND FIRST SLEEPER TO HOLD FIRST WALL LOG

6"

4'

SILL

PUNCHEON SLEEPERS

HERE SLEEPERS ARE LAP JOINTED INTO SILL (AS IN A PREVIOUS DIAGRAM) SO TOP SURFACES ARE FLUSH. END PUNCHEONS ARE CUT LONGER, SO THEIR LAP JOINTS WILL FIT COMPLETELY OVER TOP SURFACE OF END SLEEPER.

PLATE 54   PLATE 55

PLATE 56   These sleepers are lap-jointed at each end to fit the sills. A foot adze has been used to hew off their top surfaces. See also Plate 57.

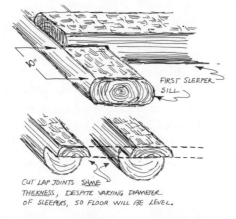

10"

FIRST SLEEPER

SILL

PLATE 57

CUT LAP JOINTS SAME THICKNESS, DESPITE VARYING DIAMETER OF SLEEPERS, SO FLOOR WILL BE LEVEL.

SLEEPER IS ROUND –
NOTCHED TO FIT OVER TOP
OF ROUND SILL.

SILL

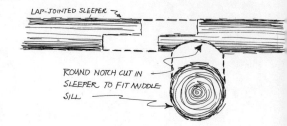

LAP-JOINTED SLEEPER

ROUND NOTCH CUT IN
SLEEPER TO FIT MIDDLE
SILL

PLATE 58   PLATE 59

that their ends extend about six inches over the sills on each side.

3. If a middle sill has been used, a notch is cut in the underside of each sleeper to fit the top surface of this sill. The middle sill itself is usually not notched as this would weaken it unnecessarily.

In Roy Thompson's cabin, the sleepers are in two pieces. Lap joints were used (*as shown in Plate 59*), their ends resting on the middle sill.

4. We have seen one floor that was nothing more than halved poles lap-jointed to fit the sleepers. This made the floor about six inches thick.

5. Sometimes the floor puncheons are hewed four to six inches thick for added warmth in winter.

WALLS ● CORNER NOTCHES

A   Choose two logs, each at least ten inches in diameter, to go across the ends of the house parallel to the sleepers. Cut them to length, and then hew off the two sides until the logs are each six inches thick. Leave the top and bottom sides rounded. Such logs will be visible many times in the plates that follow.

Now cut lap joints in the bottom ends of each. The horizontal cut should be the same width as the sill. Each joint should be at least deep enough to allow the bottom edge of the log to hide the sleeper.

Fit these two end logs into place in the six-inch spaces you have left between the first and last sleepers and the ends of the sills (*Plates 60, 61*).

You are now ready to begin cutting the dovetail notches for the corners. We recommend this particular notch both for its intricacy and beauty, and for its peculiar design which pulls each wall log toward the inside of the house locking it in place and making it impossible for one of the wall logs to kick out or roll. No pins are necessary at all. The wall will stand without support for as long as the logs are sound.

Harley Thomas, one of the finest craftsmen in the area, was taught how to cut dovetail notches by his father. In Plates 62–74 he demonstrates the almost forgotten technique.

PLATE 60 The lap joint of this end log (arrows) fits snugly over the sill.

PLATE 61 In this cabin, both the sill (the end of which is barely visible above the foundation stones) and the first end log have been lap-jointed so that their top surfaces are flush.

PLATE 62 With an axe, hew the two sides of the log back twelve inches from the end.

PLATE 63 The two sides hewed, the log is now ready for notching. The remainder of the sides will be hewed after the logs are all in place in the cabin.

PLATE 64 Slope the top surface at a 30–45° angle.

PLATE 65 Continue to hew until the top is smooth, and at the desired degree of slope.

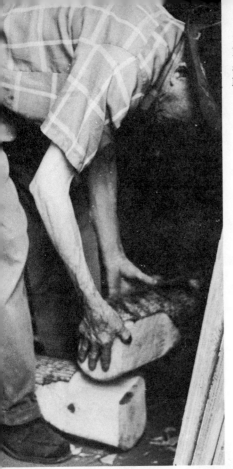

PLATE 66   Rest the next log, also hewed off on the sides, atop the first. Set it so its end is flush with the bottom log's side.

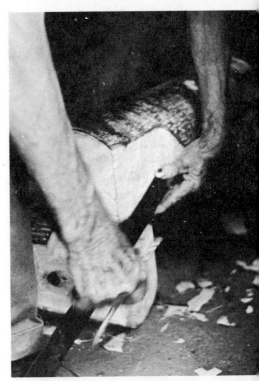

PLATE 67   Rest a steel ruler on the slope of the bottom log, and draw a line along the top edge of the ruler onto the side of the top log.

PLATE 68   Now, placing the ruler as shown, draw a vertical line on the top log which intersects with the sloping line.

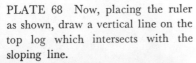

PLATE 69   Duplicate the process on the other side.

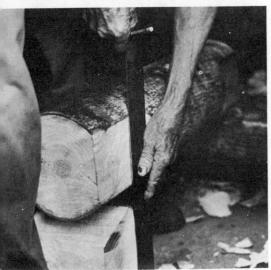

PLATE 70   Now hew out the outlined area of the top log. Hew to the line.

PLATE 71   Turn the log over as necessary to accomplish hewing.

PLATE 72   Place the two together and check the fit. If not perfectly snug, shave off the high places using the axe as a chisel. To make the top log fit farther down on the bottom one, cut the notch deeper while maintaining the same slope.

PLATE 73   Now slope the top log as before and raise a third log into place and duplicate the process just described.

PLATE 74 Here's what the finished product should look like.

Some men notch the logs as they go, one at a time, fitting each log to the next. If the top log rocks a little, they roll it off, hew out the notch a little more, and try it again, continuing in this manner until the two logs fit snugly together.

Others use a pattern that ensures that each notch will be a carbon copy of the last thus eliminating the trial and error method above. The pattern is made as follows:

First hew off the slope of one notch at the angle you desire. Taking a flat piece of one-quarter-inch thick scrap board, hold it against the end of the notched log and outline the slope and vertical edge you have cut onto the piece of scrap. Then cut out the pattern (*Plate 75*).

Duplicate this slope on every notch you cut.

Now slope the top ends of the two end logs (already in place in your wall) to fit a dovetail notch (*Plate 76*).

B   Choose two logs ten or twelve inches in diameter to go across the end of the house parallel to the sleepers. If you wish to have the ends project out about six or eight inches from the corner (as is common in many log houses), cut them about sixteen inches longer than the width of the house. Leave the logs rounded.

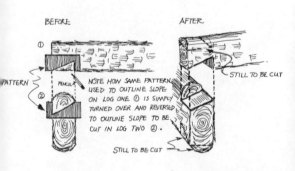

PLATE 75

PLATE 76 The end of one sill (atop foundation stone), side of first end log (arrow), and end of next wall log are visible here.

Now cut lap joints in the bottom ends of each log to fit the sill beneath. Fit the two logs into place in the ten-inch spaces you have left between the first and last sleepers and the ends of the sills.

You are now ready to begin cutting the saddle notches which we recommend for this particular cabin. As in *A*, no pins are necessary. The slopes of the notches will hold the walls vertical as long as the logs are sound. Plates 77–84 explain the procedure.

PLATE 77 Hillard Green well remembers cutting saddle notches himself as a young man. Here, despite age and near blindness, he lifts an axe again to demonstrate. First, cut a peak in the top end of the log. The peak, nearly completed, is smoothed off.

PLATE 78 Now, using a square, check the slopes. They should be at right angles. If not, shave off the high places.

PLATE 79 Next, cut a "V" shaped notch into the next log. Again, the two slopes should be at right angles. Check with the square.

PLATE 80 Check the fit. It should be snug. If it is, hew a peak in the top log and continue as before.

PLATE 81 Harley Thomas demonstrates another method for cutting the same notch. Hew a peak as above.

PLATE 82 Hew off two sides of the next log, rest it atop the peak of the first, and using the steel ruler as in the dovetail notches, trace the slopes of the bottom log's peak on the sides of the top log. Then hew out the notch using these lines as a guide.

PLATE 83   Here's how the corner should look if you followed Hillard Green's method . . .

PLATE 84 . . . or this, depending on your skill with an axe.

With Harley's method, as in Section *A*, the logs are notched one at a time without a pattern. It is simple to make a pattern, however, should you wish. Use the same method discussed in *A*—just change the slope.

Now hew peaks in the ends of the two end logs, already in place, to fit a saddle notch.

C   1. Another notch common in the mountains is the round notch, or "hog pen notch." With this variation, one simply round–notches the underside of each end to fit the top surface of the log beneath it, or vice versa.

    2. The square notch is another variation, although it is seen rarely. It is much like the dovetail except that there are no sloping surfaces. The logs intersect on flat surfaces.

    3. Variations on notches we have already seen are obvious in Plates 85 and 86.

PLATE 85 Overhanging dovetail notches on the house built by Buck Carver's grandfather a hundred and fifty years ago. The house was torn down by its new owner in 1970.

PLATE 86 Overhanging dovetail notches and two-foot wide, six-inch thick hand-split and -hewn wall logs on a house in the reconstructed pioneer settlement.

4. Either side of the log can be hewn off, leaving the other round.

5. Sometimes the first log set into place above the sill is notched at intervals along the bottom edge to accommodate the ends of the sleepers (*see Plate 41*).

6. Once in a while, the house was "built on the ground." In this variation, the sides of the logs were hewn off as in *A;* then they were laid on their sides on the ground, shuffled until the sides were as flush as possible, and then notched and marked with roman numerals to show the builders the order in which they were to be set up. If the house was later to be moved to another location, the logs were also numbered in this fashion before the house was taken down so that it could be easily reconstructed (*Plate 87*).

It is now time to choose the placement of the inside walls. If you wish to have a wall running the entire length of the house, its first log should be laid in place next. Cut a log to that length, hew it down to four inches in width, and cut dovetail notches in the ends (*Plate 88, 89*).

Don't worry about the placement of the inside doors. They will be cut after the wall is completed.

PLATE 87   The roman numeral XII originally cut into this two hundred-year-old wall log in a house being reconstructed by the Columbia, South Carolina, Department of Parks and Recreation.

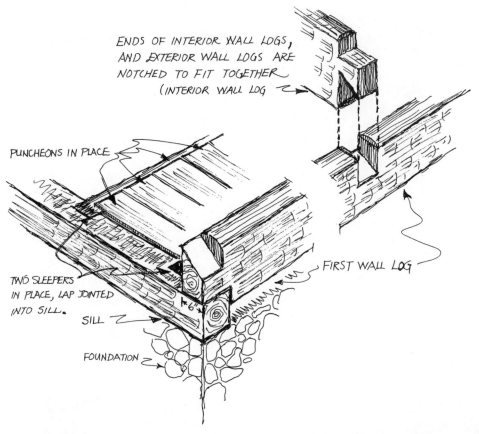

ENDS OF INTERIOR WALL LOGS,
AND EXTERIOR WALL LOGS ARE
NOTCHED TO FIT TOGETHER
(INTERIOR WALL LOG ⟶

PUNCHEONS IN PLACE

TWO SLEEPERS
IN PLACE, LAP JOINTED
INTO SILL.

SILL

FOUNDATION

FIRST WALL LOG

PLATE 88

PLATE 89 The ends of this inside wall (running from left to center) have been notched to fit similar notches cut in the outside wall (running from center right).

If no walls are to run the length of the house, choose two logs to run above the sills. Dovetail-notch the ends and fit them into place. If there is too great a gap (over two inches) between the sill and this new log, cut the notch a little deeper.

If you are using whole logs for the walls (as opposed to six-inch-thick beams split out of large trunks), you may, if you wish, leave the length between the end notches round. The entire wall can be hewed at one time when all the wall logs are up and in place. This is the method used by Harley Thomas's father long ago.

If walls are to run the width of the house, they should be started now, ends notched into the two logs you have just placed above the sills, in the manner just described.

If inside walls intersect within the house (one wall running lengthwise and another spanning the width, for example), the log spanning the width can be notched, as well as the one spanning the length, and the two fitted together.

Continue in this manner, alternating sides, until the walls are high enough to hold the ceiling beams. In building inside walls, set a new inside wall log in place with each new pair of outside wall logs (*Plates 90, 91*).

PLATE 90   The ends of an inside wall are visible on the porch of this house at "Happ'n'so" in Rabun County. The house was built in the early 1930s at a cost of less than two hundred fifty dollars.

PLATE 91 The ends of the inside partitioning walls are clearly visible in this house, located on Dog Mountain near Highlands, North Carolina. Harley Thomas helped "notch up" this house in 1926 for Colonel Sewell who died not long after the house was finished.

PLATES ● JOISTS

A   The "plates"—two logs running parallel to the sills on which the ends of the ceiling beams, or joists, rest—should be fitted next. Cut two logs that are near duplicates of the sills. Hew them down to the same dimensions as the sills. Dovetail-notch their ends. Fit the two plates into place, and drill a hole with the auger through the ends of each plate into the log below. Pin the plates down with locust pegs.

The joists, which run parallel to the sleepers, should be set on two to two and a half foot centers. Figure out the number needed, choose the same kinds of logs you used for the sleepers, and hew them in the same way and to the same dimensions with one difference—This time cut them to fit the exact width of the building. Lap-joint the ends so that the joint laps the plate completely, its end flush with the outside surface of the plate. Then, with the auger, drill a hole well into the plate beneath. Peg each joist down. This will keep the walls from bowing out (*Plate 93*).

It would be possible to stop here, as we will do in *B,* and put the roof on. If you do, leave the ends of the plates flat on top rather than cutting slopes for the next log's dovetail notch. Also put the first and

PLATE 92 Two logs were hewed and lap-jointed together to make this plate. A wooden peg through the joint ensures that they will not slide apart.

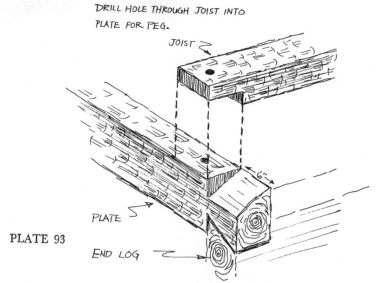

DRILL HOLE THROUGH JOIST INTO PLATE FOR PEG.

JOIST

6"

PLATE

PLATE 93

END LOG

last joists flush with the sides of the cabin rather than indenting six inches as in Plate 53.

Rather than stopping here, however, we recommend that you notch the ends of the plates completely and build the walls up at least another four feet thus making a loft which can be used either for storage or an extra room. A full second story can be added by building the walls up five to six feet above the plate (*Plate 94*).

The logs set immediately above each plate may have to be notched to accommodate each joist. This can be accomplished with a hand-saw, a chisel, and a mallet (*Plate 95*).

Hand hewn two-inch-thick boards can be set in place atop the joists as floor for the loft. Between two of the joists, leave a space five to six feet long open for a stairway or ladder from the downstairs (*Plate 96*).

PLATE 94   The loft in this building rises five feet above the joists. Note the inside wall in the foreground.

PLATE 95   In this building south of Franklin, North Carolina, the underside of the plate has been notched to accommodate each joist. Note the logs added above the plate to form a loft.

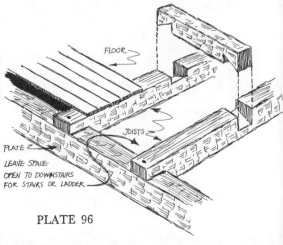

PLATE 96

B   As in *A,* cut two plates. Unlike the *B* sills, hew off the *B* plates completely. Leave no round sides. If you want a loft, cut a complete saddle notch in each end. If not, leave the top surface flat and notch only the underside of each end.

Cut joists as in *A.* Leave the joists round (unless you want a loft, in which case the top surfaces should be hewed off), and cut lap joints as in *A* to fit the plates. Set the joists in place, the first and last flush with the ends of the building, and peg only these two end joists and the center one to the plates (*Plates 97, 98*).

C   1. There are two other ways to notch the plate to hold the joists. In Plate 99, the top of the plate itself is notched for each. In Plate 100, both the plate and the next log are notched for the joists.

PLATE 98   Note how the joist (arrow) is left round except for the lap joint cut to fit the plate.

PLATE 97   The joists in Roy Thompson's cabin were lap-jointed to fit the plates. Note that the sleepers (bottom) and joists (top) are parallel.

PLATE 99 Top of plate can be notched (arrow) to hold joists.

PLATE 100 In the South Carolina reconstruction, both the plate and the log above it are notched to fit the joists.

2. The plate can be extended beyond the end wall to provide an overhang (*Plate 101*). An extra joist is not usually added on each end, however.

3. Instead of resting the joists on the plate's top surface, a cradle can be whittled out and pegged to the inside wall as in Plate 102.

4. Sometimes the plate is left completely round and the joists are cut about two feet longer than the building's actual width, round-notched, and fitted over the rounded top surface of the plate.

5. For a rough outdoor shed without walls, the plates and joists may be set in as in Plate 103. Here, the plate is held by forked logs driven into the ground, the joists are round-notched to fit the plate, and the lathing fits in round notches cut in the tops of the joists.

6. Some buildings have no joists at all. They simply consist of walls, rafters mounted on the last wall logs, and a roof.

7. If the house is large enough to have a middle sill, you may also want a middle plate. This extra plate is cut the length of the house, hewed off on top and bottom (or left round) and set in place resting on the same two end logs the plates rest on. The joists are notched on the underside to fit over the middle plate. Vertical support poles may then be fitted in from the top of the middle sill to the bottom of the middle plate (and from the top of the middle plate to the underside of the ridgepole. See below, *Plate 110*).

PLATE 101 Roy Thompson has extended his plates (between arrows) to support an overhang that will help protect the end of the cabin.

PLATE 102 The joists in this building rest in cradles pegged to the inside wall.

PLATE 103 A rough outdoor shed in the reconstructed pioneer settlement. The two plates are held by forked logs driven into the ground.

RAFTERS

A   The roofs of most of the houses we have seen have had substantial pitches—often as much as forty-five degrees. The reason for this is not because of heavy snows, but because roofs covered with hand-split shingles—as almost all of them were historically—had to have steep sides to repel water successfully and to last any length of time at all.

We recommend, to ensure the *A* cabin's authenticity, a hand-split shingle roof pitched at forty-five degrees. The rafters must be cut accordingly.

The last wall logs set in place should be the two across the ends of the house. Notch the top ends of both these logs as shown in Plates 104 and 105. If you elected not to have a loft, then you may either shape the two end joists in this manner, as well as all the other joists, or you may leave them flat on top. Just be sure you do the same thing to each joist, never allowing the top of one to be higher than the top of its neighbor. If you do, the rafters will not sit correctly.

If you *have* included a loft or second story, the rafters, spaced two to two and a half feet apart, are notched and set on the last log that runs the length of the building (*Plate 106*). This log should be pinned to the one below with pegs through the notches.

Cut the same number of rafters as joists. We recommend a one-foot overhang, so plan accordingly. Hew off all four sides (down to four to six inches square).

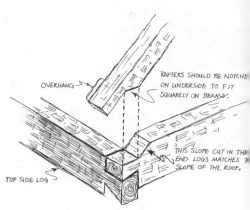

PLATE 104   The top of the last wall log can be notched to fit the rafter tightly. (See also Plate 105.)

PLATE 105

PLATE 106   The ends of these rafters are sloped and set directly on the last wall log. Note also the lathing for the roof.

Notch the peak ends as shown in Plate 107. Set them together at the correct angle flat on the ground. With the auger, drill a hole through the center of the peak and cut a peg to fit. Notch the bases of the rafters at the correct angle, leaving the proper amount of over-hang.

Then raise the rafters, a pair at a time, into place. As you go, drill and peg the base of each rafter to the wall log or joist on which it rests, and peg the peaks. Scrap boards nailed from rafter to rafter will hold them in place until you add the lathing, which will secure them permanently.

B   The rafters for B are simply poles six to eight inches in diameter notched in the underside to fit the plate. As seen in Plate 108, the ends are set beside the joist ends rather than on top of them (though you may put them on top if you wish), with the exception of the first and last pairs of rafters. In both these cases, the rafters must rest *on* either the end joists (if you have no loft,) or the ends of the last wall logs. Otherwise the gable will be slanted.

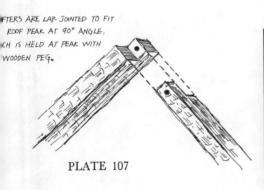

FTERS ARE LAP-JOINTED TO FIT
ROOF PEAK AT 90° ANGLE,
CH IS HELD AT PEAK WITH
WOODEN PEG.

PLATE 107

PLATE 108 The pole rafters of Thompson's log cabin are notched to fit over the plate and beside each joist.

The peak ends are cut at an angle so as to butt snugly up against a horizontal ridgepole as in Plate 109. Nail the peaks, and nail the ends of the rafters to the log on which they rest. Vertical supports may be added if desired (*Plate 110*).

PLATE 109   The peak ends of the rafters in Thompson's cabin butt up against and are nailed to a ridgepole.

PLATE 110   View of rafters, ridgepole, and vertical supports on Thompson's cabin.

C   1. "Windbeams" may be added to the rafters for extra stability. These run either horizontally about four feet below the peak (*Plate 111*), or as shown in Plate 112.

2. Another way to fasten the peaks is illustrated in Plate 113.

3. Some houses have no overhang at all. The bases of the rafters end at the horizontal support log (*Plates 114, 115*).

4. If a porch is desired, and it is necessary to use a different slope on the porch roof, here's one way it can be done:

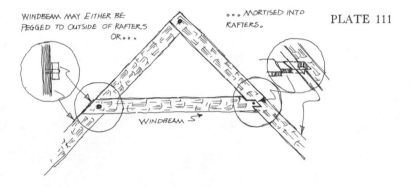

PLATE 112   Roy Thompson added the sloped supports visible here for additional strength.

Each porch rafter is set in place, one end sloped and fitted at the desired angle against each house rafter (*Plates 114, 115*), and the other on a horizontal support beam at the porch roof's edge. This horizontal beam is in turn supported by vertical poles (*Plate 142*).

The gap between the plate and the porch roof is filled by horizontal, split boards nailed against square vertical supports that lap around each porch rafter (*Plate 115*).

5. Rafters may be eliminated entirely by a special gable arrangement. See the *C* section on gables, for an explanation.

PLATE 114 Both house and porch rafters are visible here. The same scheme is diagramed in Plate 115.

PEAKS MAY BE
MORTISED AND
PEGGED.

PLATE 113

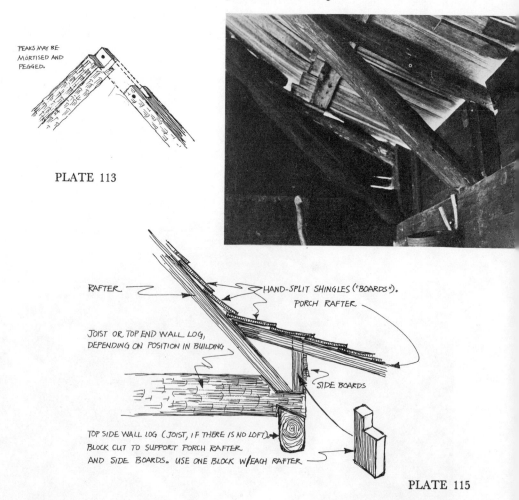

RAFTER

HAND-SPLIT SHINGLES ("BOARDS").

PORCH RAFTER

JOIST OR TOP END WALL LOG,
DEPENDING ON POSITION IN BUILDING

SIDE BOARDS

TOP SIDE WALL LOG (JOIST, IF THERE IS NO LOFT).
BLOCK CUT TO SUPPORT PORCH RAFTER
AND SIDE BOARDS. USE ONE BLOCK W/EACH RAFTER

PLATE 115

GABLES

A   Hand-hewn, four-inch-square beams are used as the vertical supports in the gables. These should be spaced two feet apart and run from the top of the end joists to the underside of the end rafters.

Cut the necessary number of beams allowing enough length (about three inches extra) to mortise the base of each into the end joist it rests on. Slope the end of each beam to fit the slope of the rafter it is joined to. If there is no window planned for the center of the gable, use a vertical support beam in the center, the top of which is cut to fit snugly into the underside of the peak itself (*Plate 116*). Nail the vertical supports in place at the top.

Duplicate the lathing style you chose for the roof in the gable end, nailing the lathing horizontally to the vertical beams. Cover the gable with hand-split shingles in either shingle fashion (*Plate 117*) or board fashion (*Plate 119*), depending on the style you choose for the roof.

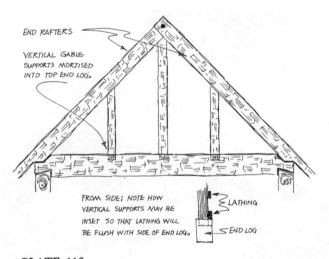

END RAFTERS

VERTICAL GABLE
SUPPORTS MORTISED
INTO TOP END LOG.

FROM SIDE; NOTE HOW
VERTICAL SUPPORTS MAY BE
INSET SO THAT LATHING WILL
BE FLUSH WITH SIDE OF END LOG.

LATHING

END LOG

PLATE 116

PLATE 117 A gable covered shingle fashion on a house near Franklin, North Carolina.

B   Use poles for the vertical supports (*Plate 118*), nailing them into place in the gable end. Space them two to two and a half feet apart.

On these supports, nail sawmill boards horizontally across the front, cutting each end to fit the rafter's slope. Start at the bottom and lap each new board over the last by about one-half inch (*Plates 119–121*).

PLATE 118 Poles can be used as the gable's vertical supports.

PLATE 119   A gable of sawmill boards on a hundred-year-old cabin on Wolf Fork Road in Rabun County. Note also the ends of the joists (arrows) and the typical absence of windows to conserve heat in winter.

PLATE 120 Richard Page and Robbie Letson examining a windowless house with a board gable. Arrow points to joist.

PLATE 121 From inside, center vertical support beam (arrow) for gable is visible. Note absence of ridgepole, and spacing of lathing for shingles.

C   1. Sometimes halved logs are nailed horizontally to the vertical supports; and sometimes vertically to horizontal lathing which is in turn nailed to vertical supports (*Plate 122*).

2. Sawmill planks or hand-hewn boards can be nailed vertically to horizontal lathing.

3. The gable can be designed to hold both windows *and* a door, if desired (*Plate 123*).

4. Several variations we have seen enable the roof to stand without joists or rafters (*Plates 124, 125*).

5. Variation 4 can be further altered to include rafters but no joists (*Plate 126*).

PLATE 123 The gable can be designed to hold a door and windows, as seen on this cabin at the Jay Hambidge Art Foundation in Rabun County.

PLATE 122 A gable of halved logs on the Jack Beasley property in Rabun County.

PLATE 124 This blacksmith shop in the reconstructed pioneer settlement has neither rafters nor joists. The gable logs support the pole lathing, as shown in Plate 125.

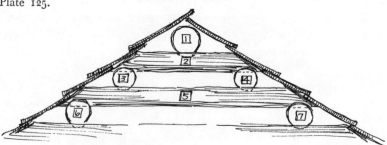

CUT ROUND NOTCHES IN *TOPS* OF LOGS. THUS: NOTCH TOP OF #2 TO HOLD #1; NOTCH TOPS OF #3 AND #4 TO HOLD #2; NOTCH TOP OF #5 TO HOLD #3 AND #4; AND SO ON. #2, #5 ETC. ARE GABLE LOGS; #1, #3, #4, #6, #7, ETC. ARE POLES RUNNING THE LENGTH OF THE BUILDING AND ACTING AS BOTH RAFTERS AND LATHING.

PLATE 125

PLATE 126 The Happ'n'so house has pole laths that are really only two feet long and serve only to help support the gable logs and the overhang. The house has a full set of pole rafters.

LATHING ● ROOF

A   Lathing for the *A* cabin may take one of two forms. Historically, if a water-powered sawmill existed in the area, enough one to two-inch thick planks were obtained to cover the entire roof. These planks were nailed side by side across the rafters with handmade nails (called "split" nails by the mountaineers).

If no sawmill existed in the area, one to two-inch thick lathing was split out of oak by hand and nailed across the rafters on two-foot centers, leaving sixteen to eighteen inches between each board. It was spaced in this manner to prevent the inescapable waste of wood that would have resulted from splitting out enough planks by hand to cover an entire roof.

Either variety you choose, therefore, will be authentic.

On top of this lathing, beginning at the bottom edge of the roof, nail hand-split shingles from which the sap has been trimmed. This sap, which is so soft that it will not stand much weathering, can be easily removed by standing the shingle on end, scoring the sap with an axe (as in the hewing process) and then splitting it off. Nail two shingles together, side by side, and then nail a third over the crack between them.

Each new row of shingles should overlap the last by four inches if you are covering your roof "shingle fashion" (*Plates 41, 86*); or by sixteen inches if you are covering it "board fashion." We have been unable to find any agreement as to which fashion is the most satisfactory. (*Plate 130* illustrates both techniques.)

At the peak, one row of shingles is allowed to overlap the other by about three inches (*Plates 41, 48*).

B   Sawmill lathing, set on two-foot centers, should be nailed to the pole rafters (*Plate 127*).

If you are able to obtain hand-split shingles, use them. If not, sawmill shingles may be used. Dip them in creosote before nailing them to the roof.

C   1. Sometimes the roof is constructed using both shingle and board fashions (*Plate 130*).

2. In place of shingles, we have seen cabins covered with tin, asbestos roofing, or tar paper.

3. Though we have not yet been able to find one, all of our informants have told us that "weight-on" roofs were common in these mountains. In this variation, shingles were held down on the roof by poles laid across them, parallel to the lathing. The two poles at either side of the peak were put on first, and they were tied together across the ends of the peak with hickory bark strips or hickory withes. Each succeeding pole was then tied to the one above it with the same material. The poles were spaced about two feet apart. Sometimes rocks were added for extra weight.

PLATE 127   Lathing (arrows) nailed on two-foot centers to pole rafters.

PLATE 128 Roy Thompson's cabin before . . .

PLATE 129 . . . and after shingles.

PLATE 130 Bill Lamb's barn illustrates both ways of affixing shingles. The style at the top of the roof is "shingle fashion," with four inches showing to the weather. The whole shingle is usually fourteen to eighteen inches long, so most of each shingle is covered by putting them on in this fashion. This makes the shingles last longer, which is why Bill used this style at the top of the barn.

The bottom half of the roof is covered "board fashion." The shingles themselves are cut to be about two feet long and you "lap it half way," exposing **eight to twelve inches to the weather.**

PLATE 131 This bear-proof hog pen in the reconstructed pioneer settlement has a solid, hewn log roof with the crack between the logs covered by planks.

4. Plate 131 shows yet another variation, but one not satisfactory for a house roof.

5. Sap was often left on the shingles instead of being trimmed off. The two sap sides would be laid together, side by side, and covered with the third shingle for protection.

WINDOWS ● DOORS

A   In many early cabins, there were few windows and doors due to the difficulty of heating during the harsh mountain winters (*Plates 119, 120*). In today's age of furnaces, however, this is not as great a problem. Thus, as we mentioned before, we will leave the number of windows and doors and their placement to you.

After the walls are up, choose the locations for your doors and windows. Allowing for the frames (each will be about two inches thick), outline the openings to be cut directly on the walls. Place wedges firmly between the wall logs just to the outside of the vertical lines you have drawn. These wedges will hold the logs level and in place after the openings are cut out.

Now with a small saw or an axe, cut out openings just to the inside of each vertical line and between two logs, big enough to accommodate the blade of your crosscut saw. With this saw, cut out the openings completely (*Plate 132*).

PLATE 132 The door opening on Thompson's cabin. Note the wedges between the logs to hold them up until the frames are added.

If the top or bottom boundaries of an opening fall *on* a log instead of between two logs, cut vertically into the log to the horizontal line. Then chisel out the remainder.

Now split out the boards for the frames. They should be two inches thick, six inches wide, and the necessary length. Dress them with a drawing knife and fit them into place.

With the large auger, drill holes through each framing board well into the center of the end of each wall log the frame touches (*Plate 133*). Cut the necessary number of locust pegs (*Plate 134*), and drive them into place in the holes you have just drilled. This will hold both the logs and the frames firmly in place (*Plate 135*). Remove the wedges between the logs.

Both windows and doors, to be authentic, should be made entirely of hand-hewn boards and hinged to the frames. Few people could afford glass for windows.

Cut hewn boards to length, place them side by side on the ground, and cut braces to fit them. Drill holes with a small auger through the braces into the boards. Peg them together. Then mount them to the walls with wrought-iron hinges (*Plate 136*).

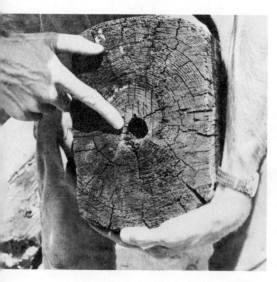

PLATE 133 A hole, drilled with an auger, into which the peg through the doorframe will fit.

PLATE 134 A locust peg over two hundred years old in the hole it was cut to fit.

PLATE 135 The peg (arrow) holding this door frame is still intact after one hundred fifty years.

PLATE 136 A wrought-iron hinge on the cabin in Plate 120.

B   Proceed as in *A,* cutting the necessary openings.

    We suggest sawmill planks for the frames, and doors, windows, and hinges purchased from your neighborhood hardware store.

C   1. We saw one house in which the windows were bordered on the outside with small poplar poles which had been quartered, cut to length, the ends slanted at forty-five degree angles, and nailed into place.

    2. Beyond this, the window and door styles varied greatly according to what the owner desired, how inventive he was, and what was available in local stores. The same, of course, would hold true today.

CHINKING ● PANELING

A   Set the inside paneling in place before chinking. This gives you
something to pack the chinking against from the outside.

If the outside walls have not yet been hewed off flush, do that now,
starting at the top. Use a scaffold if necessary.

Then shave off any high places so that the wall is as straight and
as smooth as possible. With the froe and mallet, split a quantity of
oak boards one to two inches thick and two to three feet long.
(We have heard of them being as long as six feet. Suit yourself.)
Dress what will be the outside surface with a drawing knife, and
then bevel the ends at a forty-five degree angle (*Plate 137*).

Nail the paneling on, with handmade nails if you can get them.

The chinking you use will depend on your location. In this area,
absolute authenticity will be guaranteed for the *A* cabin by the use
of pure red clay. Mix it with a small amount of water until it is
sticky and malleable, but not thin and watery. Then force it all the
way into the cracks between the logs. It should fill the entire opening
from the inside paneling out.

When you get to the outside edges of the wall logs, do not allow
the chinking to extend or bulge beyond the logs. Plate 138 shows why.

The original chinking used in houses near Columbia, South
Carolina, which lies in a geographically sandy belt, is thought to
have been one part red clay, one part lime, and one part sand—all
mixed with water as above.

B   For inside paneling, cut clapboards. These are usually the small
outside strips of wood left over after wall logs or long boards have
been split from larger logs. Today they can be easily obtained as
scrap from sawmills.

The clapboards should be nailed on horizontally on the inside
walls, covering only the gaps between the logs. If they are too wide
to use "as is," split them lengthwise (*Plate 139*). Remove the bark
and nail them into place.

Chink as in *A*, but use cement (*Plate 140*). Color it reddish for
effect if you wish.

C   1. A modern innovation is the nailing of two-by-fours to the
inside walls as braces, and then covering them with tongue and
groove boards from a sawmill. Insulation can be placed between the
inside logs and the inside paneling.

2. A variation we have seen includes chinking the logs, and then
nailing hand-split shingles to the outside walls (*Plate 141*). One can
also nail on board and batten siding.

PLATE 137

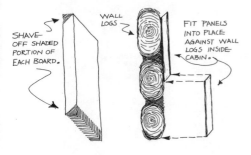

SHAVE OFF SHADED PORTION OF EACH BOARD.

WALL LOGS

FIT PANELS INTO PLACE AGAINST WALL LOGS INSIDE CABIN.

PLATE 138

RIGHT RAIN RUNS OVER CHINKING AND DOWN (ARROW); BOTH CRACKING AND CHIPPING OF CHINKING AND DECAY OF LOGS MINIMAL.

WRONG RAIN RUNNING DOWN SIDES GETS CAUGHT IN CHINKING AND RUNS UNDER LOGS ACCELERATING DECAY.

PLATE 139

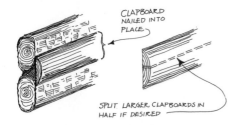

CLAPBOARD NAILED INTO PLACE

SPLIT LARGER CLAPBOARDS IN HALF IF DESIRED

PLATE 140 The house on Dog Mountain notched up by Thomas is chinked with cement.

PLATE 141 A house near Tallulah Falls, Georgia, covered with shingles.

3. Logs can be left round on the outside, hewn off approximately smooth on the inside for paneling, and then chinked.

4. It is also possible to quarter a small poplar log and chink the walls with these quarters, nailing them in place.

5. Pebbles and small rocks can be jammed into the wet clay or cement chinking to help hold the chinking in place.

6. We saw one cabin in which the outside walls were covered with shingle-sized pieces of bark nailed onto the logs.

A FINAL WORD

We don't want to give the impression that the majority of cabins built historically in this area were like either *A* or *B*. Most of them, in fact, were pretty crude structures built as quickly and as simply as possible. Setting wall logs level, for example, was done by sight rather than by levels. If a log looked right, that's the way it stayed. Round notches or extremely rough saddle notches were abundant; most of the structural logs were left round and bark-covered; the walls rarely intersected at right angles; windows rarely came out the same size; and little time was taken for cutting the intricate mortises and lap joints that a more skilled and careful builder would take the time to execute.

In fact, the only reason that most of the hundred-year-old cabins we see today resemble our *A* version is that the others have quietly disintegrated.

We have assumed that you want your cabin to last at least a lifetime, and so we have favored the *A* and *B* versions. Of course *A*, for the benefit of folklorists and historians, is the exception rather than the rule. It is the sort of building a craftsman like Harley Thomas would have built in this area either for himself or a well-paying client. The building techniques and designs given *were* used in this area, however. We verified this through both extensive interviews and personal exploration of still standing structures. It's just, as mentioned before, that they were used by craftsmen, and not by the majority of the mountain families who settled here.

The *B* cabin uses many of the historically accurate techniques of the *A* cabin; but, as you have seen, it also takes advantage of modern innovations such as easily obtainable sawmill planks, ready-made doors and windows, and cement. If you wish the *B* cabin to be as authentic as *A*, substitute techniques from that set of directions.

In any case, the best of luck to you as you use these plans. Let us know how it turns out. And if you run into problems with it, write. If we can't help, we'll try to find someone who can!

PLATE 142 And if you really get ambitious . . . This magnificent log building is part of the reconstructed pioneer settlement.

CHIMNEY BUILDING

An early cabin without a fireplace was a cabin without heat. So was a cabin with a fireplace that wouldn't "draw." Both meant a long, cold winter—or a smoky one.

Bill Lamb laughed as he talked about the first chimney he ever built. "It'd smoke a possum out'a th' house. I bet you could'a built a fire in th' *top* of it and it wouldn't of drawn. The only way that chimney would draw was *down*. The children'ud just run from it cryin' an' hollerin' when a puff'a wind come up. It'd fill th' whole house with smoke."

Building a chimney was not an easy job. If the throat wasn't exactly correct, the situation Bill described was the result. If the foundation wasn't set deep and firmly enough in the ground, the whole thing might tilt crazily away from the house. Aunt Arie often tells of the time she heard a great crash and ran into the living room to find their whole chimney lying flat in the bean patch, and a gaping hole in their wall. Others tell of struggles to bring a tilting chimney back into line—struggles that included digging under the backside of the foundation, keeping water in the hole for three or four days, and hoping it would tilt back.

Sometimes they caught fire, or a hard rain washed out some of the chinking and collapsed them. Bees often riddled the early mud

PLATE 143   A simple rock chimney chinked with red clay on a house near Toccoa, Georgia.

PLATE 144   A common problem with all-mud chinking was that it soon became the home for bees as the holes in this chinking show.

PLATE 145 A stick and mud chimney on a cabin near Highlands, North Carolina. Sticks were used only above the firebox which was of rock.

chinking with holes in which they lived. Claude Darnell can remember passing chimneys and seeing smoke pouring from a hundred perforations in the chinking.

The earliest, simplest chimneys were of creek rocks or fieldstones and red mud mortar up past the throat. Above that, wooden slats about four inches wide and finger thickness were laid on log-cabin fashion and chinked with clay so that only the wooden corners were visible from the outside. Called stick-and-mud chimneys, they were relatively easy to build, but short-lived. Few survive in our area, though many remember seeing them (*Plate 145*).

The more stable alternative (many of which survive today) was the all rock-and-mud variety (*Plate 143*).

The chinking itself was mixed in an innumerable number of ways, but usually the same way in which the owner had chinked the logs in his cabin. Sometimes the best, stiff, smooth, pure red clay was used alone, mixed only with a little water until it was about the consistency of almost-hard cement. The heat from the fires inside would bake it into hard pottery. Others, unable to find the clay that could be used alone, slaked their own lime (by letting unslaked lime boil itself out in water) and added three shovelfuls of slaked lime to every hundred pounds of clay—a trick that made the clay "set-up" harder.

To their clay, others added any of a number of things: the chaff from wheat, rye or barley, which made it set-up hard more quickly; any kind of animal or human hair; cut-up rope; hog blood; or, even one shovelful of cement for every ten shovels of clay.

No matter how you made your chimney, the trick of course was to make it draw. The almost universal solution, as shown in the following diagrams, was to make sure of two things. (*1*) The throat could be any size as long as the space behind and above it (the "scotchback") was larger. (*2*) The chimney should close down near the top to approximately the same dimensions as the throat. The top dimensions could be a little larger than the throat, but they should *never* be smaller. If they were, the chimney would be choked and would smoke.

As long as these rules were followed, almost any design or elaboration could be employed within the chimney. It could twist, slope, slant, or bulge inside; have a ledge or depression behind the throat to catch ashes or water or other solid matter that might come down the chimney; anything so long as it wasn't choked.

The following diagrams represent the four major styles of chimneys we have found in the many old ones we have tried to measure.

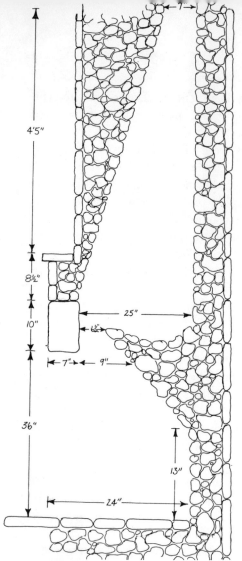

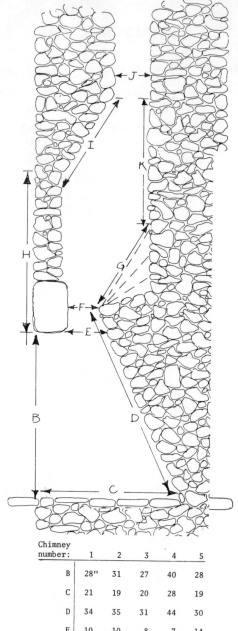

The above chimney, seen from the side, was built by Claude Darnell for the mill on Mrs. Jay Hambidge's property on Betty's Creek Road.

The design of the area above the throat (the 6 1/2" space) is unique in our experience. The chimney draws perfectly, however. The depression behind the throat was designed to catch any foreign matter that might fall down from above.

Wooden forms inside the chimney held the stone and mortar in place as it was being built. They were removed after the mortar had set up.

The following three diagrams show the three most common chimney styles we have found in this area. The charts below each of them give measurements we took from actual example of each style. The letters in the charts refer to the letters in the diagrams themselves. The dotted lines in each diagram reveal other workable design possibilities.

Chimney number:	1	2	3	4	5
B	28"	31	27	40	28
C	21	19	20	28	19
D	34	35	31	44	30
E	10	10	8	7	14
F	8	8	6	6	9
G	27	10	16	19	28
H	15	14	20		28
estimated:					
I	34	13	30		
J	10	8	10		
K		12	28		

PLATE 146

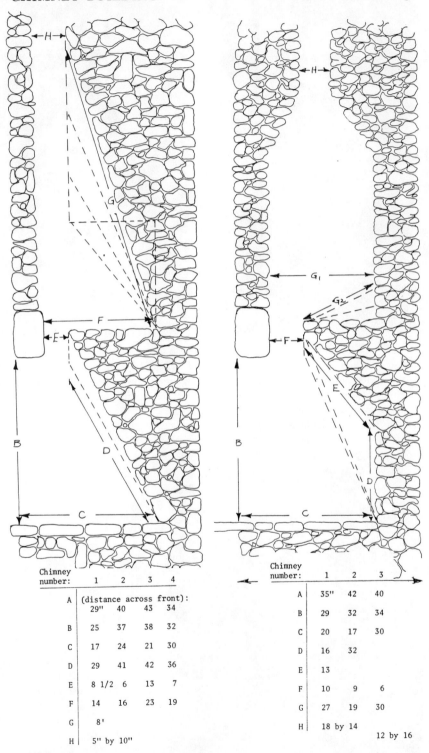

Chimney number:	1	2	3	4
A	(distance across front):			
	29"	40	43	34
B	25	37	38	32
C	17	24	21	30
D	29	41	42	36
E	8 1/2	6	13	7
F	14	16	23	19
G	8'			
H	5" by 10"			

Chimney number:	1	2	3
A	35"	42	40
B	29	32	34
C	20	17	30
D	16	32	
E	13		
F	10	9	6
G	27	19	30
H	18 by 14		
			12 by 16

PLATE 147

PLATE 148 Claude Darnell, a master chimney builder, often faces his chimneys with flagstone. The flagstone is cemented in place a round at a time, and the box thus created is filled with a "stuffing" of creek rocks and cement.

PLATE 149 Often the flagstones must be reshaped to fit. Claude measures the hole to be filled and then breaks the excess away with a hammer.

PLATE 150 Another example of Claude Darnell's work. This masterpiece, a flue for a furnace, is on the weaving shed at the Jay Hambidge Art Foundation in Rabun Gap, Georgia.

WHITE OAK SPLITS

"**S**plits" were traditionally used in the mountains for both bottoming chairs and making a variety of baskets. Lon Reid and Daniel Manous showed us how to make them so we could preserve the process on film. And the splits thus made were not wasted; we divided them up between Beulah Perry and Aunt Arie and, while we watched, each of them made a basket. Beulah's was of the large, cotton picking variety, and Aunt Arie's was a smaller one with a handle—a basket that had a hundred uses around the early farm. Both baskets now sit proudly in our office, and the photographs we took as they made them—and full directions —appear in the next chapter.

In making splits, the proper selection of timber is crucial. The tree should be a white oak sapling four to six inches in diameter. Its trunk should be absolutely straight, untwisted (check the bark lines), and unmarred by limbs, knots, or imperfections for at least seven feet. A six to nine-foot section of perfect trunk is the only piece used.

The split makers have several additional tricks for selecting the tree. Most look only in dark, moist coves on the north sides of hills and on the lower slopes, where the trees are supposedly of finer grain. If the trees are on high ground, and have shot up too tall and slim too fast, they tend to be "brash" or brittle, and hard to work.

Others check the bark carefully by rubbing their palms against it.

If it is slightly crumbly and soft to the touch, it will usually make good splits. If it is rough, jagged, and hard to the touch, the tree tends to be brash. Dan's father gave him another pointer—if the limbs of the tree droop, let it stand.

Nearly every man with whom we spoke worked his timber on the day he cut it, before it had had a chance to dry out. If he couldn't get to it the same day, he'd throw it in a nearby stream to keep it wet until he could get back to it. Most of them also gathered the timber in late summer or fall to minimize shrinkage and splitting as the splits dried. Bill Lamb, however, claims he's had better luck in the winter with a tree near water whose leaves are still clinging to the branches.

Anyway, here's how it's done.

PLATE 151 Lon Reid begins at the small end of the trunk and halves it using a mallet and froe. The butt of the tree is wedged to keep it from kicking out from under him. As the initial crack widens, he drives a wooden glut into it thus widening it even further. A second glut is driven into the crack still further down the trunk, and when the first falls out, it is driven into the crack beyond the second and so on, leapfrogging the gluts, until the trunk falls in half. Using the same process, the trunk is then split into quarters.

PLATE 152 Using the froe, the heartwood is split off each quarter, and then the bark is shaved off using either an axe, a knife, or the shaving horse and drawing knife.

PLATE 153 Now each quarter is halved thus converting the original trunk into eighths. Lon prefers using the steel wedge in this phase as its edge is sharper than that of the glut.

PLATE 154 The actual process of making the splits now begins. Beginning at the butt end of one of the prepared eighths, split it exactly in half *parallel* to the grain of the wood, or "bastard fashion." Some split them off perpendicular to the grain ("board fashion"), but most prefer Lon's method. The split can be started by driving a pocket knife blade into the bolt with a piece of scrap wood.

PLATE 155 As soon as you can get your fingers into the split, slowly work the two halves apart.

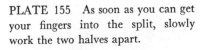

PLATE 156 Continue in this same fashion with each succeeding slice until the splits are the desired thickness.

PLATE 157 If one edge binds or catches while the splits are being pulled apart, it can be freed using the knife.

PLATE 158 Daniel Manous, who can both bottom chairs and weave large baskets out of splits he makes himself, demonstrates how to bring the split back into line if it starts to "run out" on one side. Here, the split in his right hand has started to tear off too early. He pulls hard on the *opposite* side to bring it back into line.

The finished splits can be "dressed" if desired. Lon does this by placing the end of the split flat on his knee, pressing down on top of it with a knife blade held at right angles to the split, and then, with his free hand, pulling the split through this clamp. The steady pressure exerted by the knife blade will shave off any rough places. When one side is dressed, the split is turned over and the process repeated.

MAKING A HAMPER OUT OF WHITE OAK SPLITS

S itting on her front porch hammering away at the heavy white oak ribs, Beulah Perry looked as if she had been making baskets for a long time. Actually she had never made one before, but after years of watching her father, she knew just how to do it.

Even though I had known Beulah for over a year, she still amazed me with all her knowledge of the old times, and with her stories of how she and her family lived before there were stores in which to buy canned foods, cloth, and electric lamps.

Like many of the other people we interviewed, Beulah knows what it was like to have her closest neighbors five miles away, to have a cooked possum head as a reward for being good, and to get maybe a stick of peppermint when her father had a few extra pennies.

Her house is spotless. While she was showing us how to make the basket, she served us coffee and cake. Each person had a china cup and saucer—all different. When Jan and I helped her do the dishes afterwards, we were afraid she would think us bad housekeepers if we left anything undone and scrubbed the sink and cabinets with Comet. We were sure she did it every time!

I've learned tremendous respect for Beulah and all the others who shared similar hardships, if you can call them hardships at all. Their world certainly contrasts sharply with ours of TV, cars, and mothers who do all the work. We can't go back now, but we can listen to what they have to say and learn from it. That's one reason why we asked Beulah Perry to show us how to make a basket.

MARY GARTH

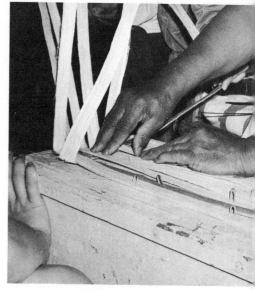

PLATE 159 The hamper requires twenty-four heavy ribs, each about an inch wide. Crease each rib, while green, in two places, thus dividing it into three sections, each twenty-two inches long. Here Beulah creases one rib. All knots and rough places should be hammered out so they will not interfere with the weaving.

PLATE 160 Now the bottom of the basket is woven, using the ribs. The first ribs may be tacked down to help hold them in place until enough have been added so that the basket will stand alone.

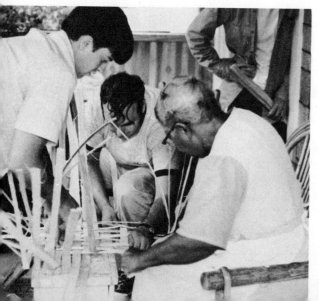

PLATE 161 Continue adding ribs, weaving the center section of each in an over one/under one pattern until . . .

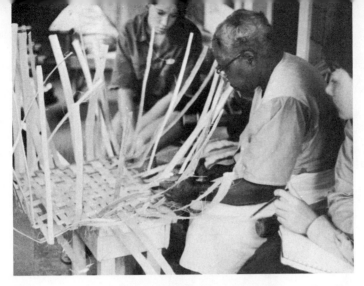

PLATE 162 . . . there are twelve ribs going in each direction, their center sections woven to form the basket's bottom.

PLATE 163 Now, beginning at the bottom of the basket, and using thin, pliable splits, weave in and out of the ribs to make the sides. Keep the splits close together and fairly tight so that the sides will stand firm when the basket is done.

PLATE 164   Continue weaving until the top is reached. This will take nearly all the splits you can make from two good oak saplings. When the end of one split is reached, simply lap a new one over the end of the old by about two inches and continue as before.

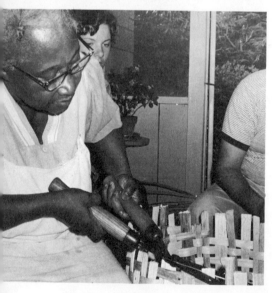

PLATE 165   At the top, the ends of the ribs will probably be uneven. Before the rim can be made, these must be trimmed off straight. This can be done with a knife or, as shown here, with a pair of hedge clippers.

PLATE 166   At the top, take two more splits and line the inside top edge with one and the outside top edge with the other. Holding them tightly in place, wrap a cord or a thin narrow split around them to make a good, tight rim. A handhole can be cut in either side, just under the rim, if you wish.

MAKING A BASKET OUT OF WHITE OAK SPLITS

"I've been a'hopin' and a'hopin' I'd have company today. That just shows you if you wish and want somethin' bad enough, God'll usually bless y'with it." With a delighted look on her wrinkled face, Aunt Arie greeted us early one hot summer day.

I first met Aunt Arie in June. My immediate reaction was one of shock. How could such a tiny, delicate woman, eighty-five years old maintain her own garden, do all her cooking and cleaning, make quilts every winter for her family and friends, and still manage to survive without luxuries? I didn't wonder long. During the day, as Aunt Arie patiently taught us how to make white oak split baskets, I realized why Mike and Paul spoke of her with such affection. She is, to put it simply, just plain good. She is full of vitality and determination, and she radiates a warmth that few people have. Aunt Arie is really hard to explain. She's downright likable and fun.

While we were making the basket, Aunt Arie talked of her childhood. Her eyes sparkled as she told us how she used to carry corn and eggs for miles in baskets like the one we were making.

At noon, she cooked dinner for us. Mary and I tried to help, but with an old wooden stove, black iron kettles, water drawn from the well, and general inexperience, we could do little more than watch Aunt Arie hustle about laughing gently at our mistakes.

With people like Aunt Arie and Beulah Perry, this work has been very rewarding for me. I've learned not only the skills required to make baskets, but also the value of sincere friendliness, honesty, and hard work—and that may be the most important lesson of all.

JAN BROWN

PLATE 167 Tommy Wilson and Butch Darnell begin by whittling ten ribs for the basket out of heavy, quarter-inch thick splits. The ribs should be about a half inch wide, pointed on both ends, and long enough to reach around half of the basket.

PLATE 168 Next, construct two hoops of approximately equal circumference out of four- to seven-foot heavy splits, depending on the size of the basket you want. Place one inside the other and nail them together at their intersecting points.

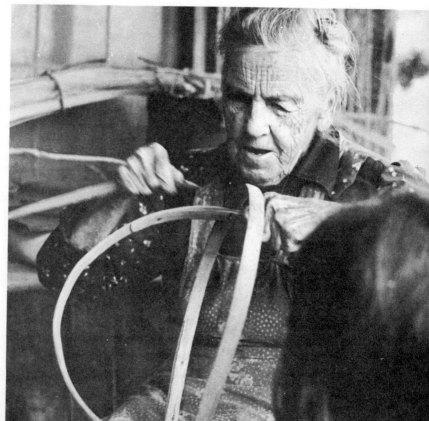

PLATE 169 The weaving is done with thin green splits. It is a simple repeating pattern, as shown here. Work from both hoop intersection points simultaneously so your weaving will meet in the middle of the basket (see Plates 177 and 178).

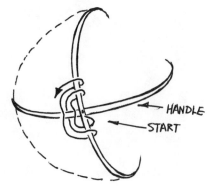

PLATE 170 The weaving begins where the hoops intersect. The following two plates illustrate the first few steps.

PLATE 171

PLATE 172

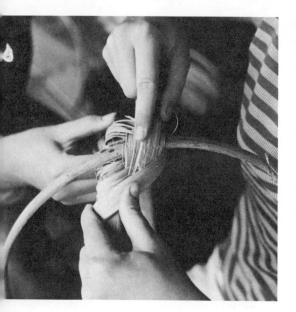

PLATE 173 When one split runs out, tuck in its end, insert the point of another into the weave, and continue.

PLATE 174 When the weaving is progressing well at both hoop intersection points, insert the first two ribs. Simply force their sharpened ends into the weave.

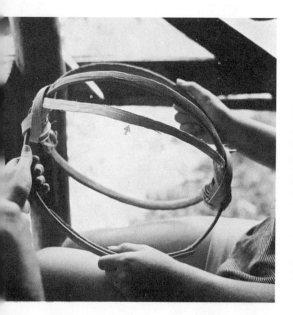

PLATE 175 The first rib in place (arrow).

PLATE 176 Continue weaving as before . .

PLATE 177 . . . inserting ribs until there are five on either side of and parallel to the main hoop.

PLATE 178 Here, the basket is well over half completed. All the ribs have been worked in.

PLATE 179 The finished product.

AN OLD CHAIR MAKER SHOWS HOW

This summer, while doing some research in the mountains thirty-five miles west of Rabun Gap, we received an intriguing lead. It seemed that near the place we were standing a trail began that led several miles up into the backwoods. We were told that at the end of the trail lived an old, reticent mountaineer named Lon Reid who almost never came out, and who, aside from being almost completely self-sufficient, still kept a number of ancient bee gums filled with active swarms of honey bees. We might make it, our informer continued, with our jeep; but those few people who cared to try to talk with him usually walked the miles in and out.

We found the trail. It was marked with a crudely lettered sign which read, "Beware of Bees." At that point, however, we ran out of time and left, determined to return. Recently, we did.

A rough, mountainous jeep track led six miles away from such civilization as a tiny country store represented. It ended far up on a mountain at a rough-hewn home surrounded by small outbuildings built of logs and poles and the shells of automobiles, evidently done in by the road we had just battled. On the front porch of the house, we were met by three curious children, their father, and two stooped old gentlemen—one of whom proved, indeed, to keep bees.

That was the first of many visits to a family that has since been added to our list of invaluable contacts. Not only did Lon keep bees, but he also crafted chairs completely by hand, carved crow and turkey calls, and, as he warmed to us, proved to be so full of stories and information that we could have filled several issues of the magazine with all he told us. This chapter, however, is limited to a set of instructions for making a chair, just as he learned from his father. The only difference in their techniques is that his father used a hand-turned lathe to round his posts and rungs, and he uses a shaving horse instead.

Plate 180 shows a finished frame. It consists of two long posts, two short posts, eight short rounds, three long rounds, and three back pieces ("backs").

PLATE 180 Lon Reid with the finished frame for one of his tall-backed chairs.

Suitable woods for the job include oak, maple, and ash. For the chair in Plate 180, the posts and backs were made of maple, and the rounds were made of white oak. The seat will be of white oak splits. The best time to gather the timber is during the fall and winter, when the sap is down. This will minimize warping. The pieces are usually shaped while green, and then set aside to season before assembly to prevent splitting.

Choose a tall maple, the trunk of which is about eight inches in diameter and slightly curved. This curve will produce the curved back. If you would rather the back be straight, choose your maple accordingly.

Saw a 42″ length out of the curved section of the trunk for the back posts, a 20″ length out of the straight section for the front posts, and a 16″ length out of the straight section for the backs.

At the same time, choose a tall, straight-grained white oak 4″–6″ in diameter. From the trunk, cut one 16″ length, two 14″ lengths, and save the rest for splits.

Quarter the maple sections to be used for posts. Split out the

PLATE 181   Lon smooths and trims the backs for his chairs using a drawing knife and a shaving horse. Merle, his brother's grandson, watches.

PLATE 182   While still green, the backs can be given a slight curve by bending them as shown.

PLATE 183 Sandra, Merle, and Donnie, all grandchildren of his brother, sometimes help out. Here Donnie drives a wedge between the chair leg and post to hold the legs in place for working.

PLATE 184 With Donnie holding the measuring stick, Lon marks the locations for the rounds on each leg.

heart. Then round the quarters off using first an axe and then the shaving horse.

Split the 16″ length into boards. Smooth and trim them on the shaving horse (*Plate 181*). For those customers who wanted their chairs to have curved backs, our craftsman's father would boil the backs in water for ten or fifteen minutes and then wedge them in a brace overnight. Now, the process has been simplified, as shown in Plate 182.

The sections to be used for rounds are now quartered, hewn, and shaved as with the posts.

Now move the pieces to the workbench. The bench, shown in the photographs, is a flat platform 7′1½″ long and 19″ wide. Four pegs have been driven into the top center. They mark the corners of an imaginary rectangle 1′1½″ long by 7″ wide.

Mount the two long posts on their sides (they should curve away from each other as shown in Plate 183) between the pegs. Drive a wedge between one leg and one of the pegs (*Plate 183*) to hold them firmly in place.

Mark the spots where holes for the rounds will be drilled. The center of the first round is 7″ off the ground; the second (or "seat round") is 17″. Put marks at these two points on each back leg's side

(*Plate 184*). At each of these four points, drill a ¾" hole 1" deep (*Plate 185*).

Now while the two long posts are still in place, mark the locations of the slots into which the three back pieces will fit. With a hammer and chisel, make a hole ¾" deep at the top and bottom of each slot's position (*Plate 186*).

Now, using the side of the chisel as a straightedge, connect the pairs of holes. This outlines each slot (*Plate 187*).

Using a knife blade and hammer and chisel, cut out the excess (*Plate 188*), thus leaving three slots in each leg for the back pieces.

The end of each back piece, before insertion, should be cut to fit its proper slot, notching the top edge (*arrows, Plate 189*). In terms of design, the effect of this is quite pleasing.

Turn the long legs over so that their front sides are up. Drill holes 8", 13", and 18" above each leg's base. These six holes will hold the side rounds of the chair. Do *not* drill the holes at right angles to those drilled previously, but at an angle which more

PLATE 185 Holes for the chair rounds are drilled while the legs are still pinned to the workbench.

PLATE 186 A hammer and chisel are used to begin the slot that will hold one of the backs.

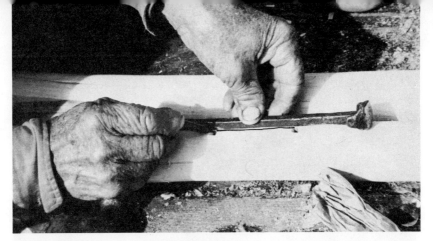

PLATE 187 With the ends of each slot marked, the sides are drawn . . .

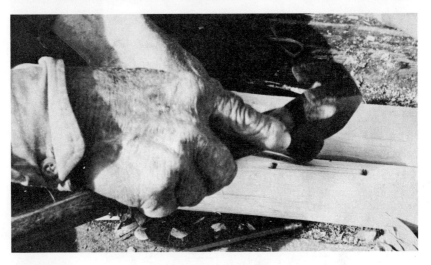

PLATE 188 . . . and cut out with a knife blade and hammer.

PLATE 189 The backs fit snugly into the slots just cut for them. Lon shapes the top corners (arrows) for decoration.

PLATE 190   The short legs are now marked for the placement of rounds.

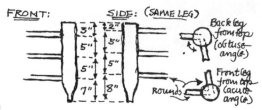

PLATE 191

closely approximates ninety-five degrees. The purpose of this is to splay the side rounds out slightly thus making the front of the chair wider than the back.

Removing the long legs from the bench, replace them with the shorter front legs. Again, with the measuring stick, mark those places where holes for the rungs are to be drilled (*Plates 190, 191*). Again do not drill the holes at right angles to each other, but drill those at the back of the short legs at about an eighty-five degree angle to those at the sides.

From the seasoned rounds, select eight 14" ones and three 16" ones. Cut one inch off each. With a pocket knife, trim down the ends of each so that they will not quite fit the holes you have cut in the legs for them. For this, you might want to make yourself a gauge such as the one in Plate 192. This gauge does three jobs at once:

1. (*Plate 193*) It shows how far into the leg each round will sink. It is this much of each round that must be worked.

2. (*Plate 194*) It indicates whether or not the top and bottom surfaces of the rounds are ready. The top and bottom of each should fit this pattern exactly. The sides, on the other hand, should be flattened off so that the round will press up and down in the leg. If allowed to press sideways, it may split the grain open.

3. (*Plate 195*) It provides a sample hole that duplicates the ones cut in the chair legs. Each round's end, as shown here, should not quite fit this hole on top and bottom. The fit should look somewhat like this:

PLATE 192 This gauge helps shape the ends of the rounds in three ways. It . . .

PLATE 193 . . . shows how far into the leg a round will sink, . . .

PLATE 194 . . . shows whether the top and bottom are rounded correctly or not, and . . .

PLATE 195 . . . gives a duplicate of the hole the round must fit.

The chair is now ready to assemble. Force the side rounds into place first; then force the three front rounds into place. Then add the two back rounds and the three backs all at once. Remember that the three longest rounds go into the front of the chair, and the short ones go at the sides and back.

Turning the chair on its back, drill ¼″ holes from the front through the upright posts into the ends of each back. One hole per end should be enough. Whittle pegs to fit these holes, force them in, and whittle the ends off flush. The pegs will hold the backs in place permanently.

Now, if you wish, you may taper the base of each leg, and the tops of the long posts, using a penknife. Then weave the seat using either white oak splits, cane, strips of hickory bark, or rope made of plaited corn shucks.

To weave a seat of white oak splits, first soak the splits in water for about a half hour to make them more pliable. This will also cause them to tighten on the chair frame as they dry, producing a good tight seat.

Begin at the underside of the frame. A satisfactory way to start is to drive a small nail or tack through the end of the first split (*Plate 197*). In the same plate, the solid line indicates that the split is passing under the bottom of the frame; the dotted line indicates that it is passing over the top. Wrap the entire frame in this manner keeping the edges of the splits close together. When the frame is wrapped, do not stop but simply go around the leg on the underside of the frame (*steps 7–8 in Plate 197*) and begin weaving. Weave on both top and bottom.

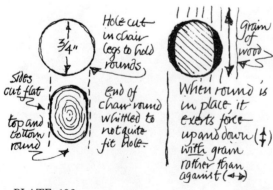

PLATE 196

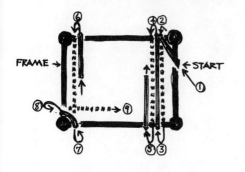

PLATE 197

PLATE 198

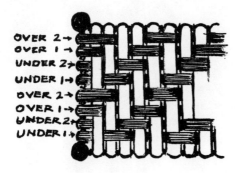

OVER 2 →
OVER 1 →
UNDER 2 →
UNDER 1 →
OVER 2 →
OVER 1 →
UNDER 2 →
UNDER 1 →

PLATE 199

At the end of each split, do not stop but simply notch the old and new splits as shown in Plate 198, tie them together, and go on.

The standard weave used is the herringbone pattern (*Plate 199*). In this plate, the splits that go from left to right have been darkened to make them easier to follow. The white splits are the ones with which the frame was originally wrapped. Pass over two splits, then under two as shown in the plate. The "twill" effect is produced by the alternation at the edges, also shown. This is called "breaking one" each time.

When the weaving is completed, either tie the end of the last split to the frame, or tack it to the frame as you did at the beginning.

It's hard to leave at the end of an interview like this one. One is tempted to stay a moment longer, wondering at the fact that here, in December of 1969, men still live as this one does, oblivious to the fact that others are bouncing about the moon.

The Twentieth Century is here, bellowing like a bull; but in quieter coves, families still make do with what they have—or do without.

It's a big country, ours is.

PLATE 200 "Take this one with you now if you want. I believe it's a good chair now."

ROPE, STRAW, AND FEATHERS
ARE TO SLEEP ON

T he early settlers in this area brought no springs, beds, or mattresses along. Forced to improvise, they made their own. Here is how it was done, largely in the words of those who did it, with several plans that include instructions, pictures, and diagrams in case you care to build your own.

The earliest mattresses were simply bed-sized cloth sacks filled with straw or feathers. These were laid over a rope netting that was attached to a simple, four-sided frame with legs. A full description of one of these "rope beds" is included in this article. For now, however, we let the people tell their own story.

❖MRS. ALGIE NORTON: "They made straw beds back then out a' rye straw. Then you raised ducks and picked 'em and made feather beds and pillers if y'had any. If you got hold'a enough sheeting or somethin', you sewed up your tick, and then when y'thrashed rye, you hauled it or went to th'stacks and filled your ticks up and carried them back—or whatever you wanted to do. A tick, well, you know it's just like a mattress only you filled it with straw. I never seen a mattress 'til I's grown.

"So we made our straw beds and feather beds, and they didn't have any springs or anything back in th'early part of my life—no such things. And I can remember seeing th'corded bedsteads and homemade bedsteads. You'd bore th'holes in th'side boards (they's about four inches square) and y'got'a rope if y'could get such a thing back then, and run it through in squares. It was as good as springs—or about—but it would sag in th'middle. You ran it [the rope] both ways somethin' like them porch chairs you see; only y'left it a little further apart."

❖ MRS. PEARL MARTIN: "I've got two feather beds and a straw bed. I'm goin't'keep that straw bed as long as I live. I take an' empty my straw out and sun it and put it back in, and it's just as clean and pretty as it ever were, you know. 'Course nobody don't lay on it only just now and then. I've got a mattress on top of it, y'know.

"We used t', when we's a'comin'up children—you see, they'd cut and thresh their wheat and rye ever'year. Well, y'see we'd fill our beds up ever'year. Ever'year. And now, since they've quit that, why I had one full and I just kep' it. Just sun it and wash th'tick'n'things, and it's just as good as it ever was. I'm keepin' it for a keepsake. I don't have to use it at all, but I just want t'keep it. And I've got two feather beds. I've got one from m'momma, and Oscar's got one from his momma. So we just swing along."

❖ MRS. GATHA NICHOLS: "She [her mother] had ducks and geese, plenty of them. Y'see, she'd set them and raise them, y'see, and she'd pick them ducks and geese and make feather beds and pillers. I've got some pillers and feather beds now that she give me when I married."

❖ MRS. HARRIET ECHOLS: "My mother had one [a rope bed], and.I helped her. We would take th'roping out and wash it in th' spring. You know how people clean house. And back then they would take th'roping out every spring and boil'em and wash'em and I helped my mother several times t'fix it back. But I don't have this any more. I don't know what become of it. They called it corded bed at that time. But for years after I grew up, she kept it; but I don't know where it is at or what become of it."

ROPE BED

The rope bed was once the only bed to be found in this area. Due to "good times" and antique collectors, we could find only one in our region that was in good enough shape to study seriously, and that was Aunt Arie's.

One Sunday afternoon, five of us piled in the jeep and pushed far into the mountains south of Franklin, North Carolina. One of our company was Aunt Arie's great-niece, but the rest of us had never met her and didn't quite know how she would react when we piled in and asked to look at the bed. But this warm, friendly, elderly lady, who had stayed home that afternoon because she said she had sensed that someone was coming for a visit, was delighted.

When we asked about the bed, she took us into a small room in the back of her home. Cooperating in every way, she let us take the straw mattresses off so that we could see precisely how the rope was threaded through the frame (*Plate 201*). Here's all you'll need to do to build one similar to hers:

Build a frame with four end posts and four side pieces to the dimensions you need. Bore a row of holes through the side pieces, spacing them nine to ten inches apart. They should be directly opposite each other on the paired sides.

Now you are ready to begin the actual rope weaving. Begin at the headboard and string the bed lengthwise as shown in the diagram. When the last hole in the headboard is filled, bring the rope around the bedpost to the first hole on the side of the bed and begin the over/under weaving as shown in Plate 202. When the last hole is filled, loop the end of the rope around the sideboard and tie it securely to one of the laced ropes.

The straw mattress can be laid directly on the ropes. No further support is needed. "I slept on straw ticks all my life," said Mrs. Lester Norton. "Best sweet smellin' bed you ever slept on. We changed th' straw every year at threshin' time."

PLATE 202

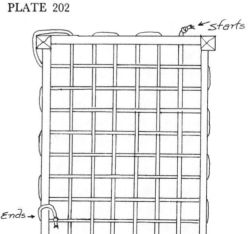

PLATE 201 A rope or "corded" bed in Aunt Arie's house. A shuck mattress fits on top of the ropes, which are woven through holes drilled in the frame of the bed.

A QUILT IS SOMETHING HUMAN

The local Harvest Festival in the fall of 1969 provided ample proof that the interest in quilts has swelled. So teams of *Foxfire* editors began to gather the necessary facts. They attended quilting bees, copied patterns from quilts that had been hidden in trunks and attics for years, and, at the last minute, turned up the most elaborate Friendship Quilt any of us had ever seen (*Plate 203*).

Originally the plan was to find all those patterns that were native to this county. That soon proved to be impossible, for quilt patterns were like ballads—they moved constantly from community to community over surprisingly great distances. Media such as farmers' journals, newspaper columns, and even quilt pattern companies spread them farther. Even more complicating is the fact that patterns which were carried from the East with the first settlers in these mountains have been around so long that many of the owners consider them Rabun Gap patterns, which of course they are not. Worse, we have at least one pattern in hand that is known by at least three different names, and no one even guesses at where *it* came from.

At last it became obvious that the only solution was to include a sizable sampling of patterns from quilts that had been made in Rabun county by the mothers of grandmothers alive here now. And that's what we've done. Each of the twelve patterns drawn for this chapter by *Foxfire*'s Bill Roland has been known in this county for at least

PLATE 203 This Friendship Quilt held by Mary Garth and Frenda Wilborn
is nearly a hundred years old and bears fifty-five names.

seventy-five years. We have not included some others that are equally authentic but are readily available in any of the numerous books on quilting patterns. These patterns include Wedding Ring, Double Wedding Ring, Attic Window, Monkey Wrench, Drunkard's Path, Dutch Doll (or Little Dutch Boy, Little Dutch Girl, etc.), Gate Latch, Four Doves at the Well, Double T, Lonely Star, Trip around the Mountain, Rocky Road, Basket, Nine Diamonds, and Odd Fellows.

But why the dramatic revival of interest? One explanation might be the statement made recently by Mrs. Claude Darnell: "They's lots of people that wants to go back to th' old times." That, perhaps, but more. The simple fact is that quilts were handmade by people for people. Every phase of their production was permeated by giving and sharing. From the trading of scraps and patterns and the actual production in "bees" to the giving away of the final finished work, quilting was an essentially human activity. There is something about a quilt that says people, friendship, community, family, home, and love.

Aside from the quilting bees themselves, many customs and beliefs grew up around them. They were passed around, shown off, and given away. Patterns were traded like bubble gum cards. Especially beautiful ones became widely known. For example, Mrs. Grover Bradley told us in a recent interview, "Aunt Bede Norton had a basket pattern—just as pretty a basket as you ever saw; handle and all!" Grandmothers made at least one for each of their grandchildren to keep, and then pass on (*Plate 204*). A belief grew up that, "If a young girl slept under a new quilt, she would dream of th' boy she was going to marry." And especially fines ones were used to cover the bed on Sundays ("Sunday Quilts") and when company came. But by all counts, the most attractive custom must be that of the Friendship Quilt, discussed in more detail later in this chapter.

Basically, the quilt itself was, and is, a pretty simple project. It consists usually of a bottom lining, a stuffing of cotton—or two to three pounds of home-grown wool—a top lining, and the top itself. But there the simplicity stops. The top was made of a number of separate squares joined either side to side, or separated from each other by cloth borders. Thus a quilt that measured sixty by eighty inches might take forty-eight 10-inch squares, sixteen 13-inch ones, or any of a number of other combinations. Each square was usually identical in pattern but distinctive in color. All the squares for one quilt might be made by the same person, or they might be made by a number of different individuals who later got together to produce the final work (*Plate 205*). Sizes varied according to the beds the

PLATE 204   Algie Norton with a quilt she pieced for one of her grandchildren. She has made four quilts for each of her eight grandchildren, three for each of her great-grandchildren. (So far!)

PLATE 205   A quilting bee on Betty's Creek in Rabun Gap. The quilting frame is suspended from the ceiling. As each row is finished, it is rolled under to enable the ladies to get to the next one easily.

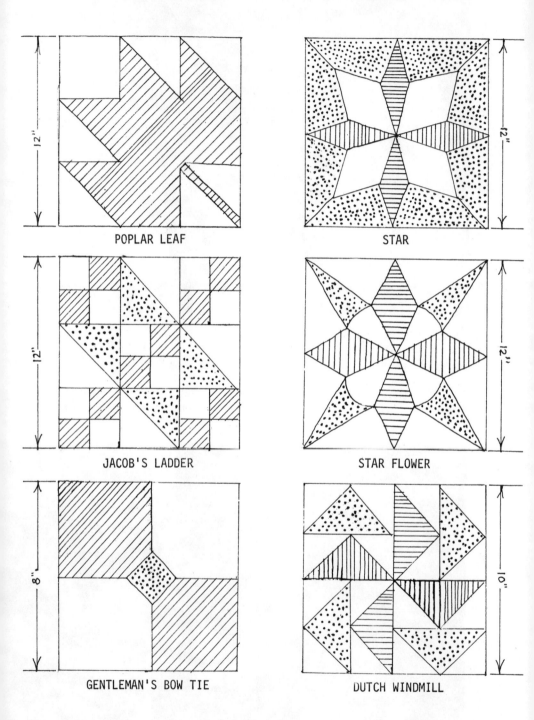

POPLAR LEAF

STAR

JACOB'S LADDER

STAR FLOWER

GENTLEMAN'S BOW TIE

DUTCH WINDMILL

PLATE 206

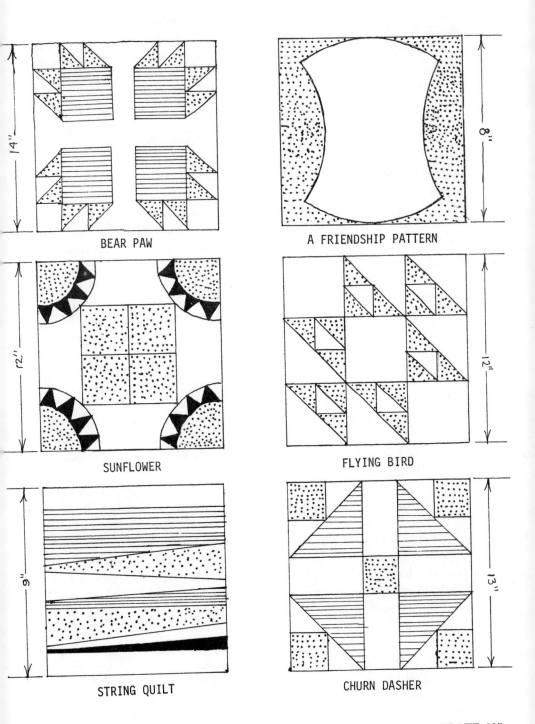

BEAR PAW

A FRIENDSHIP PATTERN

SUNFLOWER

FLYING BIRD

STRING QUILT

CHURN DASHER

PLATE 207

quilts were to fit, or the requirements of the individuals for whom they were being made.

In addition, the patterns for the squares were as numerous as the quilts they embellished, as were the number of ways each pattern could be handled. With Poplar Leaf, for example, each leaf could be set so as to point in the same direction, or they could be set in groups of four to produce an elaborate four-square pattern. The same could be done with such patterns as Gentleman's Bow. String quilts, on the other hand, were simply scraps of cloth pieced together any way they could be made to fit. Sometimes they were strips set together, horizontally, in squares. With the Friendship Pattern, the ends of each strip interlock with the sides of two others.

There was even an array of styles in the actual stitching. Tiny stitches ("fancy quilts") made it fluff up more and were the most popular. Larger ones made the job go faster. And the stitches themselves could be employed to make independent designs. Several different stitches are illustrated in Plate 208.

Emma Jean Buchanan, one of *Foxfire*'s editors, was witness to the most popular way of putting a quilt together—the quilting bee. All the women who gathered at Maggie Vinson's home had previously completed at least one Dutch Boy or Dutch Girl square. The squares had all been gathered up, and by the time the women arrived, they had been sewn together into the completed top. Mrs. Vinson had also set up the four-piece frame so that it rested on the backs of chairs, attached the bottom lining to it, and laid the cotton, top lining, and top over that. Everything was ready for the actual "quilting" to begin.

Emma Jean wrote down some of her reactions as she watched: "The women sit around the quilt laughing and joking as if it isn't a job at all. They never seem to get tired or want to go home. They all seem so content. The gossip is flowing as if I weren't even around.

"This is my first quilting, so I sit there in amusement not knowing what will happen next. As I watch them making the final stitches, I wonder, just why would these women spend their time quilting when it's much cheaper to buy a blanket at the stores nearby? Might it be that they quilt just for the social enjoyment?"

When we asked Edith Darnell the same question, she said, "It helps bring people together where they'd have quiltin'. It just seems like lot'a'pleasure. You're quiltin', you don't know you're quiltin'— a'talkin' and a'quiltin' too. And y'have lunch. I used t'enjoy goin' t'th' quiltin's."

The most captivating custom, as mentioned earlier, was that of

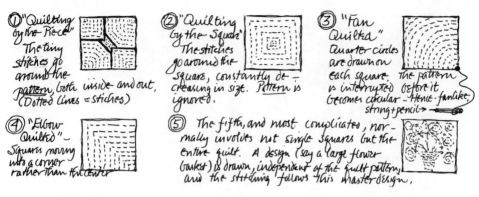

① "Quilting by the Piece" The tiny stitches go around the pattern, both inside and out. (Dotted lines = stiches)

② "Quilting by the Square" The stitches go around the square, constantly decreasing in size. Pattern is ignored.

③ "Fan Quilted" Quarter circles are drawn on each square. The pattern is interrupted before it becomes circular — Hence fanlike. string + pencil →

④ "Elbow Quilted" — Squares moving into a corner rather than the center

⑤ The fifth, and most complicated, normally involves not single squares but the entire quilt. A design (say a large flower basket) is drawn, independent of the quilt pattern, and the stitching follows this master design.

PLATE 208

the Friendship Quilt. This was a quilt much like the others—it could be any pattern—with the added feature of a number of names embroidered on the squares themselves. Often each lady who had a part in the quilt embroidered her own name in the square she had contributed. As Mrs. Tom Kelly told us recently, "The girls had a custom of making Friendship Quilts. One person would piece a quilt block, and she'd give it to another girl, and keep on till she had enough blocks to make a quilt, and then all those girls would get together and quilt that quilt. And the one that started it around got the quilt. That was a very common thing in my girlhood days. The name of everyone that pieced a square was supposed to be put on the quilt, and they valued them. It was a keepsake really."

Such quilts were made by the ladies of the community whenever a young person from that community got married, when a neighbor lost his house by fire, for a newborn child in the neighborhood, or just for a keepsake. When a boy became a man, he sometimes received one too; Edith Darnell explained: "We made 'em along when th' boy's about your age. You know, everyone sent out—their family'd send out—a square, and everybody'd piece one for it. Everywhere th' square went, everybody pieced one to go with it. When they got th' quilt done, all that pieced th' square went and helped quilt it. Then they'd wrap that'n [the boy they had done the quilt for] up in th' quilt when they got it done."

The quilt pictured at the beginning of this chapter is nearly one hundred years old. It was made of scraps gathered from friends and family, and it was pieced by one woman. After she had put the scraps together, she embroidered on each piece the name of the person from whom it had come. It bears fifty-five names. Not content with the names alone, however, she also "fancied" every single piece

PLATE 209 This detail from the Friendship Quilt pictured
earlier shows one of the panels and the elaborate embroidery
that surrounds it. The same kind of work was done around each
piece in the quilt.

by completely surrounding it with embroidery (*Plate 209*). Apparently, she used every stitch known in this area, and made up some too.
The result was the most elaborate piece of work any of us had ever
seen. The fact that something that must have taken months could
have come from an era when survival itself was difficult makes this
quilt all the more astounding.

Fancy or plain, however, the fact remains that quilts seem to us
symbolic of some of our finer human qualities. Perhaps this revival
of interest is a hopeful sign for us all.

SOAPMAKING

Whenwe talked about having an article on making soap, I remembered my grandmother saying that she was going to make some to sell at the October Harvest Festival in Dillard, Georgia. I asked Ma if she would mind having an audience. She said she'd be glad to have us, so one day right after school four of us hit it up to Ma's to watch. I was glad to have someone excited about meeting Ma. I knew she was a great person, and now I had the chance to share my enthusiasm with someone else.

She was all smiles and ready to go when we arrived. After she had added all the ingredients, she let all of us take turns stirring the soap.

Ma thought some of our questions were pretty funny, like when we asked about it being too harsh to wash your skin in. She said she'd be proud to wash in it, and that it gets you as clean as "regular" soap. When we asked about putting perfume in the soap, I thought she'd never stop laughing.

When we left that evening, we not only had some pictures and a reel of tape, but also several bars of homemade soap.

ANDREA BURRELL

The following photographs show Pearl Martin, Andrea's grandmother, demonstrating the steps involved in making soap with "store-bought" Red Devil Lye. The captions are actual portions of the tape recording made there.

PLATE 210 "You put two pints and a'half a'water and one can lye—Red Devil Lye—in your pot. You got to stir it til this dissolves good; then you got t'add th'grease to it. Then after you add th'grease, you got t'stir it for twenty minutes.

"Lye's dissolved now. Grease, this is th'grease. You just have water and grease and th'lye. This is breakfast bacon grease. You can have anything. I had a man th'other day offered to give me mutton tallow. You know—to make it out of. I think I'll take him up. I've always used hog grease myself—five or six pounds for this here."

PLATE 211 "This is beginnin' t'get thick now. Looks a lot like chicken gravy don't it? I wish this's a'little darker because homemade soap's always dark. Well, this is homemade soap, but it's not like we used t'make it because we used't'drip th' lye."

PLATE 212 Can you wash your clothes in it? "Yeah, you can. Just take that, y'know, like we used to—we took our clothes and put our soap on 'em and rub'em and boil'em. People don't do that now. And I ain't afraid t'wash my hands in it! That there lard kills th' lye." Why do you stir it so much? "It requires it. It wouldn't make if you didn't dissolve it good. You got t'get it thick like jelly, y'know. Y'can't leave jelly til it gets right." (L–R: Elizabeth Rickman, Andrea, Emma Jean Buchanan, Mrs. Martin)

PLATE 213 Did you ever add perfume to your soap? "I'll tell you, we never did care. But you know, people nowadays like yourn's ages, youn's thinks it's something terrible, but we never did care. We just had t'old smellin' lye soap. Now I could put some perfume in this, and it'd just be perfumed up like yourn's. I've got some t'put in it youn's thinks it'd make it pretty. But we never did care. We always just made it and washed with it and we never thought nothin' about it. But, of course, I guess lots of people nowadays thinks it's fancy t'sell it that ways, don't you guess? I believe I'll try this just to see—*here she breaks up with laughter*—reckon it wouldn't kill it no ways would it? If it'd do anything t'make it puny, you'd hate t'put it in there *laughing*.

"Youn's want me t'put perfume in there? I can perfume it up for youn's if you want. But I'll tell you; if for me, I like t'smell that. It smells like old times. I've washed with homemade soap s'much—it smells like homemade soap.

"Now you'd think that'd get on your hands, but that doesn't get on your hands at all t'amount t'anything. But 'course now, I wouldn't want t'comb m'hair or do anything like that. I'd want'a wash a little. But, why you can wash your hair in that! It'll bring th' dirt out just as good as anything. You needn't worry about takin'a'bath in that. It certainly won't hurt you. I've took a'bath in it many a time. If I had'n'a known what lye soap was it'd scare me t'death. You needn't be scared of that though.

"Well, don't you guess that's about enough?" *At this point, she leaves the pot. She'll stir it again in about half an hour, and then pour the thickened mixture into a shallow cake pan to harden overnight. When hard, she'll cut it into blocks with a paring knife, lift the blocks out of the pan, and put them in a basket for sale later.*

PLATE 214 "Daisy, when she went t'th' Fair last year, she got some. She got a'little piece—well, if you was t'cut off a little slice there it'd be about like she got. Her hand was chapped or somethin', and she got it t'rub on her hands, and she give a quarter for her'n. I told 'em I couldn't sell that. I cut that in two, I'd hate t'ask a quarter fer't.

"Well, of course, soap's about a quarter now. Oscar got six cakes th' other day. It'z a' dollar and a quarter. That'z nearly twenty-five cents apiece wadn't it? And them cakes, I measure them t'that, and they a whole lot littler than that. Of course, they act like they nice soaps, you know it does."

The following excerpts from recent tape-recorded interviews explain the process involved in dripping your own lye.

❖ MRS. PEARL MARTIN: "We'd make soap whenever we got out. People using a fireplace—you had t'clean your fireplace out pretty often, and when y'got'y a gum full, you's ready t'go drippin' it off.

"We used t'put th' ashes in a big wooden gum like that tree there, and it'd be holler. Then we'd drip that—just pour water on it and drip it, and then that'd be lye, y'know. We usually used hickory ashes. It takes a whole big gum full.

"Th' gum's got t'be way up on somethin'—settin' up on somethin' —and it's got t'be up high. And you've got t'drip that off and make your soap out of it. If you started that morning, you might get through by dinner; you might drip it and get it made in a day. It 'uz just like water—just poured like water, y'know. That'uz water poured in there, and water come out, except it'uz brown lookin', y'know. You'd have t'go once in a while and put th' water to it t'get enough. Just let it drip 'til y'have enough t'make your soap with.

"When y'make it with that lye you dripped, you've got t'keep a fire under it. You've got t'boil it—put it in a washpot and build a fire around it and boil it a whole long time because you've just got th' lye and th' grease, y'know, and you've really got t'boil it t'make it thick. It's just like jelly, y'know, before it's soap.

"Then pour't in a churn, you know, or somethin'other. Anything's tin rust'es.

"We'd use it ever how we had it. We used t'never have it hard. If you made just a little bunch, y'could get it hard, but if y'made a pretty good bunch, y'couldn't thicken it s'good.

"And then whenever we got out, we'd have t'make us some again."

❖MRS. ALGIE NORTON: "You have t'first build a hopper (*Plate 215*) with a spout to it—a little trough—and then put planks or boards up sloping again'it, and then y'put ashes in it, and put shucks down—or straw—in th' bottom t'keep th' ashes from goin' through. An' pour water on 'em, 'bout a gallon or two at a time 'til it gets t'drippin', and you set some kind of a container under th' spout t'catch th' lye.

"Then y'have a big washpot, and put it in that and get it t'boiling good. Put'cha in about ten or fifteen pounds of lard or any kind of grease. Then y'just keep a'pourin' your lye, lettin' it boil 'til it thickens down about like syrup, and that's what they used t'wash with (*Plate 216*).

PLATE 215   A crude ash hopper, lined with paper and filled with hickory ashes, stands ready to work.

PLATE 216 This large washpot, containing dripped lye and lard, has been heated to produce a soft soap.

"If y'wanted to, you could put any kind of perfumes or anything in it t'give it a good scent. And y'could take your mutton taller or beef taller if y'wanted to and use it in place of lard, and boil it down hard enough to cut out into blocks.

"Most of th' time they dug out a trough out of a big log t'keep it, 'cause it'd eat anything up in a year or two if y'didn't. And pour it in there and cover it up with a plank; and then y'dipped it out when y'wanted t'use it."

❖MRS. CARRIE DILLARD GARRISON: "You had t'save your ashes. We always burned hickory wood whenever we could. So when we got ready t'take up th' ashes, we had a big barrel with both ends out of it, and we had it on a slanted board. We had a trough t'catch th' lye all ready. And we'd wet th' ashes and put'em in a ash hopper and save'em.

"We usually waited until th' spring of th' year t'make our soap, and in th' meantime, we'd save up all th' old grease that happened t'accumulate around th' place—pieces of taller, suet, things that we didn't eat—and cook that out.

"And then we'd carry th' water—nobody ever had running water in those days—we'd carry th' water and throw over th' ashes and drip th' lye. Then we'd put th' grease and lye in a pot and boil it down 'til it got hard; and then we'd use that for soap.

"It sure would clean clothes too. Used t'stir it with a spicewood stick—I believe it was on th' new moon."

❖ MRS. HARRIET ECHOLS: "We'd strip up these soft corn shucks and put in t'thicken th' soap.

"If they wanted, as they called it, flavored or perfumed soap, they got th' little heart leaves from th' woods where we find th' little brown jugs in th' spring [ginger]—you remember. So that would make th' flavored soap. They would take out some of this and put it in another vessel and put th' little heart leaves in t'flavor. Just let th' heart leaves sit in th' soap; and when they cut it out, they pulled th' leaves out. That flavored th' soap—made it smell good.

"We used about two pounds of grease to a gallon of lye."

COOKING ON A FIREPLACE, DUTCH OVEN, AND WOOD STOVE

Today most people have fireplaces in their homes as an amenity rather than a necessity. Once, however, the fireplace was at the very center of home life, being used not only for warmth but also for cooking.

Cooking over a fireplace may sound simple, but in fact it requires a great deal more time and effort than using a stove. Dry kindling is used to start the fire, and green wood is cut and brought in to burn since seasoned wood burns too quickly and gives off less heat. For cooking, there must be a hot bed of coals—a process that takes a full hour for a new fire to produce. Then, as the coals die down, more wood is added slowly to maintain the temperature.

Many fireplaces had a fixed, horizontal iron bar built in, running from side to side about three feet above the fireplace floor. Others had a bar that was hinged to the side wall of the fireplace so it could be swung in and out. On these bars, pots and kettles which had a handle ("bale") would be hung with an "S" shaped hook. Pots which had a small bale on either side were hung with a pair of tongs that hooked into the bales and then into the "S" hook.

People used these pots suspended over the fire for heating soups and stews, boiling meat and vegetables, and heating large quantities of water. If the fire got too hot, or if something only needed to be kept warm, the pot could be slid along the bar to the side, or swung partly out of the fireplace.

For frying, coals were raked out onto the hearth and the frying pan set directly on them. When boiling a small amount of water or making coffee, people would set the kettle on a few coals right up against the fire. An even quicker method was to place the kettle right on top of the burning wood.

Meat was broiled simply by holding it over a bed of hot coals on the end of a long sturdy fork with a wooden handle. Popcorn was popped ("parched") by putting the shelled kernels in a covered metal box that had small holes punched in it. The box was attached to a long wooden handle and shaken directly over the fire.

Foods such as potatoes, corn, onions, and nuts could be roasted by burying them in hot ashes for insulation and then placing live coals on top of the ashes. Ash cakes were baked by wrapping the dough in cloth, placing them in a cleaned out corner of the fireplace, and covering them with ashes and coals. They were supposed to have a delicious flavor when baked this way, but it was difficult to control the heat and keep the bread clean.

Fruits and vegetables were often dried by the fire for several days to preserve them. The food would be placed on the hearth away from the direct heat, or strung and suspended from the mantle.

During the winter, fires were kept going all day. At night, ashes were heaped over the coals to keep them hot until morning. A fire would start up again "just like y'poured kerosene oil on it" when fresh wood was added. In the warmer months, the fire would be started up only when it was time to cook, and ashes would be raked over the coals to save them when no fire was needed.

THE DUTCH OVEN

One of the most useful cooking utensils was the Dutch Oven. It is a heavy, round iron pot with a handle and an iron lid that has a half-inch lip all the way around the edge. One variation looks like a large frying pan with four small legs. It is often called an "old-timey oven" or an "old bread oven."

The Dutch Oven was sometimes used out of doors, but usually it was used inside by the fireplace. It was placed on hot coals raked directly onto the hearth. The lid and oven were preheated before using, the oven being preheated on the coals themselves and the lid directly on the fire. When the oven and lid were hot enough, the bread dough—or whatever else was to be baked—was poured into the oven and the lid set on top with a pair of tongs. Coals would then be piled on top of the lid for additional heat. The lip around its edge kept them from rolling off.

One had to be careful that the coals under the oven were not too hot or the food would burn. The lid could be much hotter than the bottom as it was not directly touching what was being baked.

Dutch Ovens were usually used for baking bread and biscuits, but they could also be used for baking cakes and potatoes, roasting meats, and heating soup and stew. Here's how to bake cornbread in one:

Preheat the oven and the lid on the coals. Then carefully grease the whole inside of the oven with a piece of pork rind. Mix up the batter by combining two cups of cornmeal, one cup of flour, one cup of buttermilk, and a spoonful of salt and soda. Sprinkle a handful of cornmeal on the sides and bottom inside the oven so the bread won't stick, and then pour the batter in, making sure the oven is level so the bread will be the same thickness all around. Using some tongs, place the lid on the oven and cover it with hot coals. The bread will be ready in fifteen to twenty minutes depending on how hot the coals are. It can be slid out by removing the lid and tipping the oven, or it can be cut right in the oven and taken out with a fork or large spoon.

PLATE 217   Aunt Arie cooking on a Dutch oven.

THE WOOD STOVE

Wood stoves were considered to be an improvement over fireplaces for cooking, but they still required a lot of attention. As with the fireplace, dry kindling and green wood had to be cut to fit the firebox and kept on hand, and the fire had to be watched so that it didn't go out or get too hot.

The fire was built in the firebox located on the left-hand side of the stove right under the cooking surface. To save time, people often used coals right from the fireplace to start the fire.

At the bottom of the firebox is a coarse iron grate through which the ashes fall into the ash box. The soot which rises into the flue later falls back down into the soot tray which is directly underneath the oven. Both the ash box and soot tray are drawers that must be cleaned out once a week if the stove is used regularly.

The cooking surface of a wood stove usually has six eyes (round openings with iron lids). Sometimes they are all the same size, sometimes of varying sizes. The one at the center in the back of the stove is the hottest, the two over the woodbox are middling, and the other three are the cooler ones. The heat under the eyes cannot be regulated individually, so pots have to be moved from one to the other according to how much heat is required. Sometimes, when people wanted to heat something in a hurry, they would remove an eye and place the pot directly over the flames in the firebox.

Most of the stoves were fairly simple, though some of them got quite elaborate. One larger variety even had a flat griddle on top for frying things like pancakes, eggs, and bacon.

The oven is usually located on the right-hand side of the stove and is heated from the left and top by the circulation of heat from the firebox. The heat flows from the firebox through a four-inch high air space directly under the cooking surface to the other side. It heats more evenly than one might imagine, but if something tends to cook more on one side than the other, it has to be turned around at regular intervals. The main problem with the oven is that it is difficult to keep the temperature constant. Many varieties have a temperature gauge on the door, but this acts as a warning signal rather than as a regulator. If the oven gets too cool, more wood has to be added; and if it gets too hot, the only thing that can be done is to open the door slightly or put a pan of cold water on one of the racks. For something that takes an hour to bake, the fire has to be tended three or four times to maintain the temperature.

When cooking biscuits and cornbread, early cooks often started

PLATE 218 A wood stove

them on the lower rack of the oven to brown the bottom and then placed them on the higher rack to brown the top. Cakes, pies and roasts were usually kept on the bottom rack all the time. When broiling meat or toasting bread, the top rack was used.

About two feet above the cooking surface, most wood stoves have two warming closets. These are metal boxes about six inches deep with a door on each, and they are used to keep food warm until it is ready to be served. The stoves also have a damper that seals off the right side of the firebox and greatly cuts the circulation of heat. It doesn't put out the fire, but it cools the rest of the stove so that it can

be left unattended fairly safely. When the damper is closed, the coals
will remain hot for several hours. It has to be left open when the
stove is in use.

We asked Margaret Norton, a real chef on a wood stove, what some
of the advantages and disadvantages of using one are. Here's what
she told us—

"I've always used a wood stove because we live up here in the
woods and there's always plenty of wood. They're good in the winter-
time because they sure do warm up the kitchen. In the summer it
gets uncomfortable hot in here; 'course we can go out on the porch
every few minutes. But we're used to it. With this you have to build a
fire and wait till it's ready, but by the time you make up your cornbread or peel your potatoes, it's hot.

"Sometimes wind'll blow down the pipe hard and smoke the house,
and the soot flies out all over the place and you have to wipe off
everything. And you have to clean it out every so often and watch
that sparks don't fall out on the floor.

"And of course you have to gather your wood, and that's a dis-
advantage when you're out of it. But if the electricity goes off or the
gas gives out, you're alright if you've got wood."

DANIEL MANOUS

Daniel Manous is a loner. For the last two years he has lived on the flank of Picken's Nose in an abandoned, discarded bread truck in the back of which he has placed a wood stove and a bed. His job is to watch over a fish hatchery fed by the purest waters of Betty's Creek.

The job is a lonely one—high on the side of the mountain in a spot accessible only by foot or rugged automobile—and it gives a man plenty of time to think. Dan has two volumes of poetry with him in his truck, one by Burns and the other by Tennyson. He has read them both. The rest of his free time is spent hiking, hunting, or playing his banjo.

Dan is full of mountain stories, too, such as the following snake tale:

"Once there was this preacher on Cullowhee Mountain who had a rattlesnake on the pulpit in a box. Some preachers in these mountains, you know, hold snakes and things to prove their faith. Well, he had this snake on his pulpit. Said if the Lord ever told him that it was alright to hold it, he'd have it handy. Well, one day he was preaching away and got to feeling good and he reached right in that box in front of the crowd and grabbed that snake and pulled it out and it didn't make a sound. Tame as could be. He held it for a while and then put it back and didn't get bit at all.

"Later, all the people wanted him to do it again. He didn't much want to, but they kept at it, and finally he reached in to get it again and it bit him. He lived, but just. When he was well he said that the first time he had done what the Lord wanted him to do, and the next time he had done what the people wanted him to do, and that was what made the difference."

PLATE 219   Dan Manous in front of his old abandoned bread wagon.

MOUNTAIN RECIPES

BRUNSWICK STEW

2 pounds cooked ground
  beef
1 pound cooked lean
  ground pork
1 small cooked chicken,
  chopped
3–4 diced potatoes
1 pint kernel corn
1 cup lima beans
2–3 diced carrots

2–3 chopped onions
1 pint tomatoes or tomato
  juice
catsup
chile powder
salt
black pepper and red
  pepper
Worcestershire sauce

The vegetables may be either raw or canned. Mix everything together, and simmer a long time. If you want to can it, put in jars and place them in a boiling water bath for 1½ hours.

VEGETABLES

LEATHER BREECHES BEANS—Sometime during the winter take a string of dried green beans down, remove the thread, and drop them in a pot of scalding water. Then add "a good hunk'a meat" (ham, pork, or the like, depending on your taste) and cook all morning.

As Andy Webb said, "Now they's somethin' good ta'eat. I'd rather have them as t'have canned beans."

CABBAGE
>   1 head cabbage, chopped
>   4 tablespoons lard
>   salt and pepper to taste

Put about an inch of water in a large frying pan and bring to a boil. Put all the cabbage and lard in, season, and cover. Simmer for about twenty-five to thirty minutes.

FRIED POTATOES—Slice three or four potatoes very thin, like potato chips, put in frying pan with hot grease, and season with salt and pepper. Cover and cook until light brown, turning occasionally.

OKRA—Slice the okra about ½ inch thick, roll in meal, salt, and fry in grease until light brown and crispy.

OCTOBER BEANS—The mountain people used these beans as a substitute for soup beans, which don't grow here. They can be eaten fresh when young and tender, but people usually dried them, shelled them, and stored them for later use. To cook, parboil beans for five minutes, using about a quart of water per cup of beans and some salt. Cover and simmer until tender.

FRIED PUMPKIN/SQUASH BLOSSOMS—Make a thin batter using an egg, about half a cup of flour, and milk. Dip the blossoms in it, and fry in deep hot grease. Serve as you would any vegetable.

HOMINY—Mrs. Algie Norton told us how to make hominy:

"Well, we used t'have a big old washpot that'd hold about ten or fifteen gallons of water or anything. And we would put in about a gallon of lye from when y'dripped it down for soap or anything—or just for th' purpose.

PLATE 220   Hominy

"And y'would put that lye in, and shell y'about twelve or fifteen big ears of corn by hand so y'could get all th' sorry grains and things out of it; and y'd put it in that pot and cook it about eight or nine hours by th' fireplace in the big washpot. And when th' grains begin t'crack open and swell and get great big and begin t'get a little tender, you took it away from th' fire.

"Then y'put it in this big washpot or pans and took it to th' branch, or where they'uz plenty a'water, and washed it 'till all that outside husk and those little black things—hearts that growed t'th' cob o'th' corn—come off and out. You'd have t'wash it through maybe a dozen waters and rub it t'get all that skin [and poisonous lye] off.

"Then y'put it back in th' big pot, put it back by th' fire, and cooked it about that much longer—about all night—and y'get up and roust up your fire, put in some more water if it's needed and cook it.

"And then y'take it out when it got good and tender and done. Then y'had some good eatin'.

"Use about a third lye and two-thirds water. You keep it in a cool place. I never did try cannin' it, but y'can, I think. You always make it in th' winter time. Houses were open enough til y'had plenty of ice, and anything y'had froze in it. Out somewhere away from th' chimney or fireplace it'd keep for a week.

"White corn makes th' best. I reckon y'could make it out'a'yeller corn, but it wouldn' be as good. Use big grain corn too—big, pretty."

BREADS

CORN PONES

1 pint corn meal	1 tablespoon lard
½ teaspoon salt	milk
1 teaspoon baking powder	

Mix together meal, powder, and salt, cut in lard, and add enough milk to make a stiff batter. Form into pones with hands (or add some milk and drop from the end of a spoon), and place in a greased pan. Bake in a hot oven for about half an hour.

CORN CAKES

2 cups corn meal	2 teaspoons baking powder
1 kitchen spoon flour	1 tablespoon melted butter
2 eggs	or lard
1 teaspoon salt	milk

Beat eggs, add meal, flour, salt, baking powder, and butter. Add enough milk to make a thin batter. Pour out onto a hot griddle and flip to other side when brown. Good with butter and syrup.

HUSH PUPPIES—Mix 1 cup flour, 1 cup corn meal, and a pinch of salt and soda. Add 1 egg and buttermilk until it is the right consistency to hold its shape when rolled into a ball. Mix in 1 medium onion chopped up, roll into balls about an inch to 2 inches across, and drop into a couple inches of hot fat. Let them deep fry until they're brown and crispy; drain a bit on some paper, and serve hot.

LIGHT BREAD

1 cake yeast	2 medium potatoes
3 teaspoons sugar	2 teaspoons salt
1 pint warm water	flour

Dissolve the yeast in 1 cup of the water. Cook the potatoes, mash very fine, and add yeast along with 1 teaspoon salt, 1 teaspoon sugar, and the rest of the water. Put in a jar and leave in a warm place to rise. Sift flour, and mix it in with the yeast mixture along with 1 more teaspoon salt and 2 more teaspoons sugar. Keep adding flour until it makes a firm dough. Let rise to double, knead, and make into loaves. Let rise for one hour, and then bake at about 350° until it tests done.

BRAN BREAD—Mix together 1 quart each of bran flour, white flour, and buttermilk. Add 1 cup each of seeded raisins and molasses, and last mix in 1 teaspoon each of baking soda and salt. Put into loaf pans and bake until done.

RYE BREAD—Sift together 1 cup of wheat flour, 1 cup rye flour, ½ cup of corn meal, 1 teaspoon salt, and 1 teaspoon baking powder.

Add enough buttermilk to make a firm dough, adding ½ teaspoon of soda per cup of buttermilk. Cut in 3 tablespoons of shortening, mix thoroughly, and roll out to about ½ inch thick. Cut as you would biscuits, place on greased sheet, and bake at 450° for ten to twelve minutes.

CRACKLIN' BREAD—Prepare corn bread by using 2 cups of corn meal, 2 teaspoons of salt, 1 cup of buttermilk, 1 teaspoon of soda, and ½ teaspoon of baking powder. Mix ½ cup of cracklin's (see p. 207, last recipe) into the mixture. If it is too dry use some lukewarm water to make the right consistency for corn bread. Put in oven and cook until brown.

ASH CAKES—Mix up dough for corn bread, and make sure it's thick enough to hold its shape. Clean out a corner of the fireplace, put the "cake" in it, and cover it with a clean cloth. Put hot ashes over the cloth, then put hot coals on top of that. It takes about half an hour.

MOLASSES SWEET BREAD—Sift together 2 cups flour, 2 teaspoons baking powder, ½ teaspoon salt, ¼ teaspoon soda, 2 teaspoons ginger, and 1 teaspoon cinnamon. Add ⅓ cup melted butter, 1 cup molasses (or ½ cup sugar and ⅔ cup molasses), ¾ cup buttermilk, and 1 egg. Mix well, pour into a loaf pan, and bake at 350° for about fifty minutes.

OLD-FASHIONED GINGERBREAD

½ cup sugar	1½ teaspoons ginger
½ cup butter	½ teaspoon cinnamon
1 cup molasses	½ cup sour milk
2 cups flour	nuts or raisins if desired
½ teaspoon soda	

Mix all ingredients together, put into a large loaf pan, and bake for about an hour. (This recipe is at least a hundred years old.)

SYRUP BREAD

Mix up flour, soda, salt, and buttermilk as you would for a plain bread recipe, and instead of using sugar to sweeten it, use homemade syrup. Bake like any other bread.

CAKES

CARROT PUDDING OR CAKE

⅔ cup sifted flour	¼ teaspoon nutmeg
1 teaspoon baking powder	⅔ cup sugar
¾ teaspoon baking soda	⅔ cup currants
¾ teaspoon salt	⅔ cup raisins
½ teaspoon cinnamon	⅔ cup grated raw
¼ teaspoon ground cloves	potatoes
⅓ cup milk	1 cup grated raw carrots

Mix and sift ingredients. Add the fruits, stir until well coated, then stir in potatoes, carrots, and milk. Pour into a greased pan and cover with a lid and steam in a large pan of hot water for 2½ hours.

Serve with *Carrot Pudding Sauce,* made as follows:

Mix 1 cup powdered sugar, 1 large teaspoon vanilla or wine, and the yolks of two eggs. Beat. When ready to serve, add ½ pint cream whipped.

PUMPKIN CAKE

1½ cups corn oil
2 cups sugar
3 cups flour
2 teaspoons baking powder
2 scant teaspoons soda
1 teaspoon salt
2 teaspoons vanilla

4 eggs
2 cups pumpkin
1 cup raisins or fruit
   cake mix
1 cup chopped nuts
2 teaspoons pumpkin spice

Mix corn oil, sugar, flour, spice, powder, soda, salt, and pumpkin. Add eggs beaten well. Add vanilla, nuts, and raisins that have been mixed with ½ cup of extra flour. Bake in a loaf pan for about an hour at 400–450°.

DRIED APPLE CAKE—Mix up a regular white or yellow cake recipe, and bake it in four thin layers. Mix 1 pint dried apples with 1 pint of water, and cook until thick and the apples are mashed. Sweeten to taste with syrup and add some spices. Let cool a bit, and spread the mixture between the layers and on top of the cake. You can cover the sides if you want.

MOLASSES COOKIES

1 cup brown sugar
1 egg
1 cup molasses

¾ cup melted lard or
   butter
¼ cup boiling water
salt to taste

Add enough flour to knead. Roll, cut out, and bake in hot oven.

PIES

TAME GOOSEBERRY PIE—Mix 2 cups of berries with ¾ cup of sugar, and cook, stirring to mash the berries, until thick. Make some plain biscuit dough, roll out, and cut into 1″ wide strips. Pour the berries into a pie plate, lay the strips of dough crosswise on the berries, and bake at about 450° until the crust is done.

SWEET POTATO PIE

2 cups sweet potatoes,
   diced and cooked
⅔ cup molasses
½ teaspoon ginger
½ stick butter

½ cup sweet milk
pinch of salt
biscuit dough
other spices if desired

Mix together all the ingredients except the dough and bring to a boil. Cut rolled dough into cubes and drop into boiling mixture. Put thin slices of dough on top. Put pan in oven and bake until crust is brown.

BLACKBERRY COBBLER

blackberries, enough for one pie	butter, small amount
sugar to taste	biscuit dough, enough for several biscuits

Cook the blackberries until they come to a boil, add as much or little sugar as you want, and then add some butter. Cook until thick. Roll out the dough, cut as for biscuits, and drop into the blackberries. Then roll some dough thin, cut into strips, and place on top of the blackberries. Set the pan in the oven until the crust on top is brown.

MOLASSES CANDY—Combine 1 cup of molasses, 1 cup of water, a few grains of salt. Boil ingredients (do not stir) to hard ball stage. Remove from the fire, and let stand until cool enough to hold in well greased hands. After pulling for some time it will change from brown to a yellowish color. Cut into pieces.

BEVERAGES

APPLE BEER—Peel your apples and dry the peelings in the sun or by the stove. Put them in a crock and add enough boiling water to cover them. Cover the crock and let it sit for one or two days, until all the flavor comes out of the peelings. You may add some sugar if you want.

MUSCADINE WINE

½ bushel muscadine grapes	12½ pounds sugar

Mash the grapes with your hands, put them in a large churn, and add 2½ pounds sugar. Let it work (ferment) for about a week, until it quits.

Strain the mixture to get out the grape skins and impurities. Put back in the churn, add 10 pounds more of sugar. Let it work about eight to ten days until it quits. Makes about 4 gallons.

Recipes for hog, wild plant foods, and wild animal foods can be found in later chapters.

PRESERVING VEGETABLES

DRYING

PUMPKIN—Mrs. Tom Kelly said, "This is a recipe that was used in most families in olden times. You slice th' pumpkin around in circles, take th' seeds out, peel it, and hang it on a stick crosswise of th' joists of th' house. Let it hang there until it dries. Then store it in sacks. It took a long time to cook, and you have to cook it several hours, and they season it with hog meat and grease."

SWEET POTATOES—Boil the potatoes until done. Slip off the skins and slice. Put on a clean white cloth and put out in the sun each day. Then stack for winter use in pudding, pie, etc. Some people would just peel and slice without boiling, and set out to dry.

CORN—Corn was cut as if it were going to be cooked (twice around the cob, according to Mrs. Harriet Echols), and then spread out in the sun, sometimes on a piece of tin.

OKRA—Slice okra. Put on a piece of metal which has been covered with brown paper or on a white cloth to keep the okra off the metal or tin sheet being used. Place thinly on the sheet, and put out in the sun. Cover at night. Let dry until ready to take off the paper. Remove and put in bag until desired to use for cooking.

PLATE 221 Leather Breeches Beans

LEATHER BREECHES BEANS—String tender green beans. Fill a long needle with a long strong thread. Push the needle through the center of the bean, pushing the beans together at the end of the thread, filling from knot end to needle. Hang up the string by one end in the warm air, but not in direct sunlight. This gives the beans a better flavor. Let them remain hanging until the beans become dry. Store in a bag until ready to use.

PEAS—Pick the peas when ripe, and lay them in the sun to dry.

After they are thoroughly dry, place them on a sheet outside on a windy day, and beat the hulls off with a stick. The wind will blow the chaff away and leave just the peas. Store the peas in sacks in a dry place until you're ready to eat them.

BURYING

CABBAGE—Dig a shallow circular trench on a gently sloped plot of ground. The diameter of the trench will depend on the number of cabbages you plan to preserve. Also dig a drainage ditch leading downhill and away from the circular trench. This will serve to drain off any surface water that might accumulate and rot the cabbages.

Throw the dirt from the trench into the center of the circle, thus making a low mound. Cover the mound with straw.

Pull up cabbages root and all. Place the cabbages on the mound so that the root of each is covered by the head of another. Then cover with straw and dirt. They'll keep most of the winter.

POTATOES—Dig a hole a foot or two below the frost line. Put in potatoes and cover with straw, and pack dirt over that. Put a piece of tin on that. They'll keep all winter.

PICKLING

"Be sure that th' signs are *not* in th' bowels" (see p. 222), says Daisy Justice. "When th' moon is new is th' best time to make kraut, pickle beans, corn, or green tomatoes. If th' signs are in th' bowels they will be slimy or soft and not fit to eat. *Do not use iodized salt* for pickling."

SOUR KRAUT—Select firm cabbage heads and chop. Have a clean churn jar (usually five gallon), and pack the jar with alternating layers of chopped cabbage and a sprinkling of salt (usually a half cup of salt per gallon of cabbage). You need not add water as the cabbage will produce its own.

When the jar is filled, cover the cabbage with a clean white cloth, large cabbage leaves, or a saucer. Then place a flat flint rock or other weight on top of this to hold the cabbage under the brine. Let this stand ten days, or as long as is necessary to get it as sour as you want.

When this is completed, take the kraut out and pack it in canning jars. Then put the jars in a pot of water and bring to a boil to both seal the jars and cook the cabbage.

Old-timers used to leave the cabbage in the churn jars, omitting this last step, but it turns dark. Jars keep it in serving-size portions, and keep it fresh.

Some add a pot of hot pepper to the churn at the beginning of the whole process for additional flavoring.

PICKLED BEANS—String and break green beans. Wash and cook until tender (about one hour). Then wash them again in cold water and pack them tightly in a clean crock jar, again alternating a layer of beans with a sprinkling of salt. When the jar is full, add as much water as necessary to fill the remaining spaces as the beans will not produce enough of their own water like the cabbage. Another way is to fill the churn with beans and then add salty water to fill (one-half cup per gallon of water).

Weight down as before and let stand about ten days or two weeks. There is no need to can the beans as you did the cabbage unless you want to for convenience. Many people just use them directly from the churn. They keep well this way as they have already been cooked.

PICKLED CORN—Shuck and silk corn that is in roasting ear. Boil on cob and then pack in the clean churn jar as before, sprinkling a little salt over the ears as you pack them. Some cut the corn off the cob before pickling, but many prefer to pack the full ears into the churn.

You may also add salty water as before if you prefer this to sprinkling salt over each layer.

Others line the churn jar before packing with a clean white meal sack. Then they tie the sack at the top when the churn is filled.

When the corn is pickled, you can eat it directly off the cob, or cut it off with a knife and fry in bacon grease or butter. No need to can it in order to preserve.

It is also possible to pickle the corn and the beans together in the same churn jar. Most remove the corn from the cob when doing it this way. Then it is served fried in bacon grease or in butter.

PICKLED BEETS—Boil beets six to eight hours until soft, and the skin slips off easily. Drain the water, peel the beets, and cut them into small cubes. Put the beets into a large pot, and for every quart, add a cup each of sugar and vinegar. Bring the mixture to a boil, stirring occasionally. Put into cans and seal.

ICICLE PICKLES (*cucumbers, sweet bell peppers, and green tomatoes*)—This is a process that takes fourteen days, but is actually much easier than it sounds.

Select and cut up a peck (eight quarts) of the above, peel and all. Cut cucumbers into six- to eight-inch strips. Leave the tomatoes whole if they are small ones. Put in a crock, and pour boiling water over the top (fill the crock) and a half cup of salt per peck of vegetables. Let this mixture sit for nine days.

At the end of nine days, pour out the liquid, wash the pickles, put them back in the jar, add three tablespoons of alum (to make them crisp) and fill again with boiling water.

Let this mixture sit for twenty-four hours. Then empty the liquid again, wash the pickles again, and replace them in the jar. Meanwhile, cook the following mixture:

2 quarts vinegar	1 tablespoon pickling
9 cups sugar	spice
4–5 pieces ginger	1 tablespoon celery seed

Cook this mixture until it boils, then pour it over the pickles and leave until the same time on the following day. At this time pour the liquid into a container, reboil it, and pour it over the pickles again. Repeat this for four days in a row.

On the fourth day, the pickles are ready to serve. Keep them in the open jar in a cool place, or can them for convenience.

When pickling the above, the old-timers in the area would usually let the pickles sit overnight in a crock in salty water, then remove them the next day, boil them in vinegar, sugar, and spices to suit taste, and can them immediately. Grape leaves were often added while they were sitting overnight in the crock. These had approximately the same effect as the alum.

For spices and added flavor, they used pickling spice, strips of sassafras, and spicewood. These were called *Bread and Butter Pickles*.

CHOW CHOW

1 peck green tomatoes	2 ounces white or black
1 peck string beans	cloves
¼ peck small white onions	2 ounces celery seeds
¼ peck green peppers	2 ounces allspice
2 large heads of cabbage	1 pound brown sugar
¼ peck red peppers	1 box yellow mustard seed
4 tablespoons white	1 ounce tumeric
mustard seed	vinegar

Chop the tomatoes, let them stand overnight in their own juice. Squeeze out the brine. Chop the cabbage, peppers, onions, and beans, mix together, and add the tomatoes and the spices and sugar. Put in a porcelain kettle, cover with vinegar, and boil three hours. When cool, seal in jars.

RIPE TOMATO PICKLE

3 pints tomatoes, peeled and chopped

1 cup celery
4 tablespoons chopped red
  peppers
4 tablespoons chopped
  onions
2 cups vinegar

4 tablespoons salt
6 tablespoons sugar
6 tablespoons mustard seed
½ teaspoon cloves
½ teaspoon cinnamon
1 teaspoon grated nutmeg

Mix ingredients in order given. Put in stone jar and cover. Allow this uncooked mixture to stand a week before using.

GREEN TOMATO PICKLE

8 pounds green tomatoes,
  chopped fine
4 pounds brown sugar
1 quart vinegar

1 teaspoon mace
1 teaspoon cinnamon
1 teaspoon cloves

Boil tomatoes and sugar for three hours. Add other ingredients and boil fifteen minutes more. Let cool and seal in jars.

ICEBERG GREEN TOMATO PICKLE

7 pounds green tomatoes
builders lime
2 pounds sugar
3 pints vinegar

1 teaspoon each of cloves,
ginger, allspice, celery
seed, mace, and
cinnamon.

Soak the tomatoes in a mixture of 1½ cups lime to 1 gallon water, making enough to cover the tomatoes. Drain and soak for four hours in fresh water, changing hourly. Make a syrup of the sugar, vinegar, and spices, and bring to a boil. Pour it over the tomatoes (after the last change of water has been drained off), and let stand overnight. Then boil for one hour and seal in jars.

WATERMELON PICKLES

4 pounds watermelon rind
2 quarts cold water
1 tablespoon slaked lime
2 tablespoons whole allspice

2 tablespoons cloves, whole
1 quart cider vinegar
4 pounds sugar
10 two-inch pieces stick
  cinnamon

Remove all pink pulp from watermelon rind. Peel outside peeling from the rind. Weigh. Cut in 1 inch circles or cubes. Combine cold water and lime. Pour over rind. Let stand one hour. Drain. Cover with fresh cold water. Simmer 1½ hours or until tender. Drain. Tie spices in a cheesecloth. Combine vinegar, 1 quart water, and sugar. Heat until sugar dissolves. Add spice bag and rind; simmer gently two hours. Pack rind in clean hot sterile jars. Fill jars with boiling hot syrup. Seal. Makes about twelve half pints.

MUSTARD PICKLE

1 quart cucumbers, chopped fine
1 quart green tomatoes, chopped fine
1 head cabbage, chopped fine
4 sweet peppers, chopped fine

1 cup salt
1 gallon water
6 tablespoons mustard
1 tablespoon tumeric
1 cup flour
2 quarts vinegar

Make a brine of the salt and water, and let the first four ingredients stand in it for twenty-four hours. Drain. Make a mixture of the last four ingredients, add to the first mixture, and cook for three minutes. Seal in jars.

PEAR RELISH

1 peck pears
6 large onions
4 red bell peppers

2 pounds sugar
1 tablespoon allspice
5 cups vinegar

Grind up vegetables in a food chopper. Add vinegar and sugar, and cook for thirty minutes. Seal in jars.

CUCUMBER RELISH

12 cucumbers
4 green peppers
4 onions
½ cup salt
vinegar

1 cup sugar
1 teaspoon celery seed
1 tablespoon mustard seed
1 cup grated horse radish

Remove the seeds and skin from the cucumbers and chop. Also chop peppers and onions. Add salt, mix well, and let stand overnight. Drain, add other ingredients, and mix with enough vinegar to have moisture but not watery. Seal in jars.

TOMATO CATSUP

Tomatoes, enough to make a gallon when cooked
½ cup sugar
2 tablespoons ground mustard
1 tablespoon ground allspice

1 pint cider vinegar
3 tablespoons salt
1 tablespoon black pepper
½ tablespoon ground cloves

Select good, firm ripe tomatoes. Scald and strain through a coarse sieve to remove seed and skin. When cold, add to each gallon of tomatoes the above ingredients. Let simmer slowly for three hours. Seal in bottles or jars.

PRESERVING FRUIT

BLEACHING

❖ MRS. TOM KELLY: "Peel and core apples; cut into quarters or eighths. Fill a ten gallon wooden tub with sliced apples; then put two tablespoons of sulfur in a saucer and strike a match and set th' sulfur on fire. Cover th' tub with a clean cloth and let it stay all day. At night, take th' sulfur saucer out. Repeat the process for three days. Then transfer th' apples to large jars and tie clean cloths over them. You could eat that any time in th' year or winter without any preservation.

"Everbody nearly bleached fruits. And it was th' sulfur that whited th' apples, and they had a little sulfur flavor. But most of th' people had a big tub of that made every year."

❖ MRS. CARRIE DILLARD GARRISON: "Another way we had of preserving fruits was to burn coals until there wasn't any smoke, any fumes, or anything from it—hickory coals usually. Hickory coals would hold th' heat longer and stay alive longer, so we'd put those under a barrel [in the bottom of a barrel]; and then we'd have our fruit cut in small pieces, and put it in an open basket. We used split baskets, y'know, made out a'oak splits, and we'd put th' fruit in that and hang it in th' top a'th' barrel. But we'd sprinkle our sulfur over th' coals first; then we'd hang th' fruit in th' barrel, and then we'd cover th' fruit with a old sheet or somethin' to hold th' fumes in there, and let it stay in there about twenty, thirty minutes. Then we'd take it out and pack it in a wooden barrel usually. We didn't have churns or anything like that to put it in. They were scarce. So we'd pack ours in a wooden barrel we'd made—a homemade barrel—and we'd fix a barrel full of each fruit, and they wouldn't any insects or anything bother it. All y'had to do was keep it covered tight—keep things out of it, like mice and things like that.

"We'd make pies; cook it for breakfast. Or it just taste like fresh apples. It'd be white though—th' apples'd be white. It'd take all th' color out of them."

❖ MRS. ALGIE NORTON: "You'd take a box about two foot high and about two foot wide—a wooden box. Then y'put'cha somethin' to hold your fruit up about six inches from th' bottom; y'put'cha somethin' that ya' can put'cha some coals in—not blazin', but burnt coals. And y'have to pare your apples and peel them and core them—cut'em in about eight pieces to the apple. And y'gotta have some kind of a rack—course now y'use a screen wire to go over a little frame with about an inch or two sides around it. And put your screen over th' bottom and put'cher apples in that.

"And y'have your live coals and put about two heapin' spoonfuls of sulfur in amon' th' coals, and it blazes up for a minute. An' set your apples down, an' cover your box good, but you wanta paste that box with paper or somethin' so that no air can escape. An' cover it up an' let it set about thirty minutes an' put in more sulfur—an' do that for two or three times.

"Then y'take ya'apples out'n pack'm in jars and put a cover over, an' they'll keep til spring."

Later, Mrs. Norton added that if screen was not available, a person might use the same short-sided wooden box, but mount a slat bottom in it rather than a screen one. The bottom might even be a solid piece with holes bored in it—anything so that the fumes from the sulfur could get to the fruit. She also warned that the fruit must be stirred each time fresh sulfur was added, and that a quilt could be used to cover the box if one wished.

Mrs. Gatha Nichols added one twist to bleaching fruit for the person who wants to do it only on a small scale. For this person, she recommends the use of a churn, a teacup with sulfur and a single coal, and a cloth to cover the churn with.

DRYING

We have been fascinated by the sight of trays of sliced fruit drying in front of a fireplace. At one time this was an extremely common way of preserving foods for the winter. Now, although it is no longer a necessity, some mountain people continue the habit. Mrs. Grover Bradley, who had both a churn *and* several trays of sliced apples warming beside her fireplace when we last visited with her, said, "We *had* to eat things like that. They wadn't no other way to live. We dried everything."

APPLES—Apples are either sliced up into thin slivers, or cored and sliced into rings. One woman claimed that with a peeler, she could core, peel, and slice a bushel of apples in fifty-four minutes.

The rings were strung on a broomstick or a pole; slices were spread out on boards. Then they were set out in the sun or in front of the fireplace, depending on the weather, until the slices were brown and rubbery. This usually took two to three days. Some people say that they brought the fruit in at night to protect it from the dampness. Others simply covered the fruit with canvas at night. While drying, it was turned over frequently so that it would dry evenly.

One woman used to heat the dried slices in the oven for a few minutes at 225° to kill any germs. Other just packed them without heating. When dry, the apples were usually taken up and stored in sacks for use during the winter.

As Mrs. Grover Bradley said, "That makes th' best fried pies I ever eat."

Peaches were dried just like apples. Small berries such as *blackberries* were simply spread out on boards to dry and were not sliced.

USING SYRUP

CROCK GRAPES—Collect dry, sound fox grapes. Pack them in a churn and pour boiling hot fresh molasses or syrup over them. Take two clean cloths; dip the first in hot beeswax and the second in hot tallow, and tie each cloth separately around the top of the churn.

Make this in the fall when the grapes are fresh and ripe. Then set the churn in a cool place until winter. They can be eaten during the winter after they are mildly fermented.

JELLY, JAM, AND PRESERVES

PEAR PRESERVES

Wash pears, peel, and cut into quarters. Rinse and place a layer of sugar and a layer of pears until all the fruit has been used. Let this stand overnight. Put over moderate heat and cook until well done and a syrup has been made from the mixture. Put into sterile jars and seal.

APPLE BUTTER

Peel and slice apples, and immediately place them in a pan of cold, salty water so they won't turn brown. Then rinse the salt out and cook the apples until soft and mushy. Add one cup of sugar to every cup of cooked apples, cinnamon to taste, and cook until thick. Put in jars and seal.

MINT JELLY FROM APPLE JUICE

One cup mint leaves (chopped fine and packed tight). Pour boiling water over the clean mint leaves, cover and allow to steep for one hour. Press juice from the leaves and add 2 tablespoons of this extract to 1 cup apple juice and ¾ cup sugar. Boil until jelly test is reached. Add green food coloring. Pour into hot glasses and seal.

QUINCE HONEY

> 1 quart (2 pounds) sugar
> 1 pint water
> 3 quinces

Grate quinces. Boil sugar and water and add grated quinces and let boil twenty minutes. Seal in jars. Pear honey is made the same way.

CHURNING YOUR OWN BUTTER

The churn is usually a 4–5 gallon stoneware jar with a wooden lid and a dasher. It should be filled half, or slightly over half, full with rich milk which should be mostly cream.

Then set the churn aside so that the cream can "turn," or clabber. The time required for this step depends on the temperature of the cream. In the summer, for instance, the cream can be "poured up" one night and churned the next. The cream will be ready in three days if it is warmed on alternate sides by a fireplace in the winter.

It is important that the clabbered cream be churned when it has turned. One test of readiness is to tilt the churn to its side. The liquid should hold together in one form, separating cleanly from the sides of the container. If left too long, the cream will curdle and separate, and it will not make good butter. On the other hand, if churned too early while it is still "blinky milk," or sour milk, it won't make good butter either.

The butter itself is made by agitating the clabbered milk with a dasher which, in many cases, is a homemade affair. It consists of a stick similar to a broom handle, one end of which is nailed to the center of either a cross (two slats 4″ long, 2″ wide, and ½″ thick attached together) or a circular piece of wood 1″ thick, 4″ in diameter, containing four holes, each 1″ in diameter spaced equidistant around the center.

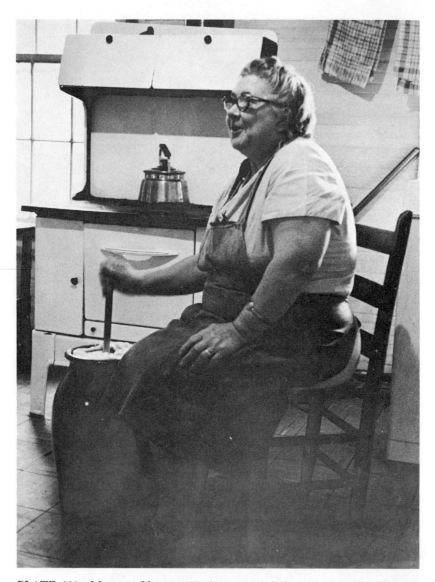

PLATE 222   Margaret Norton still churns several times a week. Her butter is
not only used by several families in the area, but also sold in the local super-
market.

The dasher is inserted into the churn, and the churn's opening
is covered by a tightly fitting wooden lid which has a hole in its
center for the dasher stick. The lid prevents splattering as the dasher
is agitated up and down. The clabbered cream must be continually
agitated by this up and down motion of the dasher for thirty to forty
minutes.

The temperature of the cream has a great deal to do with the time required in churning and the quality of the final product. If the clabbered cream is too warm, the result will be soft white puffy butter. Cold water will improve the texture.

Clabbered milk that is too cold, on the other hand, will yield specks, or small balls of butter that refuse to stick together. Hot water, stirred with the dasher into the cold liquid, will help gather the butter.

When the butter gathers adequately, remove the lid and stir gently with the dasher in a sideways motion bringing the butter together (*Plate 223*). Lift the lumps of butter out, drain, and place them in a bowl. The experts that we interviewed disagreed on the next step. Mrs. Norton next places her butter in the refrigerator overnight to chill it. Then she molds it, adding salt (¼ to ½ teaspoon per pint of butter).

PLATE 223   Gathering the butter.

Mrs. Brown and Mrs. Phillips feel that rinsing the butter with cold water immediately after taking it from the churn gives it a fresher flavor and causes it to keep longer. They also add salt to boost the flavor. The liquid left in the churn after the butter has been removed is buttermilk.

Ice and a cold mold will make butter molding easier. If you haven't kept the butter in the refrigerator overnight, drop ice into the bowl of butter and stir it through the warm butter with clean hands. Then squeeze out any water and press the butter into a mold. When it is filled, push down on the handle of the mold, which acts like a piston, thus releasing the "print" of butter. It should weight out at approximately a half pound, or a pound, depending on the size of the mold used.

Then store the butter in a cool place, ready to spread on hot breads or to use in making cakes.

To get a small amount of butter and buttermilk in a hurry, an ordinary glass jar can be used. The clabbered milk should be shaken for approximately twenty minutes in the container. Then proceed as above.

Need a diversion to make the time go faster? You might like to try the traditional chant that the churner said in time to the up and down movements of the dasher. The arrows indicate the dasher movement.

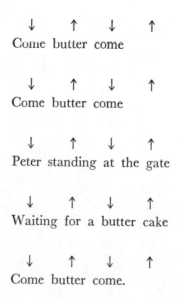

↓   ↑   ↓   ↑
Come butter come

↓   ↑   ↓   ↑
Come butter come

↓   ↑   ↓   ↑
Peter standing at the gate

↓   ↑   ↓   ↑
Waiting for a butter cake

↓   ↑   ↓   ↑
Come butter come.

SLAUGHTERING HOGS

The prime source of meat for the early family in these mountains was hogs. Part of the reason for this can be seen by a quick look at the recipes. There was almost no part of the animal that could not be used. Each farmer who kept hogs on open range in the mountains had his own identifying brand cut into the ear of each of his animals. Hogs were allowed to fatten themselves on the "mast" of the forest—acorns, chestnuts, and so on. As Mann Norton said, "My father generally kept hunnerd fifty, two hunnerd hogs in th' woods. Most ever'body did. He'd kill ten'r 'twelve at one time off th' mast just t'eat." And Bill Lamb said, "I've see'd little old-fashioned blue guineas. Little old things wouldn't grow much longer'n that [indicating about two feet]. An' I've see'd them s'fat 'til their bellies'ud drag along 'til they couldn't get over a pole in th' woods much bigger'n my leg."

Our contacts tell us that the sweetest meat came from hogs fattened on chestnuts. One problem, however, was that instead of rendering into good white lard, the fat of these hogs would boil down into a dark oil. Acorn mast made the meat taste bitter and altered the consistency of the fat. For these reasons, hogs to be slaughtered were often rounded up and brought down out of the mountains to the farms where they were fed on corn for anywhere from a few weeks to over a month. This removed any bitterness from the meat and softened the fat properly for rendering into lard.

Hogs were slaughtered, cut up, cured, and smoked at home. In fact, in many mountain homes today, slaughtering remains a family venture—the only difference being that now there is no more open forest range, so the hogs are kept and fed at the farm until killing time. The actual slaughtering is done in late November when the weather turns cold to stay. Since there were no meat freezers in the mountains, one had to rely on the winter weather to keep the meat from spoiling while it cured.

Most families paid strict attention to the phase the moon was in, and they killed on the first cold day they could get when the moon was "right." As one said, "If you kill a hog on th' new of th' moon, slice it and put it in a pan, it'll just blow you 'til you can't fry th' grease out of it hardly. You got t'kill it on th' right time of th' moon. You don't never want to kill it on th' new moon." Another said, "We'd kill hogs on th' full moon, or just about th' full moon. While th' moon was shrinkin', th' meat'd shrink. There'd be a lot'a lard an' grease if it'uz on th' shrinkin' of th' moon. If it'uz on th' new moon, you wouldn't make much lard, and th' meat'd swell up when y'cooked it 'stead'a shrink." Other farmers would kill their own hogs when the moon was shrinking, but they would take hogs to market when the moon was growing so that the meat would weigh more.

Early in the morning of butchering day, the scalding water was readied. Some farms had a cast-iron bowl about four feet in diameter set in a stone furnace. The bowl was filled with water, a fire built in the furnace, and by the time the hog was killed, the water would be hot. Other families simply had an oil drum tipped half over and filled half full with water. Into this they put heated rocks which heated the water. Others heated water in pots to pour over the carcass. The water in all cases was heated nearly to the boiling point, and ashes were often added to help loosen the hair.

Meanwhile, the hog was killed (either by a sharp blow on the head with a rock or axe head, or by shooting it in the back of the head or between the eyes), and its jugular vein (on the left side of the throat about three inches back from the jawbone) pierced immediately. As one described it, "Stick'im right in th' goozle'ere."

When the bleeding slowed, the hog was dragged to the "scaldin' place" and dipped in the hot water and rolled over to loosen the hair (by pulling or scraping), hauled out and scraped with a not-too-sharp knife, immersed again immediately, and the procedure repeated until most of the hair was off the hide. The hog

PLATE 224 Hobe Beasley and John Hopper first lift the hog's head into a tilted barrel filled with scalding water, and leave it there long enough to loosen the hair.

PLATE 225 Hobe, John, Mrs. Hopper, and Lum Williams work over the hog until it is scraped clean.

PLATE 226 Scalding water can be poured over places where a few hairs remain and then they too are scraped off, leaving a completely bare carcass. Here Hobe finishes a leg.

PLATE 227 The leaders in the back legs are exposed, and the gambling stick is inserted between leader and leg.

was not left in the water too long at any one time or the hair would "set" rather than loosen.

If for some reason the hog had to be killed and cleaned away from home, the men often dug a hole in the ground, filled it with water, added rocks heated in the fire, and then dipped the hog in that. Others simply laid the hog on the ground, covered him with burlap sacks, hay, grass, or anything that would help hold the heat, and then poured boiling water over him to loosen the hair. Another told us that they used to hang the hog up by the nose, cut the hide off in three-inch strips ("Hit'll come plumb off pertiest you ever seen"), and gut it.

When the hide was scraped clean, the hamstring was exposed on both hind legs, and a gambling stick sharpened on both ends—or a singletree—was slipped behind the exposed tendons. The hog was then strung up on a stout pole (*see Plates 228 and 229*), the ends of which were set in forked supports, or in the forks of two nearby trees.

PLATE 228   Next the supporting pole is run between the hog's legs and . . .

PLATE 229   . . . raised into place, suspending the hog head down. Hot water is again dashed over the carcass, and any spots that still may not be completely clean are scraped again.

PLATE 230   The cleaned hog is now ready to gut. Hobe prepares to make the first incision—a long cut down the middle of the underside from crotch to chin.

PLATE 231   The first incision is made taking care not to cut the intestinal membrane.

PLATE 232   Mrs. Hopper prepares to make the second cut.

PLATE 233   The second cut is made, and the intestines drop from the gut cavity and are caught in a tub.

Hot water was then poured over those places not completely clean, and they were scraped again.

Now the neck was cut around the base of the head and through the throat so that the backbone was ringed completely. Then the head was twisted off and set aside to be used as explained in the recipe on p. 202. The remaining blood was allowed to drain from the carcass, and then, with a sharp butcher knife, one long, deep cut was made down the middle of the underside from crotch to chin, being careful not to slice the envelope of membrane holding the intestines. Then the large intestine was cut free at the anus, the end pulled out and tied shut, the gullet cut at the base of the throat, the membrane holding the intestines sliced, and the entrails allowed to fall out into a large tub placed under the carcass. The liver was then cut free and the gall bladder excised from its side, and then the liver was cut up and set aside to soak for later use. Also set aside and saved, in most cases, were the lungs, heart, and kidneys. The valves, veins, and arteries were trimmed off the heart, the stomach and small intestines retrieved from the entrails, and all were drained, washed, and set in water to soak while the cutting continued.

When the inside of the carcass was completely cleaned, it was taken down and cut up. If there were enough people, one group might begin scalding a second hog, another might prepare the entrails and organs since most of them had to be used at once, and yet another might cut up the gutted carcass. A sausage pot would be started for the trimmings of lean meat, and a lard pot would be started for all the trimmings of fat which would be rendered the next day.

The cutting operation was done in several ways. Here is the most common: Remove leaf lard while carcass is still hanging. (The leaf lard is that fat which held the intestines.) Throw it into the fat pot to be rendered into lard and cracklin's. It is not salted and cured. Then make one cut all the way down the middle of the back into the backbone. Take the carcass down and put it on its back on a table or counter. With an axe, chop all the way down both sides of the backbone, close to the backbone, and lift it out. The meat then falls into two pieces. (This is the old way. Nowadays they saw the backbone right down the middle and get pork chops and fatback.) Now remove the tenderloin. It lies on either side of the backbone's cavity. Under that is the fatback, which can be taken out if you wish to use it separately in cooking. Now remove the two sections of rib cage by slicing the mesentery between the outside

PLATE 234 The large intestine is cut free at the anus, pulled out, and . . .

PLATE 235 . . . tied off with a cloth strip or cord. The gut cavity is then cleaned completely.

of the ribs and the inside of the middlin' meat. Each section should come out as one piece.

Find the joints, and cut the shoulders and hams off. What's left is the middlin' (or "side meat"). This thick slice of meat from each side, if cured and smoked, is the source of country bacon. You simply slice the bacon off the middlin' meat, cutting in the same direction in which the ribs originally ran. "Streak'a'lean" is the same lean middlin' meat as the bacon, but it is only salt cured, not smoked.

Now the ribs are placed on a chopping block and cut into two-inch sections and put aside to can, along with the backbone which is cut apart at each vertebra.

Hams, shoulders, middlin' (and jowls if you wish) are trimmed up. The trimmings are put into either the lard or sausage pots, and the rest is set aside for immediate salting.

The backbones and ribs are usually canned. Tenderloin is often cooked at once, along with the heart, lungs, liver, kidneys, and head (see recipes for hog, pp. 202–7). Sausage is ground and canned at once. Fat scraps are usually left until the next morning. Then they are cut up and the lard rendered out.

CURING AND SMOKING HOG

Meat was cured by the mountain families in several ways. Professional butchers today would probably shudder at the apparently haphazard measurements they used, but they often seemed to work.

Hams, shoulders, and middlin' meat (and the jowl if you wished) were the pieces most commonly cured. These pieces were taken to the smokehouse as soon after the slaughtering as possible—preferably while the meat was still warm, and never more than twenty-four hours after. On some farms, the smokehouse sides were relatively open, being constructed of two to three inch slats with a three-quarter-inch crack between each. Many have told us that a common sight in the spring was smokehouses with gray smoke billowing out the sides.

Others, however, claim that a sealed smokehouse (usually logs chinked with mud) is better as it keeps insects out, keeps the meat cool in warm weather, and keeps it from freezing in cold weather. Arguments could be made for either kind.

The meat was taken to the smokehouse, thoroughly salted, and then set up on waist-high shelves or down in boxes or barrels to "take the salt." Most preferred the shelf system as it allowed the meat to get the necessary ventilation more easily. Meanwhile, the winter weather provided natural refrigeration while the meat was going through the curing process.

There were different ways to begin the curing. Mann Norton's father would simply "cover each hunk of meat up good and white" with salt. Taylor Crockett preferred eight pounds of salt for each hundred pounds of meat. He mixed the salt with one quart of molasses, two ounces of black pepper, and two ounces of red pepper. Then he smeared the mix on the meat, allowing it to stay six to eight weeks depending on the weather (longer if it got very cold). "Valley John" Carpenter used simply five pounds of salt for a two hundred-pound hog. Lon Reid used ten pounds of salt per hundred pounds of meat. Lake Stiles, rather than putting the meat in a smokehouse, would take it to his cellar which had a dirt floor. He would put the meat right on the floor with the flat side down, and allow the earth to draw the animal taint out of the meat, keep it cool, and prevent souring or spoiling.

If meat was needed during the winter months, the family simply cut what they needed off the curing pork, washed the salt off, soaked it overnight, parboiled it the next day, and then cooked it. If it were left all winter, it would go through a second operation in the spring.

When the weather began to get warm (usually when the peach trees bloomed), the second phase of the operation began on the meat that was left. It was taken out of the salt mix, washed, and then treated by any of the following means:

Cover the meat with a mixture of black pepper and borax to keep the "skipper" out. (Skippers are the larvae of the skipper fly.) The meat is then hung in the smokehouse.

Wash the meat thoroughly and coat it with a mixture of brown sugar and pepper. Then put it in a bag and hang it up in the smokehouse.

Turner Enloe washes the meat, and then uses a mixture of one package of brown sugar, two boxes of red pepper, and one box of saltpeter per hog. He adds enough water to the mixture to make a syrup, coats the pieces with the liquid, and then sets them in a box to age. Lizzie Carpenter shells a bushel of white corn. She puts some in the bottom of a wooden box, puts the washed middlin' meat on top of that, skin side down, covers it with corn, adds another side, and so on until finished. The corn draws the salt out, keeps the meat from tasting strong, and gives it good flavor. Bill Lamb puts a mixture of borax and black pepper on the washed meat and *then* smokes it (see smoking section). Lake Stiles washes the meat and then buries it in a box of hickory ashes. He claims it never tastes strong this way since the ashes keep air from getting to the meat. His grandmother would bury it in corn meal which would do almost as well.

Many, however, prefer the taste of smoked meat. Holes were poked in the middlin' meat, white oak splits run through the holes, and the meat hung from the joists of the smokehouse. Hams and shoulders were done the same way.

Then a fire was built inside the house. If it had a dirt floor, the fire could be built right on the floor. Otherwise, a wash pot was set in the middle of the room and a fire built in that. The fire itself was made of small green chips of hickory or oak, pieces of hickory bark, or even corncobs in some cases. Using this fuel, the smoke was kept billowing through the house for from two to six days, or until the meat took on the brown crust that was desired both for its flavor, and for its ability to keep flies and insects out of the meat.

If you intend to cure and smoke your own meats, you might want to write the Cooperative Extension Service of the College of Agriculture at the University of Georgia in Athens, Georgia, and ask them for their booklet *Curing Georgia Hams Country Style*. It gives specific instructions such as:

The best slaughtering weight for a hog is from 180 to 240 pounds.

Kill hogs only when the temperature is 32–35° F. Souring bacteria multiply rapidly at temperatures above 40°. Cure the meat immediately after slaughtering.

Do not cure a bruised ham as it will spoil.

A good curing mixture is eight pounds of salt, three pounds of sugar, and three ounces of saltpeter. Apply the mix at the rate of 1¼ ounces per pound. Use a third of the mixture on the first day, another third on the third day, and the last third on the tenth day. Rub it in thoroughly each time.

On a ham, good salt penetration requires seven days per inch of thickness. Bacon requires from fourteen to sixteen days.

Add another day to the curing schedule for each day the weather is below freezing.

Then wash the outside coating of salt off and leave the meat at a temperature below 40° for another twenty to twenty-five days for salt equalization. Then smoke the meat, if desired. Don't allow the temperature in the smokehouse to exceed 100°. Use hickory, oak, or apple.as fuel.

Smoke hams until they are amber or mahogany in color (usually about two days). Smokehouse should be sealed and ventilated with fans, or completely screened for natural ventilation.

RECIPES FOR HOG

THE HEAD

SOUSE—(*Also called "souse meat," "headcheese," "pressed hog's head," etc.*) Prepare the raw hog's head as follows:

Trim, scrape, or singe off any hairs or bristles that are left.

If you intend to use the ears, brains, snout, tongue, or jowls for any purpose other than souse, remove them and set aside to soak. Otherwise, leave them on the head to be ground up. Note that the ears are gristly, and when ground up in the souse, they leave white flukes of gristle in the meat. This is not harmful, but some find it unattractive.

Cut out the eyes.

The bulk of the head is now halved or quartered with an axe, or left whole (depending on the size of your pot), and while still fresh, is put in a pot of fresh water, usually to soak overnight. This soaking removes the remaining blood from the meat.

We have found only a few people who cook the head whole. One reason is that leaving it whole makes it harder to soak the blood out. Bill Lamb gave a different reason, saying, "Henry'd killed a hog, and when he come in from work, they had it sittin' there cooked. Hadn't even cut th' ears out, th' eyes'r nothin'. Just cooked th' whole head like it was. Had it sittin' in a dish. That'uz th' first thing he seed was that hog lookin' at him when he come in t'dinner, an' he just turned and went back an' never eat a bite."

After soaking, rinse the head until the rinse water runs clear. Then put it in a pot of clean, salty water and cook it slowly until it is good and tender, and the meat begins to fall off the bones. Then remove all meat from the bones and run through a food chopper.

Seasoning depends on your own taste. Some use, per head, one tablespoon of sage, a half teaspoon ground red pepper, and salt and black pepper to taste. Others use one onion, one pod of strong red pepper chopped fine, and one teaspoon of salt. Beulah Perry uses a little red and black pepper, an onion, a little corn meal, and sage and garlic to taste. Evie Carpenter adds a little vinegar, along with sage, black pepper and onion.

The meat and seasoning are now thoroughly mixed, and then put into capped jars, a mold, or a plate (covered with a clean white cloth). Then, if it is not to be eaten immediately, it is put into the smokehouse where the winter weather will keep it fresh. It can either be eaten cold, or reheated, depending on your preference.

Another method—Proceed as before through the seasoning step. Then put the mixture in a skillet and place on the back of the wood stove until the grease is runny. Remove from the fire, put a plate on top of the meat, and apply pressure to make the grease run out. Repeat until all the grease is out and poured off. Remove the plate, put the meat on a clean plate, and keep in a cold place. Slice as needed.

SCRAPPLE—As told by Mrs. Mann Norton, "Take th' head, an' take th' eyeballs out, an' th' ears, an' cut down in there. Then y'got all th' hairs off of it. Y'put it in a big pot an' cooked it til th' meat just turned loose of th' main big bone.

"Y'lifted them bones out, an' laid your meat over in there an' felt of it with your hands t'see if they wadn't no bones in it. Then y'strain yer liquid through a strainer so th' little bones'd come out. Put'cher liquid back in a pot, and put that mashed meat back in that liquid. Put'cher sage an' pepper in there. Then y'stir it 'til it got t'boilin'. Then y'stick plain corn meal in there til it's just plumb thick. Then y'pour it up in a mold, an' cut it off'n fry it, an' brown it. Tastes just like fish."

Mann Norton added, "Just hold your tongue so y'didn't swaller it when y'went t'eatin'!"

HOG'S HEAD STEW—This recipe comes from the Joanne Carver family. Every harvesttime they plunge into a cooking-canning spree that goes for days and leaves them more than ready for the winter. The measurements given below yielded sixty-three quarts last time around. If you can't handle quite that much, cut proportionally, subtracting or adding other ingredients according to preference.

1½ hog's heads	1 package poultry
2 shoulders or hams of venison	seasoning
	bay leaves to taste
4 chickens	5 pounds salt (or to
1 peck onions	taste)
1 gallon Irish potatoes	Worcestershire Sauce
5 half gallons each of tomatoes, corn, peas, carrots	to taste
	pepper to taste
6 large cans tomato juice to thin	broth may be substituted for, or added to the tomato juice

Cook the meat until it comes easily off the bones. Cool, remove the meat from the bones, and grind it up (or run through a food chopper) together with the other ingredients. Place the mixture in quart jars, seal, and cook in a pressure cooker for sixty minutes at ten pounds pressure. Then store away for the lean months.

Her mother's recipe for the same stew, provided us by Brenda Carver, varies somewhat: 1 hog's head, 2 chickens, 4 pounds ground beef, 1 gallon potatoes, 1 gallon tomatoes, 4 number two cans each of peas, corn, and carrots. Chop and blend ingredients, can, cook in pressure cooker for thirty minutes.

JOWLS—The jowls are fatty, so they are often removed rather than being combined with the souse meat. Some salt them down and cure them just like hams or middlin' meat, and save them until warm weather to be boiled with vegetables. Others grind them up with the sausage meat.

Some also fry them. As Bill Lamb said, "Now you talkin' about part of a hog that I love is th' jowls. They ain't a better tastin' bite'a meat in a hog than th' jowl is. You fry it."

TONGUE—Clean by pouring boiling water over it and scraping it. Then boil until tender in a little salt water with pepper added if you wish. Slice and serve.

BRAIN—Most of our contacts put the brains in hot water to loosen the veil of skin covering them. Then they boil them in one cup of water, adding salt and pepper to taste while stirring. When cooked, they mash them with a potato masher, put them in a pan, and scramble them with eggs.

Others let them stand in cold water for one to two hours. Then they drain them and remove any unwanted fibers. Then cook as above for twenty minutes in salted water and proceed as above, using eggs, etc.

SNOUT (*also called the "rooter"*)—the snout is often cleaned and roasted. Mann Norton claims, "Lot'a people throwed away that they called th' rooter. Oh I forbid that. I'd rather have that as any part a'-th' hog. Oh that's good eatin'."

EARS—If the ears were not used in souse, they could also be boiled in salt water until tender, and eaten. Very few of our contacts used them alone, however, due to the amount of gristle they contain, especially at the tips.

INTERNAL ORGANS

LIVER—Most of our contacts used the liver for "liver pudding," or "liver mush." They made it as follows—Cut up the liver, wash it well, and remove skin. Boil until tender in salted water. Then remove and run through a colander until fine, or mash well. Mix the meat with one cup of the broth it was cooked in. Bring to a boil slowly, stirring in sifted corn meal until thick. Also stir in salt (to taste), a half teaspoon black pepper, two tablespoons sage, and a little red pepper if desired.

Pour into a mold and let sit until cold. Slice and eat. Some eat it as a sandwich, or warm the slices in bacon fat or grease before eating.

HEART—None of our contacts used the heart by itself, but none of them threw it away, either. Some canned it after cleaning, with backbones and ribs for use later in stews. Others boiled the heart, backbone, and lights (lungs) together for stew. Still another boiled kidneys, heart, tail, and tongue together for stew.

LIGHTS (*more commonly known as lungs*)—Nowhere did we run into as much difference of opinion as with this item. One said, "It's very good—*very* good." Another said, "Lots'a folks like th' lights, but I never did." Another comment was simply, "Feed'em to th' dogs!" Those recipes we *did* get—

Boil them in just enough salted water to cover them after cleaning them well. Don't use too much water or it will steal some of their flavor. If there isn't any water left when they're done, it's better.

Cook them down to the consistency of a gravy, mash, and serve. They cannot be kept.

Another chopped up the lights with the liver and tongue, added a chopped onion, red pepper, salt, and cooked until tender.

STOMACH (*also called the "paunch" or "punch"*)—Cut the stomach free of intestines, split, and wash out well. Scrape it down and soak in salt water for three days. Then rinse, cut up, and cook like chitlins. (Most of our contacts also removed the inside layer when cutting it up prior to frying.)

INTESTINES (*called "chitterlings" or, more commonly, "chitlins."*) —Sections of the intestine are put in a jar of salt water and allowed to sit for three or four days. Then they are taken out, rinsed, washed, and rinsed again. In winter, they can be lightly salted, put up in jars, and kept for a few days before cooking.

When cooking, cut up in small pieces and remove any unwanted layers of lining. Then boil in salt water with a half pod of pepper until tender. Dip into a batter made of flour, water, and baking powder (with an egg if desired) and fry; or roll in corn meal and fry in grease.

THE REMAINDER

FEET—Rake hot coals out on the fireplace hearth. Put the feet on the hearth with the hooves against the coals. When very hot, the hooves can be sliced out of the meat easily, and the remainder of the hair scraped or singed off, and the meat scraped clean. Then put in a pot of salt water and cook, or roast.

The feet can also be boiled in salty water until the meat slips off the hooves. They can be pickled too.

Mann Norton said, "Doc Neville, now he always wanted th' feet. I'd pack'em in a shoe box just as full as I could get it and mail 'em to him."

BACKBONE/RIBS—These can either be put together and stewed like chicken parts, barbecued, or canned with a teaspoon of salt per quart can. Water is not necessary when heating as they make their own gravy.

TAIL—Often the tail was saved for use in stews. One contact made a stew of feet, ears, tail, salt, and red pepper, boiled until tender.

SKIN—The mother of one of our contacts used to save pieces of skin, put them in a pan, and roast them. Then the children could "eat it all along."

SAUSAGE—Use any combination of lean meat not used otherwise.

This includes trimmings of lean meat from hams, shoulders, middlin' meat, etc. It can also include the tenderloin, meat from the head, and, if you wish, the jowls.

Take ten pounds of lean pork, a quarter cup salt, a half cup brown sugar, two tablespoons sage, two teaspoons black pepper, and two teaspoons red pepper. Many parch their own red pepper in front of the fireplace, crush it, and then add it to the sausage.

Run the mixture through a sausage grinder, fry it good and brown (but not completely cooked since it has to be reheated when served), pack into jars (half to three-quarters full) while still very hot, pour hot grease over the top, close the jars, and turn them upside down to cool. When the grease cools, it seals the lids shut, and the sausage will keep until you are ready to use it. It is usually stored with the jars remaining upside down.

Other ways to store it:

Roll the sausage into balls, pack them in a churn jar, pour hot grease over the top, tie a cloth over the lid, and set in the water trough of your spring house.

Pack the sausage in sections of cleaned, small intestine, tie the intestine off at both ends, and hang from the joists of the smokehouse for curing.

Remove the ear from a corn shuck, pack the sausage inside after washing the shuck thoroughly, tie the end of the shuck closed with string or wire, and hang in the smokehouse.

Pack in small, clean, white cloth sacks and hang in smokehouse.

FAT—The fat is trimmed from entrails, hams, shoulders, middlin', etc. It is left out all night in the lard pot so that the cold weather can solidify it and make it easier to cut up.

In the morning, the fat is cut up into pieces about the size of hens' eggs and put in a pot containing just enough water to keep it from sticking to the sides when cooked. The pot is then placed over a fire, and the fat is allowed to cook slowly. It is stirred often. By evening, the grease will have boiled out, the water evaporated, and the hard residue called "cracklin's" will have fallen to the bottom.

The grease (lard) is poured into containers, allowed to harden, and is used all winter for cooking. The cracklin's are saved for bread.

Add soda if you don't want many cracklin's. The soda also keeps it from smelling while cooking and from tasting strong.

WEATHER SIGNS

FORECASTING WINTER BY ANIMALS

It will be a bad winter if:

   squirrels begin gathering nuts early (middle or late September).

   muskrat houses are built big.

   beaver lodges have more logs.

   the north side of a beaver dam is more covered with sticks than
      the south.

   squirrels' tails grow bushier.

   fur or hair on animals such as horses, sheep, mules, cows, and
      dogs is thicker than usual.

   the fur on the bottom of rabbit's foot is thicker.

   cows' hooves break off earlier.

   squirrels build nests low in trees.

   wild hogs gather sticks, straw, and shucks to make a bed.

   animals grow a short fuzzy coat under their regular one.

   crows gather together.

   hoot owls call late in the fall.

   screech owls sound like women crying.

   juncos are feeding in the trees.

   birds huddle on the ground.

   you hear an "old hoot owl on the mountain, winter's comin'
      soon—better put on your boots"—Kenny Runion.

   birds eat up all the berries early.

FORECASTING WINTER BY INSECTS

It will be a bad winter if:
> hornets and yellow jackets build their nests heavier and closer to the ground than usual.
>
> worms are bending up and going into peoples' houses and abandoned buildings in October.
>
> there are a lot of spiders, frost worms, and black bugs about in the fall.
>
> miller moths hit the screen trying to get in.
>
> crickets are in the chimney.
>
> an ant builds its hill high.

The woolly worm tells of a bad winter if:
> there are a lot of them crawling about.
>
> he has a heavy coat.
>
> the black band on his back is wide. (The more black than brown he is, and/or the wider the black stripe, the worse the winter.)
>
> if he's black in front, the bad weather is to come; and if he's black behind, the worst weather is past.
>
> if he's brown at both ends and orange in the middle, the winter will be mild.
>
> you see him crawling before the first frost.

Three months after the first katydid begins "hollerin'," the first killing frost will come.

When butterflies:
> migrate early, winter will be early.
>
> gather in bunches in the air, winter is coming soon.

FORECASTING WINTER BY PLANTS

It will be a bad winter if:
> blackberry blooms are especially heavy.
>
> carrots grow deeper.
>
> grapes, cockleburrs, and apples mature early.
>
> sweet potatoes have a tougher skin.
>
> onions grow more layers.
>
> trees are laden with green leaves late in the fall.
>
> the crop of holly and dogwood berries is heavy.
>
> hickory nuts have a heavy shell.
>
> there's a heavy crop of berries, acorns, and pinecones.
>
> bark on trees is thicker.
>
> tree bark is heaviest on the north side.

corn shucks and silk grown thicker, and the shucks grow tighter
around, and further over the ends of the ears.
leaves shed before they turn.
moss grows heavy on the trees.
the old-time corn ear (shank) hangs downward.
laurel leaves roll up.
pine cones open early.
The darker green the grass is during the summer, the harder the
winter.

FORECASTING WINTER BY WEATHER

Two frosts and lots of rain mean cold weather is near.
A late frost means a bad winter.
For every frost or fog in August, there will be a snowy day in winter.
At least three severe fogs in June or July mean early snow.
If it snows crosslegged, it will be a deep one.
If the first snow stays on the ground for three days, another snow
will come to top it.
If it frosts before November 23, it will be a bad winter.
Lots of low rolling thunder in the late fall means a bad winter.
A long hot summer means a long cold winter—the hotter the summer,
the colder the winter.

FORECASTING WINTER BY FIRE

When you build a fire outside and it pops, it will snow in three days.
If a fire "tramps" snow coming down the chimney (in other words,
if noises are coming from the chimney that sound like boots
swishing through deep, dry snow), it will be a deep snow.
It will be a hard winter if smoke from the chimney flows toward or
settles on the ground. It will snow within twenty-six days.
If it's cloudy and smoke rises, there's a chance of snow.

FORECASTING WINTER BY THE MOON

The number of days old the moon is at the first snow tells how many
snows there will be that winter.

FORECASTING WEATHER

It will rain:
within three days if the horns of the moon point down.
if leaves show their backs.
if cows are lying down in the pasture.

if there is a ring around the moon. Count the stars in the ring
and it will rain within that many days.

if the sun sets with clouds.

within three days, if you see a black snake in a tree.

if an ant covers the hole to his ant hill.

if smoke goes to the ground.

the same time the next day, if the sun shines while it rains.

if earthworms come to the surface of the ground.

if birds fly low.

If it hasn't rained in a long time, and it starts before 7 A.M., it'll quit before 11 A.M.

If it rains on "Blasting Days" (the three longest days of the year), there won't be any "mast" (acorns, chestnuts, etc.) for animals like hogs to feed on.

If it rains on Easter Sunday, it will rain every Sunday for seven weeks.

If it begins raining on the day the moon becomes full, it will continue raining until the moon quarters.

The first twelve days after Christmas indicate what each month in the next year will be like.

The weather will be fair if:

you hear a screech owl.

smoke rises.

crickets holler. The temperature will rise.

PLANTING BY THE SIGNS

Let there be lights in the firmament of the heaven to divide the day from the night; and let them be for signs, and for seasons, and for days, and years.

Genesis 1:14

To everything there is a season, and a time to every purpose under the heaven: a time to be born, and a time to die; a time to plant, and a time to pluck up that which is planted.

Ecclesiastes 3:1–2

At the time when many of the crops planted in the spring were gathered in and preserved for the winter to come, our attention was turned to a phenomenon that had fascinated us for some time—that of planting, harvesting, and conducting a number of other activities by the moon and the signs of the zodiac. Its rules have been passed down so carefully from year to year that its practice bridges the gaps between the generations more successfully and more completely than most.

Over thirty separate interviews were conducted for this chapter, some with people who follow the signs religiously, and some with those who scoff at the idea. Many of the interviews were taped, making it possible for us to set down information just as it was given us—word for word.

THE ZODIAC

Ancient astronomers discovered that a number of the bright constellations of stars that they had studied and named were evenly spaced along the yearly path of the sun in a belt about eighteen de-

E. BLACK'S LIFETIME PLANTING, BUSINESS AND FISHING GUIDE

INFORMATION IN REGARDS TO EVERYDAY AFFAIRS COMPILED FROM 13 YEARS EXPERIENCE

INFORMATION

Check your Calendar or Almanac for the dates of month they appear each of the 12 Signs comes and every 28 days each remains 2 or 3 days. You will find most every month a little different in dates. Notice when I say root Crops I mean every thing that bears in the ground when I say above ground I mean every thing that bears above the ground. Get my new book "God's Way" Price $1.00.

Sign Leo In The Heart

This is a Fire Sign. Barren Sign favors no planting or transplanting. Good for destroying bushes and weeds and deading trees. It favors sports, pleasure, love and romance ask for jobs. Good for painting. Get hair waved, baking cakes,

3rd Sign Gemini In The Arms

This is an Air Sign. I find it one of the second best signs for planting and transplanting All Crops, root crops and crops that bear above the ground. Favors talking things over with people. Also favors making jelly, preserves and pickles.

1st Sign Aries In The Head

Known as a fiery Sign. Hot, dry and barren. Very good for planting beets, onions and tobacco. Not good for planting and transplanting other crops. Favors welding, getting hair waved, all cooking, making preserves, pickles and jelly. Also destroying weeds and bushes. Good for hunting, fair for fishing.

2nd Sign Taurus In The Neck

An Earth Sign. No. 1 for all root crops. Peanuts, potatoes, and etc. Transplanting all plants, second best for all crops bearing above the ground and all flowers. Favors buying, attend sales, deal with creditors. Very good for fishing, making pickles & canning.

4th Sign Cancer in the Breast

A Water Sign. No. 1 top sign for all flowers, planting and transplanting all crops that bear above the ground. When I say bear above the ground I mean cotton, corn, cane, tobacco, peas, beans, pepper, watermellons, squash, cucumbers, okra, wheat, rye, oats and etc., all cover crops, all grasses, all leaf crops. This sign also No. 1 for all root crops. Biddies hatched in this sign for laying hens pigs born for males & brood sows. Good for all cooking, changing jobs, moving, cut hair to stimulate growth. Good for fishing, making potato beds and seed beds.

EACH SIGN APPEARS 2 OR 3 DAYS EACH MONTH

6th Sign Virgo In The Bowels

An Earth sign Doesn't favor planting nor transplanting no crops. Barren sign very good for bus.

8th Sign Scorpio In The Loins

This is known as a Water Sign. No. 1 for all crops that bear above the ground. Also for flowers. Second best for all root crops. When I say root crops, I mean all potatoes, peanuts, chuffas, onions, beets, carrots, turnips, rutabagas, etc. Setting out plants, biddies for laying hens, pigs for males and brood sows. Set out fruit trees. Flower bushes and vines. Good for fishing and hunting.

INFORMATION: I made a 13 year test for the right signs for planting all crops, business and fishing and other things and for the correct dates I found the Ladies Birthday Almanac and others that correspond with it are most correct.

7th Sign Libra In The Kidneys

An Air Sign very good for crops that bear above the ground. Favors friendship and business.

9th Sign Sagittarius The Thighs

This is a Fire Sign. Fairly good for planting onions and cucumbers. Favors business affairs. Ask for loans, deal with lawyers, judges and bankers, work out future plans. Good for painting, Get hair waved, make cakes, make candy, preserves, jelly and pickles. Don't transplant anything.

For Laying Hens

For laying hens and brood sows 3 good signs in every month but for the best hatched off or born between February 18th and March 20th or between June 21st or July 23rd or between October 23rd or November 22nd in the sign Pisces or Cancer or Scorpio which sign appears in every month on different dates. Signs the same in every state.—

11th Sign Aquarius In The Legs

Known as an Air Sign. Very good for planting crops that produce above the ground. Except seeds are apt to rot. This is a friendly sign. Exchange ideas, seek help from friends, favors dealing with all types of people in all types of business. Favors sports and pleasure.

12th Sign Pisces In The Feet

Known as a Water sign No. 1 for planting and transplanting all crops that bear above the ground. And all flowers. Second best sign for all root crops. Biddies hatched for laying hens, pigs for brood sows. Best for pulling teeth, marking hogs, prune and set out trees, bushes and vines. Good for fishing. Wean babies and animals.

10th Sign Capricornus In The Knees

Known as an Earth Sign. No. 1 for all root crops Potatoes, peanuts, onions, beets etc. Second best for all flowers. All crops that bear above the ground, all transplanting. Pull teeth, mark hogs, prune trees and vines. Good for business. Fair for fishing. Canning.

PLATE 236

PLATE 237

grees wide. This belt also included the paths of the planets and the monthly path of the moon.

This belt was subsequently divided into twelve parts each of thirty degrees in length called "signs." Each of these signs contained a constellation of stars, and each sign thus received its name from the name of the constellation it contained. Since all the signs except Libra were named after living things, the belt was named the zodiac, or "zone of animals."

As the early wise men believed that there was an intimate relationship between the celestial bodies and mankind, the twelve signs soon became identified with various parts of the human body. Charts which illustrate this relationship have been noted as far back in history as 1300 B.C. according to the 1967 edition of *Grier's Almanac*.

Astrologers all over the world lost no time in seizing the zodiac as a guide for their predictions. With its use, they and their followers constructed everything from horoscopes to guides for good fishing days. One of their constructions which received serious and devoted attention from thousands of families was a set of rules for planting. Although the practice seems to be declining in popularity now, there are still many accurate sources of information to be found. Grier's annual almanac, "first published in 1807 and every year since," is mailed out of Atlanta and contains one of the most complete astrological calendars available. A wall calendar equally full of information of this sort is published by the Francis and Lusky Company of Nashville, Tennessee. But perhaps the most specific information comes from T. E. Black. He publishes a guide, numerous fishing and planting charts, and he even personally answers many of the letters he receives from his followers. The chart which precedes this article is from his booklet, *God's Way*, which gives complete directions for planting by the signs as tested through years of research. It is available from Mr. C. J. Black, P. O. Box 785, Andalusia, Alabama, and is reprinted here with his permission.

HOW IT WORKS

Every day of the month is dominated by one of the twelve signs of the zodiac. Each of the twelve appears at least once a month, and then for a period of either two or three days. All good planting calendars label each day with the sign that rules over it (depending on which constellation is foremost in the sky at the time), the part of the body and the planet associated with the sign, and the element it is most closely akin to. The following chart summarizes this information.

PLATE 238

SIGN	SYMBOL	BODY PART	PLANET	ELEMENT
1. Aries	Ram	Head	Mars	Fire
2. Taurus	Bull	Neck, throat	Venus	Earth
3. Gemini	Twins	Arms, chest	Mercury	Air
4. Cancer	Crab	Breast, stomach	Moon	Water
5. Leo	Lion	Heart, back	Sun	Fire
6. Virgo	Virgin	Bowels	Mercury	Earth
7. Libra	Balance	Kidneys	Venus	Air
8. Scorpio	Scorpion	Loins	Mars	Water
9. Sagittarius	Archer	Thighs	Jupiter	Fire
10. Capricornus	Goat	Knees	Saturn	Earth
11. Aquarius	Waterman	Legs, ankles	Uranus	Air
12. Pisces	Fish	Feet	Neptune	Water

The signs always appear in sequence, beginning with the Ram or Head and working their way down to Pisces, the Fish or Feet. Following Pisces, the Ram appears again beginning a new sequence.

Each of the signs is known as being either masculine, feminine, airy, dry, barren, fiery, earthy, moist, watery, fruitful, or very fruitful. In general, any activity that requires a dry atmosphere, such as painting, should be done in one of the dry signs; and an activity requiring moisture, such as some planting, should be done on one of the moist or fruitful signs.

The best time of all, of course, to conduct any activity is when a day falls on both an ideal sign *and* a good phase of the moon.

Over the years, a more specific set of rules has grown up around the zodiac which governs such activities as planting and harvesting. These rules take into account both the sign governing the day and the phase of the moon on that particular day. At the beginning of the planting season, for example, the farmer consults his calendar, picks out one of the fourteen favorable days that occur every month, and plants only on one of these fourteen "fruitful" days. Should he miss and plant his crops on one of the unfruitful days, his crops will not produce at half their ability, say the believers. T. E. Black even goes so far as to say that a few hours can make the difference between success and failure, and many of his followers agree.

THE RULES

The following rules were gathered both from interviews and wide reading. They do not represent a complete set, but they should serve to give the reader a good idea as to the nature of this system. We also included rules for butchering, cutting hair, killing weeds, pulling teeth, and others to give some grasp of the scope of the subject.

PLANTING—Planting is best done in the fruitful signs of Scorpio, Pisces, Taurus, or Cancer (when the signs are in the loins, feet, neck, or breast).

Plow, till, and cultivate in Aries.

Never plant anything in one of the barren signs. They are good only for trimming, deadening, and destroying.

Always set plants out in a water or earth sign.

Graft just before the sap starts to flow, while the moon is in its first or second quarter, and while it is passing through a fruitful watery sign, or Capricorn. Never graft or plant on Sunday as this is a barren, hot day (the sun's day).

Plant flowers in Libra which is an airy sign that also represents beauty. Plant them while the moon is in the first quarter unless you need the seeds, in which case use the period between the moon's second quarter and full.

PLATE 239

Corn planted in Leo will have a hard, round stalk and small ears.
Crops planted in Taurus and Cancer will stand drought.

Plant beans when the signs are in the arms.

Root flower cuttings, limbs, vines, and set out flower bushes and trees in December and January when the signs are in the knees and feet.

Never transplant in the heart or head as both these signs are "Death Signs."

If you want a large vine and stalk with little fruit, plant in Virgo— "bloom days."

Don't plant potatoes in the feet. If you do, they will develop little nubs like toes all over the main potato. The best time is a dark night in March.

Plant all things which yield above the ground during the increase or growing of the moon, and all things which yield below the ground (root crops) when the moon is decreasing or darkening.

Never plant on the first day of the new moon, or on a day when the moon changes quarters.

In the fourth quarter turn sod, pull weeds, and destroy.

REAPING AND HARVESTING—Pick fruit like apples and pears in the old of the moon (while it is decreasing or shrinking). This will cause the bruised spots and blemishes to dry up rather than rot. They will rot if the fruit is picked on the increase or rising of the moon, or on the new moon.

Harvest most crops when the moon is growing old. This will cause them to keep better and longer.

Dig root crops for seed in the third quarter of the moon. They will keep longer and are usually drier and better.

Gather root crops in the last quarter of the moon when the signs are in the knees or feet.

Can vegetables, cook preserves and jelly, and make pickles in the right sign during the last quarter of the moon.

MISCELLANY—Cut timber in the old of the moon. It will dry better and not become worm-eaten.

Set fence posts in the old of the moon to prevent loosening.

The part of your body governed by a particular sign is more sensitive when the moon is in that sign. People with heart trouble, for example, will have more trouble in Leo's sign, and lovers are more successful at this time. In Taurus (throat) an operation on this part of the body will be unsuccessful. Conversely, if tonsils are removed and teeth are pulled when the signs are in the knees or feet, there is less soreness, loss of blood, and danger of infection. You can easily figure others out for yourself.

Paint houses or cars in a dry sign like Leo or Aries.

Wean a child or animal when the moon is in a sign that does not rule the vital parts of the body (Capricorn, Pisces, Sagittarius).

Set eggs to hatch in a fruitful sign like Cancer. The chicks will mature faster and be better layers.

Quit habits on the second day that the moon is in Sagittarius, or on the new moon, or in Pisces.

If you cut your hair in Libra, Sagittarius, Aquarius, or Pisces, it will grow stronger, thicker, and more beautiful.

Purge with pills in Pisces and with liquids in Sagittarius.

Bake and cook in Aries.

Hunt in Taurus.

Lay foundations in Capricorn.

Don't nail shingles or boards on the growing side of the moon, or the ends will draw up and curl and go crooked.

Destroy weeds, kill trees, turn sod in the barren signs Gemini, Leo, or Virgo (especially if the moon is in the last quarter).

Slaughter while the signs are in the knees or feet, and in the last quarter of the moon.

THOSE WHO BELIEVE

The first information we gathered for this article was through interviews with those people that we knew in advance followed the

PLATE 240

signs. We knew nothing of this phenomenon before we started out.

Here, then, is the beginning of our search:

Mary Cabe, or "Granny" Cabe as she is affectionately known by her family and close friends, lives on Mulberry Road just across the North Carolina line. A tall, thin, stately, elderly woman with flashing, friendly eyes, she was the first person we questioned. Like many young people in this area, we knew nothing about the zodiac when we met her—not even what questions to ask except, "What is it?"

Patiently, with the use of several calendars, she explained its basic principles to us and gave us several of the rules. Her family had used the signs for as long as she could remember, and she spoke quietly and with complete conviction, laughing kindly at our amazement. "Take taters. On th' dark of th' moon or th' old of th' moon—that's th' last quarter," she explained, "they make less vine; and on th' light of th' moon they makes more vine and less tater. . . . Don't plant in th' flowers. A plant blooms itself to death and th' blooms falls off, and don't make cucumbers, tomatoes, squash, or stuff like that. . . . And if you kill a hog on th' growin' of th' moon, th' meat's all puffy and there just ain't no grease a'tall. I don't know why it is, but it's sure thataway for we've tried it."

Her son, Elvin Cabe, agreed, telling us the story of a man he knew who, before cutting his hay, told those helping him that they could walk right behind him and stack it as he went if they wanted to. It would never mold, but would cure perfectly because he was cutting it on just the right time of the moon.

"And you know, that stuff never molded a bit in th' world. Cut hay on th' old of th' moon," he continued, "and it'll dry a third quicker than it will on th' new. On th' new of th' moon, th' sap is still in it. It'll dry, but it'll take a lot longer. It's th' same with wood. Cut it on th' new, and when you put it in th' fire it'll spew water out both ends all th' time. It'll rot out before it'll dry. And take sand in a river. I've noticed this out fishing. On th' new of th' moon, th' water's full of sand as it can be, and if you're standing on th' edge barefooted, th' water will pull th' sand right out from you and sink you down. But on th' old, th' water's clear. It never carries sand.

"Another thing. Dig a hole on th' new of th' moon and you will have dirt to throw away, but if you dig it on th' old of th' moon, you'll not have enough to fill it back again. Look, if you don't believe me, try this, and if it doesn't work, I'll give you a hundred dollar bill. Dig a post hole on th' growin' of th' moon. Dig it ever how deep and how big around you want, and put th' post in it. It'll be loose all th' time and never settle. Dig th' same kind of hole on th' old of th' moon, just th' same size, and sink your post. It'll settle as tight as you could want —like it's took roots and growed there."

By this time, we were fascinated. Anxious to help out, Elvin took us farther up Mulberry Road and introduced us to Mr. Harley Carpenter. Speaking slowly, quietly, chuckling often, he talked about the signs and about the people who refused to believe in them.

"They're as wild as a rabbit sittin' up there in the broom sage," he laughed softly. "Get too close to 'em and they're gone. Seein', in a sense, is a great believin'. You can hear things, but if you've seen it, you've got more sense out of it. If it hadn't'a been true, it wouldn'a been handed down through the years. In other words, it speaks the signs in th' Bible, you know.

"I heared a fella' talkin' about plantin' corn. He said t'other one, he said, 'I plant mine when th' signs is in th' arms and it won't grow high, and th' ear'll come out and shank and hang down.' And th' other'n says, 'Aw, I don't plant by th' signs and by th' moon. I plant in th' ground when I get ready.' He just ain't got th' self-experience, you see. Now all these things, you'd have to go through a process of tryin' and seein'. Then you'd be a permanent believer.

"And th' same way by beans. Now you might talk to a woman about plantin' beans, and they'd just hoot at'ya and say, 'I plant in th' ground,' like I said. But there's a certain time them signs is when if you plant'm, they'll speck and rot, and it's in th' bowels. Now there's a mystery there for me and you to study about that. Why does it happen? And here's what I figure out about it—just thinkin' about my food. It goes in here pleasant and good in th' mouth, and when it comes out, its manufactured and went through a process in th' bowels. In other words, it's rotted, see? Went on out.

"And th' same way by corn now. In my comin' up, my daddy always tried to plant his corn when th' signs was in th' arms; and beans and pumpkins and so on th' same way. Well, now I've growed up and we don't have much corn in th' mountain country, you know. It's about to quit. But people back then always tried to grow enough corn to do 'em, see? Well, they'd have corn shuckin's—go in and help one another. You can't get a crowd together now unless it's for music or somethin' they're goin'ta give away. But in my bein' at corn shuckins' and shuckin' my own corn, you'd find ears once in a while that if they was planted in th' bowels, they'd be grown and matured green—solid dry rot. And th' old people claimed that that was th' signs.

"You take pigs, now—castratin' pigs. If you want a pig to do well, let th'signs be in th' feet. Gone on out, you see; gone on down past th' arms and legs and out, through th' feet."

We asked him about cutting wood. "Cuttin' wood? Oh, shucks yeah. Lots'a people just hoot at'ya talkin' about cuttin' firewood to burn good, but there's a certain time of th' moon when you cut it and it won't do nothin' but fry and hiss about and have to get red hot and maybe burn enough kindlin' to make another fire. There's a certain time in that now about deadenin'. I did know, but I wouldn't say for sure. I think it's th' dark nights in May when th' signs are in th' heart. You stick an axe in a tree, and when you cut it, it'll die."

Twenty miles away, we visited another woman known throughout this area. Mrs. E. N. Nicholson, frail but energetic and bright, is the oldest woman in the county, having watched over a hundred years go past. Did she believe in the signs? "I was brought up in that day, and I can't help from believin' in it. When I plant my garden, I wanta' plant it on the right time of the moon. But most of that's forgotten now."

When asked if she thought it ought to be preserved, she answered, "I can't help but think that it ought. There are too many things to think about today. A good home and plenty of land should make anyone perfectly happy. Too many things now that call for money. We had a good time when I was growin' up, and we got along as well as you all now."

On the way back home, we stopped in to visit Mr. Carnes whose relish, preserve, and jelly stand outside Clayton is a favorite stop for tourists and local people alike. He does not follow the signs himself as he does not plant, but his whole family did. He was able to tell us the following story, and theory.

"Some time ago, a man was castrating two hogs. He finished one, and just as he got to the second, the moon changed, and the second hog bled to death."

He also advanced the theory that you needed to plant your corn so that it would flower on the bright nights of the moon. That way, the insects could see better and pollinate the flowers more completely. This, obviously, would result in a better crop of corn.

The whole thing, being strange to us, still sounded crazy. The next day we had a new angle. If this whole thing *did* work, then there had to be a logical explanation. Margaret Norton would know, if anyone would. She was our next target.

Margaret, author of our recipe column in our magazine, is widely known and respected as one of the most successful gardeners in these

parts. Because of this, and because she has been planting strictly by
the signs for over ten years, she has become the authority in Betty's
Creek valley on the signs and how they work. Knowing Margaret
and her husband Richard better than most of the people we had
interviewed, we felt free to ask her more probing questions. Besides,
we knew a little more about the signs by the time we got to her—
more, at least, than we had known when we talked to Mrs. Cabe—
and so we felt more confident.

She and her husband Richard both talked to us freely. Margaret
explained, "It's all true, and just a few hours can make a difference.
It sure works for me. And th' ones that don't [plant by the signs]—
if they once was to get started at it, they wouldn't change for
nothin'. But they have just growed up thataway and, you know, it's
hard to change when you've done a certain thing all your life. But
I don't know why they won't try it. If they just was to fail with
something several times, they perhaps would try then, because that's
th' thing made me start tryin'. My cucumbers failed. I planted them,
and they just bloomed and bloomed and bloomed and never did any
good. I just planted 'em in an unfruitful sign."

Richard continued. "We plant Irish potatoes by th' signs, too.
They's a certain sign you can plant Irish potatoes in and they'll do
as good again; I know that. They's lots of people who hit it once in
a while anyhow though." And Margaret added, "Naturally once in a
while you'd hit it, because there's fourteen good plantin' days in
every month, see?"

Soon we were on the subject of the younger generation and
whether they were following the signs or not. Margaret commented,
"Young people aren't followin' it. They don't even know th' signs.
They perhaps just go on about somethin' else and never help their
parents in th' field; and maybe their parents don't say anything to
them, and don't say, 'Now this is th' right day to plant. Let's go and
plant.' You know, th' young generation don't work like we had to
work when we was growin' up."

What would happen with the young people not following the
lessons of their ancestors? "They'll just run into trouble. Th' farmin'
and stuff'll just be goin' out more and more every year."

Richard changed the subject. "Another thing. Now you take like
killin' hogs. There's a certain time to kill hogs too. You kill a hog on
th' new of th' moon and take a slice of it and put it in a pan, and it'll
just bow up. You don't want'a never kill it on th' new of th' moon."

Just before we left, we finally got to the question that had been
bothering us for days. If it was true that it *did* work, then *why?*

Why did it work? Margaret supplied an answer—"Well, it must have been in th' plan when th' world was made. Because you know in Ecclesiastes it says, 'There's a time for everything. A time to be born and a time to die. A time to plant and a time to harvest.' That's God's book, you know, so that's the reason."

THOSE WHO DOUBT

It was not long before we came across first one, then another and another who refused to believe in the signs. Seeking some semblance of balance after so many days of living with the zodiac, we were glad to find them and talk with them.

Most of those we talked to were educated people. Most had college degrees, and held positions of great respect in the community.

Dr. Harry Brown of Mountain City, for example, was County Agent fifty years ago. Later he was Farm Bureau president, and then Under Secretary of Agriculture in the administration of Franklin D. Roosevelt. He stated, "My yield's as high or higher than anyone in the county, and I've never used the signs. I don't even know how they work. There's no scientific evidence for it at all."

Pope Bass, overseer of the Rabun Gap-Nacoochee School's dairy, has been farming for forty years without using the signs. He said that he had never been able to see any difference between his crops and the crops of those who used the signs.

James T. Burden, Professor of Agriculture at the Rabun Gap school, said essentially the same thing. "There's no scientific proof at all. Look. If someone's going to be careful enough to plant by the signs and watch and harvest the crop that carefully, then the chances are he *will* have a good crop, regardless." He plants by the weather and the season. When the soil is warm enough, and the danger of frost is gone, it's time to plant, signs or not.

Mr. Burden realizes the importance of the signs to many of his students' families, however, and he is very careful not to turn them against their parents' beliefs. He tells the students that they are perfectly free to use the system if they wish, cautioning them only with the statement that there is no scientific proof for it as yet.

Barnard Dillard, owner of the local drugstore, added another dimension to the subject with a story he remembered about a family who played a trick on one of their elderly relatives who could no longer see well enough to read the planting calendar. Knowing beforehand what he considered to be the right time to plant corn, the boys in the family asked his advice, but planted on a day whose signs were exactly opposite of what he recommended. "They had a fine crop, too," he recalls.

SO?

Two points of view. We are in no position to judge which is correct. But we can't resist a parting shot.

The times are turning against the practice of planting by the signs. Younger people, now exposed to a different type of education, are turning to new ways of doing things and often discarding the old in the process. Sometimes this is good. But with planting by the signs, there remains a lingering mystery that refuses to be silenced.

It would be nice to be able to dismiss the whole thing with a wave of the hand as "fogeyism," but it's hard to dismiss like that the unshakable beliefs of generations of people older and presumably wiser than we will be for some time.

Besides, there are two stories we haven't told you yet—those told by Wilbur Maney, County Agent, and R. L. Edwards, owner of Edwards Photographic Studios in Clayton. Knowing these men and their reputations, we have every reason to believe the truth of these stories.

While cutting a field of waist-high, bothersome brush one day several years ago, Mr. Edwards noticed an older man watching him at work. He stopped his tractor and went over to say hello, at the same time complaining good-naturedly about the job that still lay ahead. "Well, after this you won't have to worry about it any more," said the older man.

"Why, sure I will," answered Mr. Edwards. "Next year I'll just have to cut it all over again."

"Nope. After this it won't ever come back," the other stated. "Know why? Because you picked exactly th' right day to cut that brush. Th' moon and th' signs are just right. You're killing it, every bit. Go ahead and finish th' job today and you'll never have to worry about it again."

"You know," said Mr. Edwards, "that old man was right. I cut that brush several years ago and it hasn't come back up *yet*. My only trouble now is that for the life of me, I can't remember which day I cut it on."

Mr. Wilbur Maney had a similar experience while attending a funeral in Hiawassee in August 1967. The corpse of the large man to be buried was enclosed in a huge, steel, waterproof vault. As is normal at funerals a dump truck was standing by to carry away the excess earth after the services. Usually one full load would do the job.

During the service, an elderly gentleman standing nearby spoke to Mr. Maney. "See that dirt?" he asked. "You watch when they get done. Because of the day they dug that hole on, they'll hardly have a wheelbarrow load left to cart away."

The vault was lowered into the ground, the dirt replaced, and all the remainder carried away in one wheelbarrow.

Mr. Maney still does not plant by the signs, and still does not really believe in it—and yet . . .

One of these days we intend to dig those two post holes Elvin Cabe told us to dig. We'll keep you informed.

THE BUZZARD AND THE DOG

as told by Bill Lamb

Used t'be th' very best pro-ducin' land we had in them days would be out in some rich cove—black dirt. Why, it'd be a sight at th' beans, corn, pumpkins—and what potatoes we growed, we growed without fertilize. It'uz just whatever th' earth made'uz all you made on it. When they first come out with fertilize, they'd even put it out in th' hill with a teaspoon.

They'uz an old man lived back over in yonder other side'a High-lands; had a little dog that'ud stay with ever'thing that he laid down. If it'uz his coat, he'd stay with it 'til 'at man went back.

Well, he went down t'South Carolina an' got'im a bag a'fertilize, and it'uz old fish scraps. Smelled about as bad as a dead fish. He had some old straw stacks there, and he'uz so particular with his fertilize he went an' laid it down in th' sack on that waste straw around them stacks.

Well, his dog laid down with it. And he had a spoon a'puttin' it out fer his corn—out across th' field. An' he got out away from them stacks, an' he looked around an' he see'd an old buzzard come; an' that bussard flew 'round an' 'round an' 'round. Hit sailed 'round an' 'round an' drawed his 'tention. His dog was a'layin' there with that sack a'fertilize. Said that old buzzard flew 'round an' 'round, an' directly it lit out from th' dog some eight'r'ten foot. Said that old buzzard'uz standin' there'n looked, standin' there'n *looked;* an' then he'd walk a little piece. Walked on up an' that dog'uz a'layin there asleep with that fertilize. Said directly that there old buzzard just hauled up an' *pecked* that dog! Said that dog riz, an' on after th' buzzard, an' down through th' field, an' him about t'catch it, an' hit'uz just'a'floppin an'flyin'; an' he just stood there an' laughed t'hisself about what that buzzard thought about that dog stinkin' thataway an' him not dead!

HOME REMEDIES

The scarcity, until very recently, of medical facilities in the remoter rural areas of this country has been so well documented that it needs little repetition here. Nevertheless, despite the lack of facilities, people *did* get sick and often needed help. The fact that help wasn't there didn't eliminate the need.

And so, as with everything else, they were forced to make do with what they had on hand. As Harriet Echols told us, "People, y'know, didn't have a ʼhance of runnin' after doctors back in these mountain areas. They weren't close, and where I was raised, it was twelve miles *by horseback* to thʼ nearest doctor. They got a cut and it was too bad. They used thʼ turpentine and sugar or kerosene oil as an application to kill infection; and of course kerosene oil in those days was scarce because people had to burn it for light, y'know. That's all thʼ lights we had except thʼ pine knots in thʼ fireplace."

The end result was a staggering body of lore, a portion of which is included here. Some of the remedies undoubtedly worked; some of them probably were useless; some of them—and for this reason we advise you to experiment with extreme care—were perhaps even fatal (taking large quantities of whiskey for snake bites, for example). "It was a chancy business," as Molly Green said of her remedies. "If it hit, it hit; and if it missed, it missed."

But the remedies themselves stand as a weighty testament to the ingenuity of an all but vanished race.

ARTHRITIS

Drink a mixture of honey, vinegar, and moonshine.
Make a tea from either the seeds or leaves of alfalfa.
Drink powdered rhubarb dissolved in white whiskey.
A magnet draws it out of the body.

ASTHMA

In one pint of gin, place several pieces of the heartwood of a pine tree. Leave them in the gin until they turn brown. Then take one teaspoonful of the mixture twice a day.
Suck salty water up your nose.
Smoke or sniff rabbit tobacco.
Swallow a handful of spider webs rolled into a ball.
Keep a Chihuahua dog around the house.
Smoke strong tobacco until you choke.
Drill a hole in a black oak or sourwood tree just above the head of the victim, and put a lock of his hair in the hole. When he passes that spot in height, he will be cured. (Another person told us that if the person died, the tree would also.)
Drink a mixture of honey, lemon juice, and whiskey, using about a tablespoon of each.
Gather leaves from ginseng, dry and powder them. Put the powder in a pan, place a hot coal on top of it, and inhale the smoke.

BLEEDING

Place a spider web across the wound.
Apply a poultice of spirit turpentine and brown sugar to the wound.
Apply lamp black directly to the wound.
Use a mixture of soot from the chimney and lard.
If the cut is small, wet a cigarette paper and place this over it.
Use kerosene oil, but be careful not to add too much or it will blister the skin.
Use pine resin.

BLOOD—BUILDERS

When the sap is up, take the green bark of the wild cherry and boil it to make tea.
Take leaves of the lady's slipper, dry them, and beat them to a powder (you can wrap them in a rag to do this). Put this powder into a can, add water, let sit, and then give a spoonful three times a day.

Take the young leaves of the poke plant, parboil them, season, fry, and then eat several "messes."

Make sassafras tea, using the roots of the plant.

Put some yellowroot in a quart can of whiskey, and let the root soak it up. Add some cherry bark for flavor (*Plate 241*).

BROKEN ARM

Make a mixture of red clay and water. Put splints on each side of the arm and plaster it up with the clay. When the clay dries, put the arm in a sling.

BURNS

Put hot coals on the burned place and pour water over them. The steam will draw the fire out.

Powder hot coals and put this warm powder on the burn.

Boil chestnut leaves and place the resulting ooze on the burn.

Take table salt and dissolve it in warm water. Wrap the burn in gauze and keep it constantly warm and moist with applications of the salt water.

Bind castor oil and egg whites around the wound with a clean cloth.

The scrapings of a raw white potato will draw the fire.

Linseed oil will draw the fire out.

Scrape the inside of a white potato. Put the scrapings on the burn and leave them there until they turn black and the sore turns white. Then add a salve made of talcum powder and Vaseline.

If the person has never seen his father, he can draw the fire by blowing on the burn.

Use lard and flour.

Use a mixure of Sloan's salve and Japanese oil and petroleum jelly.

Put axle grease on the burned area.

CHEST CONGESTION

Make a poultice of kerosene, turpentine, and pure lard (the latter prevents blistering). Use wool cloth soaked with the mixture. Place cheesecloth on chest for protection, and then add the wool poultice.

Heat mutton tallow and apply it directly to chest.

PLATE 241 Harley Carpenter holds a yellowroot plant he has just pulled up from a stream bank near his home.

Place a large quantity of rock candy in a little white whiskey to make a thick syrup. Take a few spoonfuls of this several times a day.

Apply a mixture of camphor, mutton tallow, soot, pine tar, turpentine, and lard to chest.

Make an onion poultice by roasting an onion, then wrapping it in spun-wool rags and beating it so that the onion juice soaks the rags well. Apply these rags to chest.

Eat raw honey.

Render the fat of a polecat. Eat two or three spoonfuls. This brings up the phlegm.

Mix up hog lard, turpentine, and kerosene. Rub it on chest.

Rub groundhog oil and goose oil on chest. Then cover with a hot flannel cloth.

Wear a flannel shirt with turpentine and lard on it all winter.

COLDS

Make a tea from the leaves of boneset. Drink the tea when it has cooled. It will make you sick if taken hot. Leaves of this plant may also be cured out and saved for use in teas during the winter months.

Make a tea from powdered ginger, or ground up ginger roots. Do not boil the tea, but add the powdered root to a cup of hot water and drink. Add honey and whiskey, if desired.

Boil pine needles to make a strong tea.

Take as much powdered quinine as will stay on the blade of a knife, add to water, and drink.

Parch red pepper in front of a fire. Powder it, cook it in a tea, and add pure white corn liquor.

Put goose-grease salve on chest.

Drink lamb's tongue and whiskey tea.

Drink whiskey and honey mixed.

Drink red pepper tea.

Eat onions roasted in ashes (good for children).

Eat a mixture of honey and vinegar.

Make a tea by putting some pine top needles and boneset in boiling water. You can sweeten it with honey or syrup.

Drink tea made from wintergreen fern.

Make a combination tea from boneset leaves and horsemint leaves.

Take a three-pound can of pine twigs and rabbit tobacco. Boil together and strain. Drink some every three hours, taking no more than one full juice glass within a twelve-hour period.

Drink some of the brine from kraut put up in churn jars. It makes you thirsty, and you drink lots of water.

COLIC

Tie an asafetida bag around a baby's neck for six months to keep away six months' colic.

Take one pinch of soda in a spoon of water.

Drink Sampson's snake root tea.

Feed the baby breast milk with one drop of kerosene or one drop of asafetida in it.

Chew some camel root and swallow the juice.

Massage stomach lightly with warm towels or warm castor oil.

Chew ginseng root.

Drink some asafetida and whiskey mixed in milk or water.

Boil two or three roots of ginseng in a pint of water, then strain and drink (*Plate 242*).

PLATE 242   Harv Reid with one of the ginseng plants from the patch near his home.

CONSTIPATION

Gather the roots of mayapple, cut out the joints, and dry the middle of the root. Place in a cloth and beat to a powder. Add a few drops of castor oil and roll into pills. They keep very well. You can also put a pinch of powder in food, or put in some syrup.

COUGH

Mix one teaspoon of white whiskey with a pinch of sugar, heat over a fire, and drink.

Eat a mixture of honey and vinegar.

Put some ground ginger from the store in a saucer and add a little sugar. Put it on the tongue just before bedtime. It burns the throat and most of the time will stop coughs.

Take some rock candy with tea.

Take a teacup of roots and stems of red horsemint, boil in a pint of water for two or three minutes, strain, and drink.

Dissolve four sticks of horehound candy in a pint of whiskey and take a couple of spoonfuls a day. This is also good for TB.

Boil one cup of wild cherry bark in a pint of water. Add some syrup and cook until it gets thick.

Make a cough syrup using the roots of about six lion's-tongue plants. Boil them in about a teacup of water, sweeten with syrup, then simmer until thick. Take a spoonful a few times a day until your cough is gone.

Boil a handful of mullen roots and leaves in a pint of water to make a light tea. Add sugar or syrup to sweeten. Take only a spoonful at a time.

Parch leaves of rat's vein and grind them to a powder. Put a pinch on your hand and snort it.

Make a cough syrup by boiling a handful each of wild cherry bark, black gum bark, and whole rat's vein plants in a half a gallon of water. Simmer for one to two hours; strain, add one pint of sugar, and boil again until it makes a thin syrup.

CRAMPS

To cure cramps in the feet, turn your shoes upside down before going to bed.

CROUP

Squeeze the juice out of a roasted onion and drink.

Render out some mutton tallow, add beeswax to this, and place it on the back underneath the victim's shirt.

Add a little vinegar, lemon, or onion to honey and eat.

Put a drop of turpentine in a spoonful of sugar and eat.

Drink a thick syrup made of onion juice and honey.

For a baby pour a mixture of turpentine and white whiskey into a saucer and set it afire. Hold the baby over the smoke until he breathes it deeply. This loosens him up.

Take homemade lard, turpentine, and kerosene and make a poultice which is bound in a wool cloth over the chest and around the neck.

Put some groundhog oil on some hot flannel rags and place the rags on the child's chest.

Boil an onion, some turpentine, and some lard together. Pour the juice on a cloth and put it on the chest.

Get a pine knot, split it up fine, and light it. Hold fat meat over the fire. Take the resin and fat to cure the cough.

DIARRHEA

Take a tea of red oak bark.

Drink some blackberry juice.

DROPSY

The following is a remedy that Dr. John Fowler found handwritten, carefully folded and tucked away in an old book. It is presented here as written. "A receipt for the dropsy   3 qts of apple vinegar   nine bunches of black snake root   three bunches of sinaker snaker root   three hanful of stare root   three hanful of cammil flours too hanful of worm wood   forty five new nails   put them all in a iron oven set them in the coroner by the fier   let it stand nine days till it works   then rige out ["rige," sometimes spelled "rench," means strain or remove foreign matter] and in the same oven add one bottle of rum   one pound of sugar then set on a slow fier   simer it down four days to too bottls full   one spoonful at a dose   eat no fat meat and no sweat milk   keep out of the rain and dew."

DYSENTERY

Take high proof liquor, put it in a cup and set it afire, and after it burns and goes out, drink what's left.

Drink some blackberry juice.

Drink a tea made of strawberry leaves.

Peel off first layer of bark from a persimmon tree. Take the next layer of soft bark and swallow three mouthfuls of the juice. You can also use white oak bark.

Dig up two dewberry root vines and boil the roots in a quart of water, strain.

Make a tea of willow leaves. "It cures the dysentery nine times out of ten"—Aunt Arie.

EARACHE

Pour drops of juice from the buddie blooms (sweet shrub) into ear.

Dissolve table salt in lukewarm water and pour this into ear. This dissolves the wax which is causing the pain.

Put either wet ashes wrapped in a cloth, or hot ashes in a sack on ear and hold there.

Save the liquid that boils out of the ends of hickory and persimmon wood when burned, and pour this liquid into ear.

Pour castor oil, or sweet oil, or British oil into ear.

Put several drops of sewing machine oil in ear. (One person claimed that the reason this worked so well was that our body is a machine too.)

Roast cabbage stalks and squeeze the juice into ear.

Break apart a Betty bug at the neck, and squeeze one or two drops of blood into ear.

Warm a spoonful of urine and put a few drops in ear.

Hold your head close to a hot lamp.

Put a few ashes in an old rag. Dampen it with hot water and sleep with your head on it.

EYE AILMENTS

Put a few drops of castor oil in eye.

A sty can be removed by running the tip of a black cat's tail over it.

FEVER

Tie a bag containing the sufferer's nail paring to a live eel. It will carry the fever away.

Snakeroot tea will bring it down.

Boil two roots of wild ginger in a cup of water, strain, and drink.

Boil a cup of pennyroyal leaves in a pint of water and drink.

FLU

Gather some boneset, put the leaves in a sack, and put it in the sun to dry. Make sure it has air or it will mold. Then cook the leaves in some water, strain, and drink.

Chew rabbit tobacco.

FRETFUL CHILD

Boil catnip leaves to make a tea, and give the child about a quarter cup. Use one cup of leaves to a pint of water to make him sleep.

GALL BLADDER TROUBLE

Take a spoonful of pure corn whiskey and Black Draught.

HEADACHES

Bind wilted beet leaves on the forehead.

Tie a flour sack around your head.

Put several ginseng roots in a piece of brown paper and tie to your head.

Put turpentine and beef tallow in a bandage and tie it tightly around your head.

Pour hot water over mustard leaves to rouse their odor and strength. Bind these leaves in a poultice to head with a cheesecloth strip.

Smear brow with crushed onions.

When you get your hair cut, gather up all the clippings. Bury them under a rock and you will never have a headache. Old-timers would never allow their hair to be burned or thrown away as it was too valuable.

Use a poultice of horseradish leaves.

Rub camphor and white whiskey on head.

HEART TROUBLE

Make a tea of heartleaf leaves and take two or three tablespoons three times a day. One person said she would boil the heart leaves together with leaves from the rat's vein plant.

Take root of a bleeding heart, break it up, and make a tea of it.

Eat ramps and garlic. You can eat them cooked or raw.

HICCUPS

Take a teaspoon of peanut butter.

Put half a teacup of dried apples in a teacup of water in a pot. Bring to a boil, stirring occasionally. Strain out the remains of the apples, and drink the juice while hot.

INSOMNIA

Make a tea of boneset leaves, using one tablespoonful. You may use them fresh or dried.

IRRITATION CAUSED BY INSECTS

BEE STINGS—Chew or mash ragweed and put it on sting to deaden pain and reduce swelling.

Put moist snuff, mud, tobacco juice, or red clay on it.

Put castor oil on it.

Take seven different kinds of leaves. Wad and twist them together, tear the wad in half, and rub the sting.

Place either turpentine, chewed tobacco, tobacco juice, kerosene, or a mixture of sugar and dough on the sting. Any of these will relieve the pain and draw out the poison.

Crush a few chrysanthemum leaves and rub the juice on the sting.

PACKSADDLE STINGS—Chew or mash ragweed and put it on the sting to deaden pain.

CHIGGER BITES—To relieve itching and infection, rub chewed snuff or tobacco over the bites.

Make a mixture of butter and salt to stop itching.

SPIDER BITES—If bitten by a black widow spider, drink liquor heavily from 3 P.M. to 7 P.M. You won't get drunk, you'll be healed.

BUGS—For head lice (cooties), shingle hair close and use Kerosene. For chinches or bed bugs, burn sulfur in a closed house.

IRRITATIONS OF THE SKIN

HIVES—Boil chestnut oak leaves and apply the resulting dark juice to the affected areas. Or take any of a variety of teas to break them out. These teas include catnip, ground ivy, a tea made from the mashed up berries of the tread-save, red alder leaves, raw alder bark scraped uphill, or a tea from cockle burrs. Wrap the latter in a rag and make the tea by straining.

Make a catnip tea using ten leaves of catnip. Boil it in one and a half or two cups of water. Take a teaspoon three or four times a day. Especially good for babies.

POISON IVY—Use a mixture of buttermilk or vinegar and salt.

Make a strong brown tea by boiling willow leaves, and put the tea on the affected area.

Take some witch hazel and add all the boric acid that will dissolve in it. Apply to all affected parts of the skin.

Rub wild touch-me-not on the area.

Rub the infection with the inside surface of a banana.

Slice open a green tomato and run the juice over the affected area.

Apply either linseed oil, a mixture of epsom salts and baking soda, white shoe polish, or the water drawn off cooked oatmeal. One can also blister the irritated spots with turpentine, or add half a teaspoonful of soda to half a pint of buttermilk and bathe the affected areas.

OKRA STING—Put four ounces of good live copperas in one quart of boiling water and let cool. Wash affected areas with water as hot as you can bear it for twenty minutes about four times a day.

ERYSIPELAS (skin disease)—Use a poultice of peach tree leaves and corn meal.

Make a salve of balm of Gilead buds fried in mutton tallow. Add Vaseline if you wish. The best tallow to use is McQueen's Pure Mutton Tallow which is available in many A&Ps.

ITCH—Use sulfur and lard.

Use gunpowder and sulfur.

Wash some yellowroot and put it on the affected area.

INFLAMMATION—Bind salty fat meat to a stone bruise or a thorn in the foot to draw out the inflammation. A poultice of clay will do the same thing.

To kill infection, pour some turpentine or kerosene mixed with sugar on the affected area.

Make a tea of poke roots by boiling them in water for a couple of minutes. Dip a cloth in it and rub on the affected area. (Be careful not to get any in your mouth.)

FRECKLES—Buttermilk and lemon juice mixed together and put on freckles will remove them.

Put sap from a grapevine on them.

Put stump water on them.

Make a poultice of eggs, cream, and epsom salts, and spread on the freckles. Take off after it dries.

CHAPPED HANDS—Rub pine resin on them.
Rub hands with mutton tallow.
Wash or pick wool. The lanolin in it will be good for the skin.

ATHLETE'S FOOT—Wrap a wool string around the toe, or step in cow dung that is fresh.

SWEATY FEET—Boil dried chestnut leaves until you have an ooze. Apply this to the feet.

KIDNEY TROUBLE

Make a tea from dried trailing arbutus leaves.
Eat one or two pokeberries a day for a couple of days.
Drink some red alder tea.
Take one root from a queen-of-the-meadow plant. Boil it in one pint of water until it makes a dark tea. Strain and drink a cup a day until you are well.

LIVER TROUBLE

Make a tea of lion's tongue leaves by boiling a few leaves in water, then straining. Add syrup if you want to sweeten it.
Wash a couple of roots from the spignet plant, boil them for a few minutes in a pint of water and strain. Drink about a cup a day when your liver is acting up.

MEASLES

Any herb tea will break them out.
Make a tea of sheep dung to break them out.
Boil red alder branches and drink the tea.
Keep the person home and out of the cold. Then give him some whiskey to drink. Use a few drops for tiny children and a tablespoon for adults. It will make the person sweat.

NAIL PUNCTURE

Put some old wool rags into an old tin can, pour kerosene over the rags and light. Then smoke the wound.
Take a hammer and draw the nail out. Grease the nail and put it away somewhere to prevent lockjaw.
Pour kerosene oil over the cut, or soak it in same three times a day. This will also remove the soreness.
Mix lard with soot from the chimney, thin with turpentine, and pack around the wound.
Pour pine oil over the wound.

Mix biscuit flour with buttermilk until a dough forms. Pack this dough in a poultice of sugar and turpentine.

Tie it up in a poultice of sugar and turpentine.

NOSEBLEED

Take a small piece of lead and bore a hole in it. Put a string through the hole, tie it, and wear it around your neck. Your nose won't bleed again.

Place a nickel directly under the nose between the upper lip and the gum and press tightly.

Lie down and put a dime on your heart.

Sniff devil's snuff box or some puff balls, and it will stop.

Hang a pair of pot hooks about your neck.

Place scissors, points up, on your neck.

PAIN KILLER

Roast some poke roots by the fire. Scrape them clean with a knife and grind up. Make a poultice out of the powder and apply to the bottom of the foot. It will draw pain out of anywhere in the body.

PNEUMONIA

To bring down the fever, put some quinine and hog lard on a cloth and put it on your chest.

Give the person two teaspoonsful of oil rendered from a skunk.

Make an onion poultice to make the fever break. Then give the person whiskey and hot water.

Make a tea of butterfly weed, add a little whiskey, and drink it.

RHEUMATISM

Roast a poke root in ashes in the same manner as you would roast a potato. While it is still hot, apply it to the inflamed joint. This eases the pain and reduces the swelling.

Drink a mixture of pokeberry wine and whiskey.

Let rattleroot, ginseng, red corn root, wild cherry bark, and golden seal root sit in one gallon of white whiskey. Drink small portions of the resulting liquid as needed.

Rub some wildcat oil on the skin.

Drink a tea made from the seeds or leaves of the alfalfa plant.

Cook garlic in your food to ease the pain.

Carry a buckeye or an Irish potato until it gets hard.

RISIN'S

Place an elm bark poultice over the bump.

Scrape the white of an Irish potato and place the scrapings on the bump. Bind them on with a clean cloth. This will draw the risin' (boil) to a head.

The inside surface of the bark of the lind tree (basswood) will draw it to a head.

Take raw fat meat (the fattest you can get), cut a thin slice of it, and bind it over the bump with a cloth bandage. This draws it to a head, and when you pull the cloth off, a tiny hole is left in the center of the lump. Make a thread loop and ease this loop into the hole and twist several times; then yank the core of the risin' out with a swift motion.

Eat sulfur mixed with honey.

Take the skin out of eggshells, and place it on the risin's.

Put a wilted running briar leaf on it, wrap with a cloth, and leave on overnight.

Scrape some bark from a sevenbark (wild hydrangea) bush, grind it up, boil it in enough water to cover for a few minutes. Make a poultice of it, put it on the risin', and it will draw it out very quickly.

SORES

Put butter around the sore so a dog will lick it. The dog's saliva will cure it.

Put a little lard or something equally greasy on the sore. Then dust the sore with sulfur. The grease will hold the sulfur on.

Make a salve of white pine resin and mutton tallow.

Don't ever burn the cloth bandage from a sore; you must bury it for the sore to heal.

Mash up yellowroot and put it on the sores.

Use a salve made from mutton tallow, balm of Gilead buds, and fresh turpentine from pine trees.

SORE THROAT

Bake onions in an open fireplace; then tie them around your throat.

Make a poultice of kerosene, turpentine, and pure lard (to prevent blistering), and place this on your neck. In five minutes you will be able to taste the kerosene in your throat, and the cure will have begun. Then take two or three drops of kerosene oil in a spoon with a pinch of sugar and swallow this to complete the treatment.

Gargle with honey and vinegar.

Rub pine oil on your throat.

Gargle with salty water.

Put a drop of kerosene on a lump of sugar and eat it.

Gargle with a half cup water, two tablespoons vinegar, and a half teaspoon of salt.

Take a sock you have worn inside a boot and worked in for almost a week so that it has a bad odor. Tie it around your neck.

STOMACH TROUBLE

Make a tea of wild peppermint and drink it.

Drink some blackberry juice or wine.

Drink some juice from kraut left over after cooking.

Chew calamus root or yellowroot and swallow the juice.

Make a tea of golden seal roots and drink it.

To stop vomiting, grind up some peach trees leaves in a rag. Put the rag with the ground leaves in it on the person's stomach.

To settle the stomach, place five small flint rocks in a glass of water. Let it sit for a few minutes and drink.

TONSIL TROUBLE

Gargle with tan bark tea made from chestnut leaves.

Smear balm of Gilead salve all over the person's chest.

Gargle with salt water.

To burn out tonsils, paint them several times a day for several months with iodine and turpentine.

TOOTHACHE

Make a small amount of wine from pokeberries, and mix one part of the wine with eight parts white whiskey. Take a small spoonful just a couple of times a day. It's also good for rheumatism and muscle cramps.

Put drops of vanilla straight from the bottle on the tooth.

Buy some Bluestone in a store and put a drop of it on the tooth. It kills the nerve.

Use burned alum.

Put some homemade tobacco in a corncob pipe. Light it, and draw the smoke over the tooth.

Hold whiskey or turpentine on the tooth.

Put some damp ashes on a cloth, and hold against the sore tooth.

Put a few ashes in an old rag and dampen it with hot water. Sleep with your head on it.

WARTS

Stick the hand which has warts on it into a bag and tie it up. The first person who opens it will get your warts.

Get something like a penny that someone would want to pick up. Put some blood from the wart on it and throw it into the road. When someone picks it up, the wart will go away.

Wet your finger and make a cross on the wart.

Take a persimmon stick and put as many notches on it as you have warts. They will go away.

Count them, touching each one as you do, and say a verse which is secret and known only to you, the conjuror.

Tie a horsehair around it.

Rub the wart with the skin of a chicken gizzard, then hide the skin under a rock. The wart will disappear.

Count the warts. Tie as many pebbles as there are warts in a bag and throw this bundle down in the fork of a road. They will soon go away.

Steal a neighbor's dishrag. Wipe it across the warts and bury it in the woods.

Wash the affected area with water from a rotten chestnut stump for nine mornings in a row before breakfast.

Rub the warts with a rock and put it in a box. Whoever opens the box will get the warts.

Rub a flint rock three times over the warts and put it back where you got it from. They will disappear.

Cut the wart, make it bleed, and put one drop of the blood on a grain of corn. Feed the grain of corn to a chicken or rooster and the wart will disappear.

Put the juice from a milkweed on it every day for two weeks.

Put a small piece of bacon or salt pork on the wart. Wrap it up and sleep with it that way. In the morning the wart will be gone if you have faith.

Pick the wart with a needle, and put a few drops of the blood on some fat meat. Bury the meat, and when it rots the wart will go away.

WHOOPING COUGH

Take a half cup of brown sugar, the juice of three lemons, two egg whites, and one bottle of olive oil. Mix these up together and give one teaspoonful of the mixture.

Drink mare's milk.

Boil chestnut leaves in water, drain, add honey, and drink.

WORMS

In the early spring, pick the small tender leaves of the poke plant. Boil the leaves, drain them, and cook in grease from fatback. Eat a mess of these.

Take "worm syrup" which is made by boiling Jerusalem oak and pine root together.

Take the shells of a hen's egg and bake them until they turn brown and brittle. Crumble them up fine and mix the particles with syrup and butter. Feed this to the sick person every morning for one week. The particles cut the worms to pieces. This remedy also works for dogs and other animals.

Eat tobacco seeds.

Eat a head of garlic every day until they are gone.

For ringworm, crack open green walnut hulls, crush, and apply the juice to the affected area with cotton.

Put three or four drops of turpentine in a teaspoon of sugar and eat it.

Put some charcoal in a quart of water and drink it.

For tapeworm, starve it. Then hold some warm milk up to your nose and sniff deeply. The tapeworm will stick his head out of your nose to get the milk. Hold the milk farther and farther away from him, thus drawing him out.

YELLOW JAUNDICE

Scrape a cow's horn, boil the scrapings, and drink.

PREVENTIVES, CURE-ALLS

SPRING TONICS—Take wild cherry tree bark, yellow poplar bark, and yellowroot boiled, strained, and mixed with white liquor.

Mix together some sulfur and molasses, and eat it.

Eat rhubarb once a week.

SALVES—Take about two tablespoons of mutton tallow, and heat it up in a frying pan with about six balm of Gilead buds. Mash the buds up while the mixture cools, and when the grease is all out of the buds, strain the mixture. Put it in a jar and cover it. The salve is clear, and will keep for years.

Take one cup of pine resin, about one ounce of camphor-phénique, one cup of mutton tallow, and ten to fifteen balm of Gilead buds. Put it all in a frying pan and heat until liquid. Mash the buds until all the juice is out of them. Strain and put into jars and cover. Makes about a pint.

For bed-wetting, feed the child a couple of elderberries or red sumac ("shumate") berries before bedtime.

For any serious child illness, take some blood from the child's arm, put it on a grain of corn, and feed it to a black hen.

To prevent taking contagious diseases, tie asafetida around the neck.

A piece of nutmeg tied around the neck will prevent neuralgia.

Place a Bible under your pillow, and you will never have nightmares.

Give a grouchy person a tea made from violet blossoms.

To help hair grow, break a section of a grape vine, set in a bottle, and let the juice drain. Rub the juice in your hair.

HUNTING

Since most early families had hogs, it was not really essential for them to hunt wild game. Many did, however—to supplement their diets with fresh meat, to supplement their incomes with the money they could get from selling the hides, and for the fun and sport of hunting itself. As Mann Norton said, "They really didn't have to hunt, but they liked the taste of wild meat." Lon Reid agreed, "They didn't have to hunt. They had hogs and a garden. But they enjoyed it. They liked the chase, and they liked a change and fresh meat."

They also hunted to protect both themselves and their stock, for the early forests, with their unbroken miles of virgin chestnut trees and their paucity of settlements, were also filled with wildcats, bears, panthers ("painters"), and other predatory animals. It is easy, for example, to see how the early morning trip to the barn to find your cow slaughtered or all your chickens gone might be a disquieting experience—especially if your survival depended on your stock. It is also easy to understand the irritation caused by a polecat or fox who ate the eggs and young of prized fowl. And it is easy to see how the ringing squall of a panther on a lonely, starless night from the mountain just behind you might be a very real cause for alarm. Many of the stories we gathered from the nearly sixty people we interviewed concerned this aspect of early survival in the forests. Here is a sampling:

❖ MRS. ALGIE NORTON: "Before the War between the States, my grandparents lived on the edge of North Carolina. They had a little boy about three or four days old, so my grandfather's sister had come to stay with them for a while.

"He had to be away from home one night, and they was a painter began t'holler up above th' house on the rock. They closed th' doors and put things against them t'keep him from comin' in.

"He come on down and scared th' dog so he run under th' house a'hollerin', and they heered it climb up on th' roof of th' house. Back then, th' houses was built out of logs, and th' roof was weighted down with poles—split boards weighted down with poles—and he begin t'try t'scratch and tear in.

"They was scared, and they didn't know anything else t'do but burn some powder. They'd always heered it said they'd run from th' scent of powder. So they burned some powder on th' hearth and got th' scent—and they still heered it scratchin'.

"So they built a big fire t'keep it from comin' down th' chimney, but it finally went away.

"And this tale was handed down by my uncles and aunts. The baby was Uncle Columbus Garland that used t'live on Betty's Creek, and th' other baby was Uncle Hannibal Garland—the one that was about two years old."

❖ BILL LAMB and BUCK CARVER

Bill: "I've been scared s'many times I couldn't mention that!"

Buck: "Bill used t'tell me, 'I've seen plenty a'men could whip me and make me like it, but I'm not afraid'a them. I *am* afraid t'stay out of a night by myself—especially in th' big laurels around Nantahaly.' So I said, 'What'r' you afraid of, Bill?' He said, 'Boogers! Th' same darn thing *you* are!'"

Bill: "I always *was* cowardly of a night. After I'uz married, I used t'be awful bad t'sleep with m'head covered up. M'chickens roosted up in th' swamp above th' house. Possum had got inta'em— 'course I never heered it. M'grandaddy was'ere wi'me, an' he hollered, 'Bill, Bill!' I throwed th' cover up over m'head an' rared up an' said, 'What!' He said, 'Somethin's eatin'up ever'one'a yore chickens!' An' I heered 'em goin', 'Cow! Cow! Cow!' I run out on th' porch. Had a awful good dog. I wondered that he hadn't heered it hisself at first. I run out—called. Then tried t'whistle an' couldn't! M'chin kep' jerkin'. I see'd that wouldn't work, so I set in callin' an' here he come, 'n got after that possum. Ran'im along th' rails a'th' fence. You never heered rails fallin' s'much—possum runnin' th' rails a'th' fence an' th' dog tryin' t'catch'im.

"Directly he treed it, an' I tried again t'see if I could whistle,
an' I could whistle just as good as you want! I wadn't cold either.
I had just run out there'n'called that dog, an' m'chin had jerked
'til I couldn't whistle!

"You ever see'd a dumbull? Piece a'board about that long [about
six inches]—right thin—y'cut'em off sort'a in th' shape of a old
fashioned coffin—diamond shaped. He'd made'im [Buck] one, and
I heered it, an' I thought it'uz somethin' in th' river at th' start. I
thought it'uz a dog takin' a fit.

"I hollered at m'wife t'get th' children in th' house, I heered a dog
takin' a fit up there. There'uz an old pole fence runnin' down through
there, an' I jumped up b'th' side where I could run up a bush an'
I looked fer't. Meantime I heered it again, an' boys, I thought
that'uz th' time fer me t'get t'th' house too. I took up through
there—corn was up about a foot high I guess—an' m'wife'uz down
there th' next day. I see'd her stop an' look. Sometime she'd look up
there, an' look down here. I didn't know what was th' matter. She
said, 'I'uz just lookin' at how fur you jumped!' Took me about
three steps t'make home!

"It'uz that old dumbull. It'd just goin' 'Whoo, whoo, whoo!' A
dog'll just leave out from'em. They just can't stand'em. They just
go like th' biggest old dog ever you heered growlin'n'ever'thing else.
It goes plumb scarey! Boys, you c'n just make it growl and mutter
and cut up!"

❖ CALVIN TALLEY: "Back years ago, I've heered my daddy tell
about when he was young. He had this little shack over by th' post
office. He said one night that he'd been t'church, an' he come in.
He was there by hisself that night. This other feller'd been stayin'
with'im, but he happened not t'be there that night.

"And where th' shack set, he had t'walk through this laurel thicket,
up this trail. An' just as he was fixin' t'go in th' shack, he heered
somethin' kind'a whine up on th' side a'th' mountain—make a funny
noise—an' said it didn't make him feel too good, what he heered. So
he went on inside an' lit up th' lamp.

"An' directly th' noise that he heered kept gettin' louder, an' come
into a big rock that stood right behind th' winda', an' he said that it
screamed out. It sounded a lot like a woman that was scared of
somethin' that screamed at th' top of her voice. He said he knew that

it was a painter, an' it didn't make him feel good at all. He said that he was kindly uneasy, and he left a lamp burnin' all night t'keep it from comin' in th' window on'im.'

Traditionally the mountain people kept several different kinds of dogs around their homes. Many had at least one "plantation dog" whose whole job was to keep the hogs and cows out of the corn.

❖BILL LAMB: "Used t'be open range. You fenced in your gardens instead of fencin' in th' stock. Lots of times cows would push over th' rail fences and turn th' whole herd into your corn. Or hogs would slip in. Dogs would grab'im, and he'd squeal like he'd not come back for a year after they turned them loose, and then he'd be back th' next day. I've been awful aggravated in my time at stock in my fields."

Since cows and hogs were grazed on open range, mountain families often trained "ketch dogs" also. Their job was to help round up the stock when the time came to bring it in for slaughtering or for sale.

And then there were the hunting dogs—the pride of many families. Stories abound concerning this dog or that, legendary in a community because of their ability. Often different breeds were used, depending on the game to be hunted. Blue ticks, black and tans, and redbones, for example, were popular coon dogs. Plots, curs, and Airedales made fine bear dogs. Feists were used by many for both squirrel and deer, bulldogs for boar, treein' walkers for fox, beagles for rabbit, and so on. Others, however, were not so particular. One old man told us that when he got a new dog, he'd take him out, and whatever he ran, why, "That's what kind'a dog it'uz goin' t'be."

Training dogs was an intricate process for the avid hunter, and some men were exceptionally skilled at it. We have heard more than once, for example, that if one was having trouble with a wildcat, he'd go see a Waldroop because they had the best cat dogs in the mountains. And the hunting stories reveal that sometimes a man would be invited along on a hunt, not so much because of *his* hunting skill as that of his dog.

The easiest way to train a dog was simply to take it along on a hunt with several other skilled dogs and let *them* train it. "That helps awful," said Mann Norton.

If you had to train say a coon dog, yourself, however, there were several methods. The most important rule was to go with him

PLATE 243 Ray Connor, an avid hunter, stands with one of the plots he uses for bear hunting. In the background are skins from a few of his kills.

on a hunt, *stay* with him, and get what you were after. If he got on a track, treed the animal, and couldn't find where the coon had gone, the hunter/trainer would point up in the tree, show him, and then shoot it out. Once they got one coon, the dog would see what he was after, and he would be a coon dog for life.

❖ MANN NORTON: "You just got t'go rag'lar with'im. Get a live coon'r a house cat'r somethin', an' put'im up a tree an' get'im started barkin' at it. If he c'n tree a house cat, you're in business. Or get'cha a live coon an' put'im up on a stump where th' dog can just nearly reach'im. Well, if he's a young dog, don't matter if'n he does—won't kill it nohow. Or take a coon an' drag 'im around an' take it somewhere an' tie it up on top of a stump or a tree'r somethin' like that. Just take 'at coon with a chain on it, or a string, an' lead'im. An' he'll track'im. Lot'a folks keep a coon around t'train their dogs with.

"And lot'a people don't have th' patience t'train a dog. If he trees an' y'have't'dig two or three hours t'get'im out, why, it pays t'do that. Dig in there to'im an' let 'im fight an' drag it out. An' he'll stay with'im when he finds out you'll go too."

And deer? "Your trouble is keepin'em *from* runnin' a deer," said Bill Lamb. "They'll run a deer natural, like a dog runnin' sheep. Some dogs, you never *can* break'im hardly from runnin' deer."

Many of the rules above apply to training a dog for other game also. In addition, most dogs were trained to answer to the hunter's horn. The horn might be a cow's horn, or even one barrel of a shotgun. The latter, when broken open, makes a great trumpet. One problem: you can't "blow a good dog off" if he's running anything.

The more we researched this chapter, the more valuable an asset we found a good dog to be. Nine times out of ten we found the dog to be at least half responsible for the success of a hunt. That's one reason why dogs are now outlawed in our part of the country for deer hunts. They just got too good at it.

Of course, there's always the hunter who would rather *not* use a dog, preferring to pit himself against the quarry. And then there's the old man we know who takes his dogs to the woods in the evening, builds a campfire, cooks supper, turns the dogs loose, and then just sits down with his back against a tree to listen to them run in full cry out over the mountains. And we suppose that's as valid a reason for training a dog as any.

There is a prevailing belief in the mountains that an animal tastes only as good as what it eats. For this reason, animals such as coon and possum, if they were going to be eaten, were hunted by many only when and if the corn, chestnut, acorn, and grape crops were good. When the mast was good, so was the flesh of the animals that fed on it. For the same reason, many shunned possum, polecat, and other "nasty" animals that sometimes feed on carrion "karn").

In any case, here's how the hunting was done according to instructions given us by older men in our county who have hunted all their lives.

RACCOON

A good place to find "sign" was around branches and the heads of little springs where they had been turning over rocks looking for crayfish and spring lizards. Often their tracks could be found along sandbars, and in soft damp places beside creeks. Sign could also be found around oaks and other trees where they'd been scratching for nuts.

A hunter would find fresh sign and bring his coon dogs to the spot that night. He could also simply set his dogs out in a likely spot and let them try their luck. Right before daylight was also a good time.

He'd then follow his dogs as best he could when they "struck," and when they had "treed" (which could be in any place from a hole in the ground to a rock cliff to the top of a real tree), he'd hurry to the spot, call the dogs off, and make his kill.

Coons were tricky, however, and sometimes if the dogs were at the base of one tree, the hunter would find the coon three or four trees over. If it was in a tree and it was night, the old hunters would light pine knot torches or build a brush fire at the base of the tree. The coon would look at the fire, and the hunter would watch for his eyes to shine and then shoot. If that failed, they'd wait until daylight so they could see it.

Several people had told us that when the moon was shining the coon would look at the moon and not at the fire. Others tell us that on a moonlit night, a coon would always head for a sinkhole, so it was best to hunt them on cloudy nights. Others of our contacts deny this, however.

If the coon was holed up in a cave, some would try to smoke it out:

❖ BILL LAMB: "Get your dogs out. Then build a fire in front of the hole and fan the smoke in. You have t'be careful. Sometimes you'll make th'smoke s'hot they'll die in there. You'll smoke'em too hard. Just give'em smoke along'n'along 'til it worries'em so they'll come out. And when y'smoke'em hard, when they first come out an' hit th'fresh air, they'll just blare their mouth like a possum grinnin' an' they'll fall over. It knocks'em out somehow when they hit fresh air. You c'n pick one up then.

"If they die in there, sometimes y'can get'em out after they've died. Y'twist'em out with a withe—take a long, green pole like a fishing pole, split one end, stick the pole in the den, and then try to get th'end twisted in the fur and hide so you can drag it out."

Some also trapped coons. One told us that if you build a wooden box with a hole just large enough for a coon's arm to go through, and put a dime inside, he'd reach in, clasp his fist around the dime, and then not be able to get free. "They're stingy about shiny stuff," he said. "They won't let go."

POSSUM

This animal was noted for staying close to settlements, chicken houses and fields. Usually they were hunted at night—often with coon dogs—while they were out and feeding.

❖ MANN NORTON: "One good thing about it: possum won't go fur. He'll climb up in a bush or sull up (curl up and lie still playing possum) somewheres. Lots just catch'im in a sack to train coon dogs with. They won't climb high. Usually climb out on th' first limb they come to. You can just climb up there an' get'im live."

Some trapped them by building a pen out of rocks, putting sardine bait in back and a trap in front.

The problem, according to many, was not catching them, but "Gettin' shed'a them."

GROUNDHOG

It is a simple matter to find a groundhog burrow in an open field. Again, as with possum, the problem was getting rid of them. Hunters would simply wait until they were feeding, which they do during the day, or sunning beside their holes.

If one went into his burrow, the hunter would simply wait several minutes.

❖ LAKE STILES: "He'll stick his head out an' look for y', but if he sees y' a second time and goes back, he'll not come back anytime soon. They'll rear up on their hind feet an' pop their teeth at'cha like they're goin't'eat'cha up."

They could also be "twisted" out of their holes like coon.

SQUIRREL

Most hunters "still hunted" (found a likely tree, sat down in a fairly concealed spot, and waited) for squirrel. The early morning or late evening, when they were cutting nuts in a hickory, oak, or chestnut, was a favorite time. The hunters would either tree them with dogs, or simply find a good tree while walking through the woods and conceal himself there, or wait until later. Sometimes when a hunter came on a squirrel and noticed it run to the side of the tree away from him, he would stop, get his gun ready, pick up a rock and throw it to the ground just *beyond* the same tree. The noise would scare the squirrel back around to the hunter's side and give him a shot.

RABBIT

A good beagle was often used in rabbit hunting. He could jump the animal for the hunter and give him a quick shot. The hunter would sometimes walk the fields and scare them out himself also. And he might try to track them in snow, but they were hard to find in cold weather as they took to brush or their holes.

Rabbits and other small animals were sometimes trapped in a home-made box like the one in Plate 244. This box measures 39¾″ long by 13″ high by 12½″ wide. The supports for the gate are 28″ high, and the trigger stick is 36½″ long.

PLATE 244   A rabbit box

DEER

A good place to find deer sign was in the gap of a mountain where they'd been feeding on leaves of plants or acorns. There the hunter would look for tracks, a trail, droppings, and for "horning bushes" that they'd used to rub the velvet from their horns. Some hunters also looked for places where they had bedded down on a ridge and for watering places beside streams.

In spots such as the above, many hunters built tree stands (crude wooden platforms A-framed between trees, or even old chairs nailed up in a tree) ten to twenty feet off the ground. They built them up-wind so the deer would not smell them, and since they were above the line of vision, they were rarely seen by the deer. The hunters would return to their stands every morning and evening and still hunt, waiting for them to return and feed or sleep.

Stalking was done, but was tremendously difficult. As Bill Lamb said, "You needn't get in a thicket after one, thinkin' you'll see it in there. He'll stay a hundred yards ahead of'y'all th' time. You just have't wait for them t'come past you."

Most old hunters, however, used dogs—a method now illegal in many areas. Sometimes men would get on either side of a gap or swag, set the dogs loose, and let them drive the deer through between them. Another way was for one man to take the dogs and drive the ridge. Other men would go to gaps or stands at the lower end of the ridge in a low gap and wait.

Usually, according to most of our contacts, when a dog got after a grown deer, it would head straight for water. If the deer didn't "run over you," the hunter wouldn't get a shot unless he followed this procedure of Mann Norton's: "You just as well, if you know where he'll hit th' river at, t'put a man down there, fer that's where he'll go when th' dogs gets atter'im. One feller we had 'ud hear th' hounds on a deer an' run t'th' river where he thought th' deer would come out. When it did, he'd jump on'im an' drown'im. When that deer hit th' water, he hit it with it an' took it by th' throat."

Deer could also be penned. One man who owned a large piece of property that was fenced in built special trap gates in the fence. The deer would walk into a chute after bait, and when he pulled it, a gate would fall shut behind him pulling one in front of him open as it went thus turning the deer unharmed into the fenced acreage.

BEAR

One sure sign of a bear was a group of nervous hogs. Other signs were tracks, signs of their climbing or clawing trees, raking out bare patches under chestnuts in search of mast, a rotted log broken open where they searched for grubs and insects, and so on. Another popular place to look for tracks was around laden huckleberry and blueberry bushes.

Bears usually feed at night and sleep during the day. Many hunters started just before daybreak and held the dogs until they found a fresh track and started pulling and barking. Then they'd deploy several men to either side of the top of a nearby likely gap, set the dogs loose, and then wait for them to drive the bear through the gap past their stands.

Dogs were also used to tree or bay a bear. They would hold the bear in one spot until the men got there and finished it off. Often the bears were fierce fighters and killed or maimed many a good dog before being killed themselves. Their reputation made many men cautious about hunting them at all. When Buck Carver, during one of our interviews, asked Bill Lamb if he hadn't ever backtracked a bear, Bill's reply was, "No! But I guess that's th' track I'd take —th' back track. I'd see where he slept th' night before!"

Some men also constructed large log pens in likely spots, and used green withes to set the trap. When the bear took the bait, it was caught for the gate fell behind him.

Several interesting practices among early bear hunters were related to us by Taylor Crockett. According to him, when a bear was killed and skinned, it was then cut into as many piles of meat as there were men. Equal portions of each section of meat were put in each pile. Then one of the men was blindfolded and pointed so he faced away from the piles. Another man would point at a pile of meat at random, ask whose pile of meat he was pointing to, and the blindfolded man would call out one of the hunter's names. In that way, no one's feelings were hurt. If the bear got away and someone else killed it just before you showed up, you got the hide and half the meat. If you got there after the other had already skinned it, you got "a mess a'meat," but usually not as much as half. If your dogs had been running it, the other man killed it and you didn't show up at all, and the other knew that they were your dogs—if he was an honest man he'd bring you a portion of the meat anyway.

TURKEY

The turkey was a very popular food before its almost total disappearance from this area. Signs the early hunters looked for were places that looked like chicken scratchings where they had been feeding on acorns, grapes, and various grasses. They would also listen for the sounds of gobblers flying up into their roosts in the evening and yelping.

Some hunters sought them only in winter, feeling that if you destroyed the hens in the spring, you'd be doing real damage to their potential numbers. As Lon Reid said, "If you're destroyin' th' hens, you're destroyin' th' turkeys."

Others preferred early spring ("gobblin' time") when the turkeys were listening for the hens to gobble. Most found the roosting places the night before, and then returned early the next morning. They'd get into a blind, get into position, gobble to the turkey, and then wait for him to answer and investigate.

Surprising as it may seem, every one of our contacts said that it was imperative that if you were not in a blind, then rather than being behind a tree you should be on the side of the tree *facing* the turkey. Apparently, if you were on the side facing them and you didn't move, they'd look beyond rather than at you.

All turkey hunters we talked to used a call to attract birds to their hiding place. These calls were of many sorts. One of the most popular was the small bone from the turkey's wing. Sharp sucking intakes of air through this bone produced a series of turkey-like yelps. The same effect could be achieved with the hollowed stem of an easter flower bush or a new cob pipe. Others used blades of grass or leaves stretched between the thumbs and placed vertically against the lips and blown through.

PLATE 245   Jake Waldroop crouches in a pile of brush similar to the blinds he has made in the woods for turkey hunting.

PLATE 246　Jake holds his favorite turkey call—the small bone from a turkey's wing. This particular one is fifty years old.

PLATE 247　Here, he demonstrates how the call is used.

PLATE 248　To make this crow call, Harley Carpenter split the end of a green dogwood branch, forcing half a laurel leaf into the split, and trimming off the excess leaf. Blowing through the split produces the desired sound.

❖GRADY WALDROOP: "Th' real old hunter uses what they call a lion's tongue. Cut's'em in half an' lets'em wilt an' puts'em in their mouth, and they just make a hen ashamed of itself."

Others used a wooden box with paper-thin side walls. Drawing a small whetstone across the top edge of one wall produced a low, rasping crooning call that was a dead ringer for a hen. You could also yelp by pulling the stone with a jerking motion.

Another old hunter we talked to used to take the big end of a cow's horn, cut off a two inch section, and plug one end of it with a wooden plug or "head." He'd drive a nail in the center of the plug so that the nail was inside the horn with its head projecting above the open end. Stroking the nail head with a whetstone produced the desired sounds.

Turkey calls had to be handled with exquisite care, a fact revealed in the following tape-recorded passages.

❖GRADY WALDROOP: "When y'call to'im an' he gobbles, put' cher call in yer pocket, never say another word, an' directly he'll come slippin' up. Might be an hour, mebbe quicker, mebbe longer. If you call another time, he'll suspicion somethin'. After he quits gobblin', he'll make out like he's goin'th' other way, an' he'll slip back. That's th' nature of a turkey. Most of th' turkey hunters calls too much. If he's a half a mile off, an' y'call to'im, he won't miss th' place two foot when he come out, and that's right."

❖LON REID: "In winter, scatter them and call them back. If it's lost and winter, they'll gobble. If you see him before he sees you, and he's goin' away from you, you can circle around and wait fer'im. He'll go in a straight line. Don't give too many yelps at once when y'call. If you make a little bobble when you're callin', them ol' gobblers'll go th' other way. They'll detect it."

❖JAKE WALDROOP: "Get in that blind and sort'a lay a little brush out in front of y' an' slip yer gun through that. Now y'can't move that gun. Y'can't bat an eye now. That turkey gobbler can really see'y'. If he answers y' when y'yelp to'im, an' he gobbles as much as twice, why, y'can be assured if y'don't get'im excited he'll come right t'that spot. But y'can almost bat'cher eye an' 'fut!' —he's gone.

"But if you keep still, why he'll walk up in shootin' distance, an' y'can just drop'im."

HOGS

Hogs were hunted, like bears, with specially trained dogs who would bring them to bay and hold them until the hunter arrived. Hogs usually sleep during the day and roam at night, but they were hunted any time since the dogs could find them and run them out.

Often hogs were not killed, but caught and taken to the farm to be fattened, and slaughtered and sold at a later date. In order to take them alive, the hunter would employ specially trained catch dogs. The trail dogs would run the hog down and bay it, and then the catch dogs would be turned loose and told to catch. One would latch onto the hog's ear and get as close to its side as he could to stay out of danger. Then the hunter would lasso the hog, put one rope on his front leg and one on his back, and lead him out.

Hogs, like bears, could be formidable foes. Minyard Connor tells the story of a man he went hog hunting with once. The man's hands were so crippled up that it was difficult for him to do much of anything with them. They got a wild boar trapped, and "They's an oak tree there—I bet it'uz two or three foot through. An' th' old man's hands'uz crippled—he'd try t'draw'em thataway. An' that old big hog made a dive at that old man an' he just scaled up'at tree like a squirrel!"

We should not leave this chapter without one final word about hunting in general. At this point in time, our mountains have been so logged over and our game so depleted that we would be totally irresponsible if we encouraged our readers to head for the woods at once and kill everything that moved. Conservative hunting, skillfully managed, at times serves a valuable purpose. But wanton destruction of what little game we have left must not be tolerated.

Marie B. Mellinger, a naturalist who has written several articles for us in the past, made the following statement especially for *Foxfire* as a word of caution, and a plea:

"The days of the pioneers when each man had to provide food for his own household are over. So too are the days when the woods held an abundance of game and the rivers teemed with fish. Now it would be difficult to find enough wild animals in our forests for survival were such hunting necessary.

"The need to protect and save our few remaining animal species becomes imperative."

DRESSING AND COOKING WILD
ANIMAL FOODS

RACCOON

SKINNING AND DRESSING—Many hunters cut the jugular vein
and bleed the coon as soon as they have killed one to prevent the
meat from spoiling. Then they either bring it home and skin it, or
skin it in the field. It is done as follows:

Ring the hind legs and the front legs at the foot joint. Split the
pelt on the inside middle of both hind legs from the ring to the
crotch.

Repeat on front legs, splitting to the middle of the chest.

Then split the pelt up the middle of the underside from the crotch,
through the split from the front legs, and up to the end of the bottom
jaw.

Cut around tail on the underside *only*. Connect split. Skin out both
hind legs, and make a small slice between bone and tendon and
insert a gamblin' stick. Hang the coon up. Take two small sticks, and
grip them together firmly so that the base of the tail is between.
Pull carefully while holding the sticks tightly clamped together, and
the tail will slide off the tail bone (*Plate 249*). If you want to keep
the skin, be sure not to pull the tail off.

Work the pelt off to the front legs, slicing the mesentery between
skin and muscle when necessary (*Plate 250*). Slice up to front legs,

PLATE 249   U. G. McCoy clamps the tail between two sticks and slides the pelt off the tail bone. The coon is hanging upside down from a gamblin' stick.

PLATE 250   Now he works the pelt up to the shoulders slicing the mesentery, where necessary, with his pocket knife.

and then skin the front legs out. If you want to eat the coon, remove the two pear-shaped musk glands from under the forearms.

Skin around the neck until you get to the head (*Plate 251*). Cut the ears off even with the head. If you make a bad ear hole, the pelt's value will be reduced by fifty cents. Skin right around the eyes leaving only the eyeballs. Then go down the snout, cutting off the end so that the nose button is still attached to the pelt.

Now split the flesh down the middle from throat to crotch and remove intestines and organs. Cut off the head, tail, and feet, and soak the carcass in cold water (preferably overnight unless you have just killed it) to get the blood out.

PLATE 251   Carefully, he works the pelt off over the coon's head.

COOKING—The most common way of cooking coon is to put it in a pot of salted water (one spoon of salt per pound), one or two pods of red pepper or one tablespoon of black pepper, and let it boil in a pot with no lid until the meat is tender. Remove, put in a greased baking pan, and bake until golden brown.

To parboil, add either broken spicewood twigs, an onion or two, a teaspoonful of vinegar, or some potatoes to the water to remove the wild taste. Take out, roll in flour, salt and pepper, and bake in a greased Dutch Oven turning the meat often. Another method is to rub the parboiled coon with salt and pepper, and dot it with butter. Place quartered sweet potatoes around the meat, and bake it in an oven at four hundred degrees until the meat and potatoes are tender. The meat can also be parboiled, cut into pieces, rolled in corn meal, and then fried in lard.

Another contact told us that his method was to sprinkle the skinned carcass all over with salt and leave it overnight on a pan that was tipped so that as the salt drew the water out, it would drain. The next morning he packs it in ice and cools the meat, then parboils it, cuts it into two halves, and bakes it like a ham, basting it with a sauce containing poultry seasoning. Still another woman told us that rather than skinning the coon, her family always dipped the coon in boiling water to which ashes had been added to help loosen the hair. Then the coon was scraped clean, gutted, and the chest cavity filled with sweet potatoes. It was then baked until brown and tender.

Apparently it is also possible to salt the scraped, gutted carcass and smoke it like a ham for later use.

POSSUM

DRESSING—Few people in this area bother to skin the few possums they eat. The prevailing tradition is to scald the possum in boiling water containing a half cup of lime or ashes. Then it is scraped until hairless, gutted (it should have been bled immediately after caught), the musk glands under the forearms removed, and either the head or at least the eyes removed. The carcass is then soaked, preferably overnight, before cooking.

COOKING—The most common way of cooking possum is to parboil it in water containing salt and red or black pepper to taste. It is boiled until tender, and then put in a greased pan surrounded or filled with sweet potatoes. It is then baked until golden brown (about two hours if you're using a wood stove).

Another contact lines the bottom of the baking pan with sassafras sticks instead of grease. Then she bakes it. Some prefer to skin the possum, parboil the meat in salty water until tender, cut the pieces up and roll them in red and black pepper and flour and fry them in fat.

Beulah Perry said, "Lot a'times, when I was a kid, th' possum head was my favorite, an' my mother would always pay me to do things. And she'd say, 'Now Beulah, if you do so and so, then I'll leave th' possum head on.' And when th' possum would get done, she'd cut that head off and give it to me. You know, as little as you think, why, they's right smart a'meat on those. You eat th' tongue, brains, everything in th' head except th' eyes." You could also dry, salt, and smoke the carcass for later use.

RABBIT

SKINNING AND DRESSING—Some hunters in this area gut the rabbit as soon as they have killed it. Many carry it home and gut it that evening, however. They do this by making one short slash in the belly parallel to the backbone, and removing the entrails through this cut. At home they skin it, often making a cut *across* the middle of the back, inserting their fingers, and pulling both ways. The legs are lifted out of the pelt as with the squirrel.

COOKING—There are several popular ways. First cut the rabbit into sections. Remove the legs, and separate the ribs and back section by cutting up the rabbit's sides vertically. Parboil the pieces in a covered pot in salted (two tablespoons) water to make it tender if it's not young and tender already.

For frying, put the parboiled pieces in a greased pan and fry until brown on all sides, seasoning with a half teaspoon pepper. Some roll the pieces in meal or flour before frying.

For baking, dip the parboiled pieces in a breaded solution consisting of two eggs, four tablespoons of flour, a quarter cup milk, and a half teaspoon pepper. Put pieces in an oven and bake until brown (about thirty minutes).

Others prefer the meat simmered in the salted water until tender, and then eaten. Another contact used to make rabbit dumplings similar to those described in the squirrel section.

GROUNDHOG

DRESSING—Skin the groundhog, remove the glands from under the legs, gut, and soak overnight in salty water. The hide was often placed in a bucket of ashes over which water was poured. After the ashes had taken the hair off, the hide was removed, dried, kneaded, and cut up in strips for shoe strings.

COOKING—Parboil with spicewood twigs (to take the wild taste out) until tender. Pepper and put in a greased pan to bake until brown.

Another way is to parboil the groundhog until tender in water containing two carrots, garlic, and a piece of fat meat "about the size of a baby's fist." You can also add pepper and a tablespoon of salt if you wish. Then the groundhog is browned in an open baking pan in the oven.

The carcass could also be dried, salted, and smoked for later use.

SQUIRREL

SKINNING AND DRESSING—The most common way of skinning a squirrel in the mountains was to ring the back legs at the feet, and cut around the top of the base of the tail. The hunter then put the squirrel on its back, put his foot on its tail, grabbed its back legs firmly, and pulled. The hide would come off just like a jacket right up to the neck. Then the front legs were pulled up out of the skin and cut off at the feet, and the pelt cut off at the neck. Usually the head was not skinned out, but if you wanted to, it would be done about the same as with the coon.

Cut off the head, back feet, and tail. Then gut.

COOKING—After soaking the squirrel long enough to get all the blood out, cut it into pieces and roll the pieces in flour, salt, and pepper. Fry until tender and brown. If the squirrel is old, you may want to parboil it in water containing sage to take out the wild taste.

Another contact used to cut the squirrel into pieces after parboiling, and cook the pieces in a gravy made of milk and flour.

Another made squirrel dumplings. Cut the squirrel up and parboil the pieces for five minutes. Then remove the meat and cook it in fresh water until tender. Add to the broth a quarter teaspoon of pepper, one tablespoon of butter or cooking fat, and some milk. Prepare the dumpling dough, and cook by dropping the pieces into the boiling broth mixture. Cover and cook for ten minutes and serve hot.

BEAR

SKINNING AND DRESSING—Cut jugular vein and bleed, or cut head off. Slice down the middle of the underside from the neck to the back legs, sliding the knife between the hide and the flesh. Roll the bear from side to side while cutting until the hide is off.

With the axe, cut off the legs below the knees, cut through the breastbone, and cut between the buttocks to the backbone. Cut the end of the large intestine and strip out the innards. Cut on either side of the backbone (as in the hog) separating the meat into two halves. Cut out the hams and shoulders for curing in salt. Cut the neck, flank, and lower part of the shoulder into small pieces for stewing at once.

COOKING—Many of our contacts cooked bear roasts and steaks in the same fashion as beef or venison. One suggested parboiling the fresh meat until tender, and adding several large apples to the water. When the apples fell apart, the meat was ready to be taken out, seasoned, and baked.

DEER

SKINNING AND DRESSING—After killing, remove the scent glands (on the hind legs at the inside of the knee joint), the testes, and cut the jugular vein immediately. Then hang the carcass up by its hind legs, and ring each of the back legs below the knee. Cut down the inside of the back legs to the crotch, cut down the belly to the center of the chest, and ring the front legs in a manner similar to the back. Cut down the inside of the front legs to meet the cut in the chest. Peel the hide off the back legs, down the body, and off the front legs up the neck to the ears. Cut off the head right behind the ears with an axe.

With the same axe, chop down between the hams. Cut from the hams to the chest with a knife, and then separate the ribs using the axe again. Cut down to the brisket with the knife, cut around the anus, and then remove the entrails. Save the heart and liver if desired.

Another method also used by local hunters was to make a diagonal cut just behind the chest cavity about twelve inches long. The entrails were removed through this cut, which was plenty large enough and yet small enough to prevent dirt and leaves from entering the cavity.

CURING—Sometimes hunters would salt the entire carcass with about twenty-five pounds of salt, let it dry, and hang it in the smokehouse. When they needed pieces, they simply stripped them off and cooked them.

Others cut the deer into pieces very similar to those that a beef is cut into (legs, ribs, rump, loin, etc.). These pieces were either dried in the sun until all the moisture was out and then put in the smokehouse; put into a fairly thick salt brine and left; or salted down (about one inch thick) and put in the smokehouse to cure in the same manner as pork.

COOKING—Before cooking meat from the smokehouse, soak the pieces overnight in clear water. If you kept them in brine, simply cook without adding salt.

For steaks from the smokehouse or brine, slice into pieces a half inch thick, four inches long, and three inches wide. In a skillet, brown in butter and simmer until tender depending on the toughness of the meat. Salt is not needed since the meat was salted during curing. For fresh steaks, roll in flour, pepper and salt until covered, and then put in a frying pan with a half cup of shortening. Fry slowly until tender, or until both sides are browned.

One woman told us to pound the steak, and soak it for an hour in a mixture of a half cup vinegar, one cup water, and a teaspoon of salt (for two pounds of steak). Remove from the liquid, dry, and roll in about a cup of flour. Season with salt, pepper, and garlic salt, and brown in shortening at a high heat. Cover, and simmer at a low heat for forty-five to sixty minutes.

For fresh roasts, some put a four-pound roast and one pod of red pepper (to kill the wild taste) in water and parboil, uncovered, until tender. The meat should be completely covered with water. When tender, take out, wipe dry, sprinkle salt and pepper to taste, and then brown in an oven.

To cook without parboiling, rub with a teaspoon each of salt and pepper, and place in a roasting pan. Add one cup water, one medium diced onion, and one half cup chopped mushrooms. Cover and bake at a low heat for around three hours.

For pot roasts, soak a four-pound roast in salt water overnight. Remove from water, dry, and rub with a mixture of one half teaspoon each salt and pepper, and one half cup flour. Heat one half cup fat, add five or six chopped onions, and brown meat on all sides. Add a cup of water, cover tightly, and cook on top of stove until tender. If you wish, add two or three chopped potatoes and carrots half an hour before the roast is done.

For venison loaf, mix together 2½ pounds ground deer meat, 1 pound ground hog meat, 2 eggs, 2 teaspoons salt, 1 teaspoon pepper, 1 large chopped onion, and 1½ cups breadcrumbs dampened with a little water. Shape into a loaf, and bake for about an hour at 400°.

For stews, cut two pounds of meat into one-inch cubes and brown on all sides in a small amount of fat. Then, in a stewing pot, add the meat, two cups water, four potatoes, six large carrots, four medium onions, one quart of tomatoes, one tablespoon salt, and one teaspoon pepper. Bring to a boil and simmer for three hours. After three hours, thicken with three tablespoons flour and one half cup water. Eat then, or store in a cool place and heat as needed. Another person told us to thicken with flour, three tablespoons bacon drippings, and a pint of tomato juice.

TURKEY

DRESSING—Most early cooks in our area scalded and plucked the turkey leaving the skin on, but one said that he skinned them many times. Then the fuzz was removed by singeing in the fire, the feet cut off at the joints, the head cut off, and the entrails removed. The latter was done either by severing the backbone from the base and pulling the entrails out through the tail end, or by cutting up the middle from the legs to the breastbone and removing them. The gizzard, liver, and sometimes the heart were saved.

COOKING—After cleaning, some then cut off the legs and breast (saving them for frying like chicken) and stewed the rest. Others rubbed the outside with lard, sprinkled it with two tablespoons of salt and one teaspoon of pepper, replaced the liver and gizzard, and baked it for about three hours on low heat. After baking, two cups of the resulting liquid were sometimes mixed in a saucepan with two tablespoons flour and a quarter cup water and heated to make gravy. Chopped liver and gizzard could be added.

Lon Reid's family used to cut off the wings, spread them out and dry them in front of the fire. When stiff, they were used as fans for the fire.

QUAIL

DRESSING—Pull the skin off the bird without bothering to pluck the feathers. Cut off the feet and head and remove the insides, saving the gizzard, heart, and liver if you wish. Rub it all over with butter, salt and pepper, place in a roasting pan, and cover. Bake in a moderate oven until tender, then uncover and let brown.

TURTLE

DRESSING—When cleaning mud turtles, most people chopped the head off first (some by holding a stick in front of the turtle, coaxing him to bite down on it, and then chopping), and then dropped it shell and all into boiling water.

Then the meat was cut loose from the shell, gutted, and cut into pieces, sometimes three inches in diameter and one inch thick, and sometimes just chunks.

Others simply skinned the turtle without boiling by cutting the bottom plate off first, then cutting between the meat and the domed shell, and then gutting the turtle, cutting off the legs, and cutting the remaining meat into pieces. Some took the meat off the legs, and cooked it along with the rest of the meat.

COOKING—The meat was soaked overnight in salty water (some with a little soda also) to remove the wild, strong taste. It was cooked according to any of the following directions:

Parboil (if desired) and roll in flour. Put three tablespoons of flour, one tablespoon salt, and one teaspoon pepper in a covered skillet, and fry the meat until brown on all sides.

After parboiling (with salt and hot pepper if desired), cool, and dip meat into a batter made of one cup plain sifted flour, one half teaspoon salt, one teaspoon baking powder, two beaten eggs, and one half cup milk. Fry in deep fat until golden brown.

Stew in sweet milk and butter, pepper and salt just like oyster stew.

FROG

Mrs. Lake Stiles: "First, after y'get'em dressed [cut the legs off and clean them and throw the rest away], get your grease not too awfully hot—if y'get it too hot, when y'put'cher legs in they'll jump out. Roll'em in flour an' salt an' pepper like chicken, an' fry'em; or either y'can take buttermilk'n'an'egg an' whip it t'gether, and then roll th' legs in it an' either bread crumbs or cracker crumbs, an' fry it."

HUNTING TALES

I nevitably, conversations about hunting turn to hunting tales. "The biggest bear I ever saw . . . ," "The best dog I ever had . . . ," and so on, are preludes to stories filled with expressions not heard in any other context. When an animal is "treed," it is not necessarily "put up a tree," but "holed up" anywhere—be it in a hollow log, a hole in the ground, or a cave. When a hunter says, "I cut down on him," he means he opened fire. When dogs "open on a track," they find the scent they're looking for and charge ahead. A "painter," as mentioned in a previous chapter, is not a person who paints houses or portraits, but a panther.

The stories provide instruction and detail on many aspects of mountain life. And, perhaps most important of all, they are filled with the spirit of the hunt, the dedication of the hunter to his task, and the sense of sharing and generosity implied in getting food for others.

❖NATE CHASTAIN and BOB CARPENTER: "I trailed one coon from five o'clock t'twelve o'clock that evenin'. Went up on Keener's Creek an' struck on up'ere. Trailed him out across on Rickman's Creek, all th' way up th' backside of th' mountain up above Hopper's on Betty's Creek, and back out into th' Joe Gap, back down Keener's Creek, back out on th' face of th' mountain; an' 'bout two o'clock that day it got s'cold, m'dogs couldn't trail it no fudder an' they just blowed out on it an' I had t'quit.

PLATE 252

"I went over in Blue Valley one time. Camped over there in an old road'n'cooked m'supper. Settin' there—got done eatin' supper, an' all at once m'dogs tore off out down towards th' creek, an' they commenced treein'. So I hung up m'bucket'n'fryin' pans an' things on a limb'ere. Thought I'd go off over'ere to'em—see what they'uz barkin' at. Had a coon treed up a tree. An' they'd bark down here at this tree fer a little bit, an' then they'd run back up here t'another place'n'bark. Just about th' time I shot one out, th' other'n jumped out an' here they left me. Then they treed it again up on th' face of th' mountain.

"So I got that one pulled out an' got up'ere just about to'em, an' out it jumped again. Here they went again. I went on again. They treed it again. An' I got nearly to'em an' it jumped out again. So I had t'hike'em again after'em.

"They treed it again, an' I got to'em. They treed it in a little old black oak. Had a little holler in th' top of it. Well, I cut it down, an' just about 'fore it hit th' ground, why that coon bailed out' a that thing an' here he went again.

"And they run that thing right up next t'th' Broadway Gap an' treed it up a big hem pine, an' I run that coon all night that night. They treed him up there about four that mornin', an' I stayed there till daylight with that tree; but I never could find that coon. Never did find him!"

TURKEY

❖ ANDY WEBB: "Used t'be, back when I was a boy growin' up, we'd go out there in th' woods, take y'r gun, be gone a hour, kill all th' squirrels y'want'a carry inta th' house t'eat. Now you can't hardly see one in thar—just onct in a while.

"An' turkeys? A-w-w-w, I never see'd th' like. Go out through th' woods there and get inta'flock maybe twenty-five'r'thirty of 'em in one bunch.

"One time, me'n'm'father—right funny t'me—he never did kill one; a gobbler, y'know. Me'n him had been out lookin' fer our hogs. It was in th' fall a'th' year. Th' leaves had all fell down. We'd gone walkin' along th' trailway, an' I heered one. I said t'him, said, 'Pap, did you ever hear that turkey?'

"'Why, no,' he says. 'I didn't hear it.' He says, 'Y'know,' he says, 'Andy,' he says, 'turkeys won't gobble in th' fall of th' year.' I says, 'They will too, if 'ey get squanderin'. A young one.' I said, 'You never killed one.' I says, 'I'll give you my gun, an' you set down on the holler of this tree an' I'll get behind'y'an' call it up an' let'cha kill it.'

"Said, 'All right.'

"So he set down in th' holler of th' tree, an' I got around behind him an' gave'im m'gun. And that turkey was just as plain as that house down yonder when I called it up. One a'my uncles had made me a turkey call. He took a piece of a little cow's horn, an'he put a nail through it an' a little piece'a wood and stopped it, y'know, right real good. I could take me a little old rock an' I could just call one as pretty as you ever seed. An' 'ey'd answer y' too.

"Well I called that turkey up, and it got up on a log an' walked that log backerds and forrerds. I kep'waitin' thinkin' t'm'self, 'You'll see it.'

"Finally at last I happened t'think that maybe he didn't see it; an' I said t'him, said, 'Pap?' Said, 'Don't you see 'at turkey?'

"'Why, no,' he said. 'I don't see it.'

"'Well,' I said. 'Be right real still an' hold up yer arm.'

"He held up his arm, an' I had one a'these old-fashioned rifle guns we used t'call'em. I just eased it back; told him t'hold his arm up.

"Crack a'that gun he seed th' turkey fall off'a that log, an' that's th' first time he seed it.

"I killed lots of 'em. Killed one on th' back of th' mountain; called it up an' killed it. Fifty long steps off—I stepped it off—an' I

PLATE 253   Andy Webb with one of his grandsons at the door to their home.

shot hits head square light off. An' hit had a beard *eleven* inches long."

❖ GRADY WALDROOP: "They was one up'ere at what they called th' Lightnin' Stump. Man that stayed there said he'd shot at him time'r two an' never got'im.

"Well, I decided I'd go up. They's some hogs up in'ere, an' I says I'll just go up in'ere. An' this boy went wi'me. I went an' located this old gobbler right at roostin' time, just before dark. Then we took a lantern an' got up t'this stand, an' I hid this old boy an' said, 'Don't shoot at nothin' less it's a turkey. An'if a turkey comes out, you shoot; an' if it don't, why you just lay there 'til I tell y't'get up, or you hear me shoot. Then y'can get up.'

"He'uz hid off under th' gap, an' I got again' a white oak tree on top'a th' ridge, an' I got out m'turkey caller—had a old weed'r somethin'—an' give a yelp'r two. God, he gobbled an' just jarred th' ground.

"I just put m'call in m'pocket an' set there, an' he come a'walkin' an' went like he's goin' t'Georgia!

"'Well,' I said, 'I guess he's a gone cat.' An' I set there till I just got nearly petrified. Set there s'long an' it so cold. An' in a while, I heered a brush crack. I hadn't heered him gobble in a long time. I said, 'It's gonna' somethin' happen directly!'

"So he come steppin' out directly. I seed that old red head come up over th' hill, an' he stretched as high as three'r four feet above th' ground. I drawed at that head an' then just cut down.

"So he got off in a sink hole where a tree had turned up, an' this old boy run up an' said, 'What'd y'shoot at?' I said, 'Get down in that sink hole an' you'll find out.' An' that old turkey's down in there just'a floppin' up a storm. Had spurs a inch an' a half long!

"That old boy got down in there an' got him by th' neck. I said, 'Lay with him now! He might get loose'n'get away!'

"An' we took him out t'an old shack'uz out there an' took his entrails out an' washed him out good, an' he weighted twenty-three pounds an' a half after we took his entrails out an' cut off one leg.

"Went down to a camp where an old man had been after him fer a year. Cut off a foot an' tied a note to it said, 'Been a good old rambler, but he's been here an' gone!'"

❖ JAKE WALDROOP: "I was up at th' head of Dismal—see if I could hear a gobbler—an' I could howl like a hoot owl. So I howled, an' this old gobbler answered me way down—he go, 'Chobalobalob, chobalobalob.'

"So I went back up th' ridge sort'a opposite to where he'uz at; an' up to about th' time th' sun went down, I laid there in a beech thicket. An' directly he went t'gobblin' right down under me, an' I heered him fly up, an' he went on his roost. Well, when he went up on his roost, why I yelped a time or two like a hen turkey, an' he was just a'rarin' a'gobblin'.

"So I went back th' next mornin' an' got in m'blind, an' got t'where I'uz goin't'call'im out. And th' owls hooted and th' robins singed and different rackets took place, an' I heered nothin' out of'im.

"Directly they'uz some hogs down off in th' cove, and they'uz bells on'em. Th' old sow, she got up an' she shook her head an' rattled that bell. 'Ting-a-ling-a-ling-a-ling,' that bell went.

"So that old gobbler, he went t'roarin' then, an' he flew from me way over on another ridge, an' he hit th' ground. An' when he went down, he went t'gobblin' again. Why I called to'im—yelped like a hen—an' he answered me twice, 'Chobalobalob, chobalobalob!' An' I just got ready and laid still. I knew he'd come right t'that spot.

"It wuz about ten or fifteen minutes, an' I heered him a-comin', struttin' out, y'know, 'Vuh-duh-yuh-yuh-yuh,' like footsteps, them wings on th' ground. He walked to about twenty steps of me, an' I give'im a load in th' head, an' that was hit fer him."

❖HARLEY CARPENTER: "I'd bought a little old coon-footed mule that I's tryin' t'make a crop with. Paid fifty dollars fer'im; an' I's tryin' t'make a workin' with my uncle an' his brothers. They said they'd come help me. So my wife's brother was up there th' evenin' before we's goin't'have th' workin'. Said, 'Let's go turkey huntin' in th' mornin'—have turkey fer dinner.'

"So we pulled out before day an' went up above Barker's Creek there a piece, an' got up there before crack a'day. An' it was just begin't'crack day when th' gobbler settin' on a roost a'raised up an' gobbled.

"We heered it, an' I placed him out on th' side here, an' I got right up in th' head a'th' holler an' se'down. I had a leaf then, buck tongue or deer tongue. When it first grows up it makes a *real* leaf t'call with.

"So I got up there so's when I called an' they started t'come, they'd come up by *him*. He'd never killed one. So when I commenced callin', why directly here they come. One was a good'eal

PLATE 254   Harley Carpenter in the middle of one of his hunting tales.

bigger than th' other'n, an' th' big'n kept th' little'n sorta whupped back, y'know, like a rooster would.

"So they got out, I thought right out even of him, an' he was just about ready t'fire, an' he moved or somethin'—or they made a booger.

Anyway, they just wheeled an' broke t'run around th' hillside, an' out'a sight they went.

"Well, that knocked that hunt in th' head.

"But they didn't fly. They just run around th' hill. An' we got up in th' other gap an' set there awhile an' called an' called an' thought they might come back out again, but they wouldn't come back n'more t'that callin' cause they'd got scared, y'know.

"So we took off back down toward Mulberry Gap, an' back an old trail startin' in fer home. Just got'own nearly inta th' gap, and right up on th' high part of this mountain up here, we heered one gobble.

"I said, 'Let's go fer'im!'

"He said, 'Y'reckon it won't be too late?'

"I said, 'No.' I said, 'He'll not fly off'a there. He'll be right up there.'

"So we started out an' trotted part a'th' way, an' got about half up th' mountain, an' he kind'a give out on me. Sun was gettin' way up, an' he said it was gettin' kind'a late; he'd just sit'own an' wait. So I said, 'Well, I'm gonna go on an' try'im.'

"I went on 'til I just come up on th' top there like on th' high part, an' he was right off out there a little off on this side. Th' very minute I put m'leaf t'm'mouth an' clucked, why he answered. Well, he'uz just right down under me, an' before I could call again, I seen'im comin' up through there just runnin' like a blue streak. I went up an' got behind some bushes an' clucked again, an' when I done that, he seen where I was, an' he'uz comin' right square t'me just as straight as he could be. I just squatted down right in th' trail, an' I feared t'move—feared he'd see me, y'know. An' so I just set there, m'gun layin' across m'lap.

"Well, directly he come out an' got near t'a bunch a chestnut sprouts, an' I just said t'myself, 'Now if he'd just go in behind somethin' an' stop, I'd get ready.' Well, sure enough, he run out pretty close an' stopped an' gobbled again; an' when he done that, why, I got m'gun ready an' got it right on th' trail that he'uz comin' on.

"Well, he didn't do nothin' more, an I didn't call n'more, an' he just started t'runnin'. He got up close enough fer me t'fire, but I thought, 'I'll just let'cha run over me an' I'll shoot'cher head off.'

"An' he got right up pretty close to this big oak tree. I's just sittin' right out there, y'know; an' he just wheeled an' run across an' stopped right behind that tree there. And when he stopped, he doubled that neck up like he does when he goes t'gobble; an' when he done that, I had m'gun on him, an' I dropped'im. An' that beard was eleven inches long!

"So I hoisted'im an' took off back th'hill, an' got down pretty close t'where he was, an' he got up an' called, 'D'ja get'im?'

"I said, 'Yeah!'

"'Aw, you never!' I had him hid best I could on m'back, y'know. 'Whad'ja shoot at? Squirrels?'

"I said, 'No. A turkey.' I says, 'I've got'im!'

"'Naw you didn't,' he says. 'You shot at a squirrel.'

"I just sort'a wheeled thataway, y'know, an' rolled him around where y'could see'im. *Hot Dang!* he said. 'Sure did, didn't cha?' He took right up th'mountain toward me. Glad I didn't have t'tote'im th'rest of th'way home. His spurs was two inches long. He was an *old* booger. Twenty-four pounds.

"We got back an' nobody hadn't come. Back in them times, if somebody'uz a'comin' much, they'd a'been there. Quick as we could get th'feathers off of'im an' cut'im up, why one come.

"It was too late t'try t'boil it, so we just took part a'that breast, sliced it thin like bacon, an' just fried it.

"Then th'others come; an' just before dinner time, why, th' preacher come, an' us right ready t'eat, y'know. So we never let on t'im 'bout th'turkey, y'know. Just asked him t'stay. Directly Uncle Bill says, 'Preacher, did'ja' ever eat any mud turkle?'

"An' he said, 'Certain'n'declare no. I don't believe I ever did.'

"An' he said, 'Well, have a piece an' see if y'like it!'

"An' that preacher took out a piece an' cut it up an' he eat it, y'know, an' all th'rest of us lookin' at one another, y'know, just a'bustin'.

"An' directly old Bill picked it up an' said, 'Have another piece! Do y'like it?'

"An' he said, 'Certain'n'declare I do. I like t'go back home,' he said, 'an' tell m'wife that I eat mud turkle fer dinner.'

"So he went on eatin' on that piece, an' directly old Bill got tickled s'good he sort'a leant over to'im an' said, 'Aw, preacher,' he said. "That wadn't mud turkle!' He said, 'That's turkey gobbler!'

"'Certain'n'declare,' he said. 'I'm glad y'told me. I'd a'went home an' told m'wife a great tale about eatin' mud turkle fer dinner!'"

WILD HOG

❖TAYLOR CROCKETT: "On one occasion, we were on a trip t'feed our hogs. In cold weather when th'snow'uz on th'ground, food got a little scarce. T'keep th'hogs doin' well, 'n'keep'em from starvin', an' keep'em gentle, we'd take a little feed out there.

"We were on a trip like this one time. Found a bunch'a old sows'n'shoats. An' we found an enormous big wild boar with'em. Well, we didn't want him with'em because we were afraid he'd lead th'young hogs off an' make them wild too, so we had t'figure t'get rid'a'im. We'd like t'do it in a way t'have some fun out of it, so we went back t'get two or three of our ketch dogs. Th'dog we had with us that day was just a little ol'dog we used t'hunt fer th'tame hogs; an' if they'uz a *wild* hog, we had t'get a little rougher dog.

"So they'uz a feller that'uz wi'me, 'n'he had one that'uz pretty rough, 'n'I had one too. So we went'n'got'em an' came back, an' th'dogs took th'track an' we heard'em bayed.

"Feller wi'me said, 'That's bound t'be th'big hog.' Said, 'Ol' John wouldn't bay if it wadn't. He'd just ketch it.'

"So we let out runnin' 'til we caught up t'where we could hear th'dogs barkin', an' shore enough, they had th'big boar bayed. He must'a weighed three hunnerd'n fifty, four hunnerd pound, an' had a'great big bristles. Wicked lookin' fella'. He'uz standin' there chompin' his teeth—poppin' his teeth. An' old John, he'd caught'im all right, but he'd cut old John. He'uz standin' with a big gash in his side.

"Gener'ly they jus' depended on catchin' one of'em an' tyin' him with a rope—then take'im in an' keep'im a while, y'know, an' mebbe use'im. But that was just a little too much of a customer for that. So we studied 'bout what we'll do.

"About that time, th'hog decided *he'd* do somethin', so he took off right across th'ridge'n we heard th'dogs bay again. We took off again. Heretofore we'd gotten ever' hog we'd got after perty easy.

"This feller had'a short club kind'a like a baseball bat. He'd made th'brag that he'n ol'John an' that club could handle any hog that they wuz. He had his club, so we lit out.

"We got over'ere, an' th'hog had got under a little rock cliff there. They'uz a little narrow trail leadin' inta it. Th'ol' dog'uz in th'trail at th'mouth—it'uz a kindly semi-cove—barkin'.

"An' th'young dog had gone down below an' climbed up an' was peepin' over through some bushes barkin'. An' I thought, 'Well, now, that dog's got sense. I'll do th' same thing in place a gettin' right where that hog might run over'ya'.'

"So I climbed around an' peeked in, an' I noticed that m'buddy'uz standin' right in th' bend of th' trail; an' I said, 'You better watch! That hog'll get you directly!' 'Bout that time I said, 'Here he comes!' An' he ran out, an' my friend, he didn't have anywhere t'go— standin' right there on th' side'a that little rock cliff—an' he just went t'runnin' straight up an' down in place. He wadn't goin' any-where, but he was goin' through th' motions! He forgot about his club, an' th' big hog passed'im an' just made a pass at'im, an' his big old tooth hooked inta his overhaul bibs an' just cut his over-hauls in two!

"I asked'im why he didn't use his club, an' he said he forgot about it. An' th' last we saw a'that hog, he was jumpin' a big old tree lap with his big old tail standin' out behind'im. An' so we just gave'im up fer that day.

"Later on, though, we got'im. Got another dog'r two that were real good, an' they caught'im, an' I ran up wi'my knife an' cut his throat. We figgered he was too much t'tie an' drive in. Just too much t'handle. An' yet we didn't want'im leadin' off our tame hogs. So I decided t'kill'im, an' so I cut his throat. I just straddled him t'do that. About that time, th' two dogs that was holdin' him turned him loose, and there I was a'straddlin'im, holdin' on one ear, an' them a'goin' down th' mountain. I rode'im about a hundred yards 'til he threw me off in a brush pile an' laid over an' bled t'death."

BEAR

❖ MARVIN WATTS: "Up around Bryson City, there used to be a lead mine pure enough t'melt bullets, and they'd get bullets for them old hog rifles back then. And we lived wi'an old fella', Parker. He said he lived with an old man when he's a boy. He figgered if he could work all summer fer a hog rifle, they could kill their meat and they could make their bread. So he worked all summer.

"Long 'at fall he says, 'Well, we 'bout got th' crop made. Gone let'cha go.' He went an' got his rifle, an' he got his bullet mold, powder horn, an' turned it over to him. Parker took this an' went on home; worked all summer fer this.

"One evenin' he decided t'go out an' still hunt; try t'kill 'im a bear or somethin'. Sittin' at th' head a'th' swamp an' there's three bear come walkin' out. A small little bear in front, and they's a big he bear in th' center, an' then they's a little cub behind this'un.

An' he waited 'til this big bear got betwixt him an' a tree t'shoot it wi'his hog rifle so he could save his bullet—go cut it out of th' tree. And when he shot this big bear, th' big bear just wheeled around an'grabbed th' cub an' squz it t'death. An' he went home an' got he'p an' come back an' got th' big bear an' th' little bear, an' took a axe an' cut th' bullet out. He'd take it back an' remold it. Lead was hard t'get, so that's th' way they'd try t'save their bullets."

❖MANN NORTON: "One time Uncle Jeff treed up on Wild-cat Branch over there. He treed a bear. Well, his old dog went up; he peeked in—it'uz kind of a cave in there. Said he could see some-thin's eyes shinin' in there. He just had two loads a'amminition, an' one a'them was a head off'a one a'these old nails. They'd go out —them bears an' painters around at that time—with two loads'a amminition fer them old muzzle loadin' guns!

"He shot; cut down inside an' shot. An' he put this nail head in an'shot again. He said he never could see his eyes n'more. Ever-thing looked dark in there. So he said he hauled off his old shot pouch an' went crawlin' in, an' in, an' in. Finally he said he felt somethin'. What about a man crawlin' in on a bear now! He didn't know. Mebbe it was just crippled up in there. So he crawled in there, it just as dark as a dungeon an' no light n'r nothin'. Said he finally got a'hold'a his hind laig. He said he kep' pullin' an' pullin'. Finally he got out his knife. He'd got 'im a hick'ry withe 'fore he went in there. Popped it through his ham string on his hind laig. He said it never moved. He knowed it was dead then.

"He twisted his hick'ry withe in that hind laig an' drug him out'a there. Biggest bear! Weighed about four, five hunnerd pounds.

"One time he's tellin' it t'a school teacher up there on Betty's Creek. 'Why,' she said, 'Mr. Hopper, wadn't you afraid it'd *bite' chew?'*

" 'Why, no, madam,' I said. 'I wadn't afraid at all fer I knowed I wadn't a'holt a'th' bitin' end I wadn't!' Oh, he'uz a dandy!"

❖TAYLOR CROCKETT: "This fella' come an' told me, said, 'I found where a big bear's been a'feedin'. What about you gettin' your dogs and let's see if we kin go kill 'im.'

"Well, at that time I have five perty good dogs, so I met 'im down there. We started through th' woods leadin' th' dogs. It'd rained about twenty-four hours before, an' I found these tracks that'd been made right a'ter th' rain. Th' dogs trailed'im a little, but I didn't turn'em loose 'cause it wadn't a real good track.

"So we followed along 'bout a half a mile'n found where th' bear had bedded down right above a rock cliff. They always try t'find a place that's way back in rough where they kin hear an' smell in all directions. Up on top a'this rock cliff, there his bed was where he'd laid. Th' leaves around it were wet, an' th' bed was dry, so we knew he'd laid there when it'uz rainin'.

"An' I turned th' old dog loose. He was smartest, an' he knew th' most about tracks, an' he checked th' track out one way'n'another way—th' bear had been there two or three times—finally decided which one was th' right one an' started out. I turned th' other dogs loose. That bear'd been all around, an' he'd had plenty'a time t'ramble. Th' dogs trailed back'n'forth'n'here'n'yonder, an' finally went way out'a hearin' over on another big mountain.

"I said, 'Well boys, we won't get that bear. He's left th' country.'

"'Bout that time I heard th' old dog come back to us, an' before he got t'me, a little down th' mountain below me, I heard th' dogs go t'barkin' real excited, so I knew that they'd jumped'im. I headed out down thataway, an' they passed right under me. But I knew th' bear'ud get past an' I hollered, 'Sooooo–ey pig! Git'em!' 'At's 'e way I'd holler when I wanted'em t'catch a hog. They all just fell in, an' here they went as hard as they could; an' directly I heard'em ketch'im.

"I caught up, an' shore enough, they were catchin' a big bear. He'uz tryin' t'climb up th' steep side of a mountain'n'get over th' mountain, an' they wouldn't let 'im climb. He'd start up an', why, a dog'ud grab'im an' jerk'im back.

"I got I guess, oh, a hunnerd'n'fifty feet, mebbe two hunnerd feet. Th' bear was standin' right above a little ivy thicket. One'a'th' dogs grabbed'im an' they rolled down th' hill a piece, an' th' bear came out on top.

"Well, I had t'do somethin' 'cause he had my dog. I wadn't quite as close as I ought'a be, but I shot anyhow. I could hear th' bullet hittin' his side. He turned th' dog loose, an' he headed right straight to me just as hard as he could come.

"Well, I thought, well that's fine. I'll just shoot you dead right now. So I leveled down an' shot again. That bear never stopped a'tall—didn't faze'im.

"So I thought, well, I've got enough time t'shoot again. Well, I must'a been gettin' a little excited 'cause I worked m'gun a little hard 'n'jammed it, 'n'by th' time I got that shell out an' another'n in, why he was too close. I had t'jump out of his way.

"When I jumped, th' bear, he turned an' went right straight down th' mountain, an' I wheeled an' shot' im from behind—right between his shoulders. I thought I'd break his back, but I missed his backbone just a little bit.

"By that time, th' old dog that th' bear had hold of first, he'uz a awful greedy old dog—if I'uz there he'd ketch one—he ran around an' got in front of him. He thought I'uz tryin' t'catch th' bear I guess. He made a pass'r two at'im, and then they just locked jaws.

"Well I ran down there'n I said, 'Well I'll finish you this time!' I just put m'gun up against th' bear's head and pulled th' trigger, an'nothin' happened. I'd shot all th' shells.

"First I grabbed m'huntin' knife. Then I figured, well, that won't be quick enough. So I decided I'd make'im turn'im loose by hittin'im with m'gun butt. So I rared back t'hit'im with m'gun butt, but 'bout that time another big dog they had just come right between me'n th' bear an' grabbed th' bear kind'a by th' side, kind'a in th' soft part of th' stomach, an' jerked him two or three times. That made'im turn th' dog loose.

"Then th' other dogs all got there an' rared up on th' bear an' were grabbin' at'im, so I couldn't a'shot again if I'd a'*had* a bullet.

"One a'th' fellers with me on th' hunt, he'd caught up by that time, an' I looked up'n'there he stood. Y'could'a stuck yer fist in his mouth an' his eyes were as big as saucers. He had his gun stuck out in front of'im, an' looked like he was just ready t'pull th' trigger, but he didn't. He must'a had presence of mind enough, I guess, t'figger he'd hit a dog. So he'uz gonna' wait till he could shoot.

"Directly th' old bear just rared up an' flopped over'n gave a gasp, an' that'uz th' end of'im. I told that old boy t'go ahead an' shoot'im 'cause he might slap a dog'r somethin', so he got t'help kill th' bear anyhow!"

❖ MINYARD CONNER: "Once my grandfather's huntin' over on Tennessee side. They's an' old summer man come up'ere an' stay with him, y'know. They'd go huntin' ever'day. Well, it'uz about th' time th' blueberries'uz ripe, an' they begin feedin' on'em. And they went up on top a'th' mountain and got on a trail on top a'th' ridge, an' one of'em went one way, an' one th' other.

"An' m'grandaddy said he's sittin'ere, an' said it'uz real early— just crack a'daylight when he got'ere—an' said he hadn't done his mornin' job, an' he just pulled his britches down an' set down in th' trail—just laid his gun down, y'know, an' set down.

"Said while he's settin'ere, said he seen a bear comin' right down th'trail! Said he forgot about bein' out of his britches, an' he just raised up an' took his gun an' whistled right low. An' just as he whistled, y'know, th'bear raised his head up. When th'bear raised his head up, he shot'im right in th'heart—shot him right in th'stickin' place like you'd stick a hog in.

"Said th'bear just throwed his mouth open way wide, made a high dive fer'im just like he's gonna get'im; an' said he didn't have time t'chamber another load, an' said he give a jump an' seen what he'uz into—had his britches down around his feet; an' said he just drawed his gun back an' hit him. He turned off just 'fore he got to'im an' run down a big rock cliff there. Said just as he went out'a sight behind that rock cliff, said that bear said, 'OOOOOO Lord,' just as plain!

"Th'other feller, he come on down. Said, 'What did'ja shoot at, Bill?'

"An' said he's done scared t'death, an' said, 'I shot at a bear.'

"He said, 'Where did he go?'

"Said, 'He went right under that rock cliff there.'

"He went on under, an' says, 'Here he lays! Dead'r'n hell!'"

SNAKE LORE

It is difficult to say what variety of mountain wildlife holds the place of honor in fireside conversations. The more challenging game animals like deer certainly rank high. And of course there are the more dangerous ones like panthers and bears with which nearly every hunter has had his moments of terror. Few living things, however, occupy the place of respect and awe that snakes enjoy. Time after time we have been on field trips with seasoned mountain people who refuse to enter an abandoned house or meadow or cave because it looks so "snakey." And time after time we have been amazed at the quality and variety of tales evoked by the mere mention of snakes.

There was that snake, for example, that, hours after its head had been cut off, bit a dog. There was the copperhead that lay along a limb, its head resting on a "thresher bird" nest slowly swallowing the young. Then there was the snake that stuck its feet out when it was held close to a fire; and the milk snake that would come to the barn each night and milk the cow; and the rattlesnake that was found frozen stiff as a stick and was taken inside where it soon thawed out and began to sing. And then there are those that swell up inside their holes for protection—and get wedged in so tightly that you couldn't "pull one out with a tractor."

There are snakes that won't bite during dog days. And then there was that snake two summers ago that bit a woman in the throat

PLATE 255 "They never have been a snake try t'bite yet. You can have one mad out there in th' yard, and I can walk out th' door and tell him t'lay down, and he will lay down on the ground flat. I can take an axe and walk right up and chop his head off. I've done that a'many of a time."
—Hillard Green

while she was leaned over picking beans. They found her dead in the field, one hand clutched so tightly around the snake's neck that it too was dead.

And the one Marvin Watts told us about: It seems there lived a frail girl who was given milk with bread every day in an attempt to strengthen her. She went off behind the barn each time to eat it, and once she was followed by a man who, to his horror, found her sharing her meal with a snake that would stick its head out from a hole in the barn's foundation. He killed the snake, and not long after, the girl also was found dead.

It's not surprising they have so many enemies. Men go on "snake hunts" every fall, walking into the middle of rattlesnake dens with limber poles and killing twenty or thirty at a time. Aunt Arie burns old shoes in a Dutch oven to keep them away, and she's killed her

share single-handedly. Once one crawled up through a crack between
the boards in her kitchen floor, and she crushed it underfoot. Joe
Arrowood has seen hogs eat them. He says they put their hooves
on the snake's heads and strip them clean. Many say that's why
you don't often see snakes around hog lots. Richard Norton has seen
places where deer have killed them, too. Apparently they whirl around
and around on top of the snakes and "just job'em full'a holes."
Supposedly goats also kill them. And sometimes snakes even kill each
other. There are numerous stories that tell of black snakes fighting
rattlesnakes, or king snakes swallowing copperheads whole.

We have put together many of the snake stories we have had on
file, and we present them here just as they were told to us. Some
of them are hard to believe. One thing's for sure though; when the
mountain families tell you these hills are full of rattlesnakes and
copperheads, they aren't kidding. We've seen them—and killed them
—ourselves, and we know they speak the truth.

PLATE 256 Wayne Mason, one of the students working
with *Foxfire*, brought in this photograph, yellowed and
stained with age. It shows his grandfather posing with a giant
rattlesnake.

COACHWHIP SNAKES

❖LAWTON BROOKS: They're about five feet long and an inch to an inch and a half around. They look normal except for the tail that's plaited "pretty as a leather whip." The plait doesn't unbraid, but stays together and is hard and firm and "keen as a needle." The snake wraps itself around a person, cow, dog or whatever else it happens to be attacking. Then it kills it either by whipping or running it to death. "I don't know if they kill it to eat or not. It's hard to imagine one eating a cow."

❖HOYT THOMAS: "They're like a black snake, and th' end of their tail looks just 'zactly like th' end of a whip plaited. They say they can get around a cow's leg and just run her t'death a'whuppin' her with th' end of their tail. I saw one. It looks just 'zactly like it was plaited on there. They're a flat land snake."

❖HILLARD GREEN: "Whip snakes are not so poisonous. They look sort'a like a black snake only their tail looks like a black whip— looks like it's been plaited. And they can sling that an' hit you an' cut you just like a knife."

❖LON REID: "They look like a black snake. I don't know if I've ever seed any or what, but I've seed one I believe was one over yonder on that big mountain. Might'a been over there 'sang huntin'. I forget. Anyhow I seed one. I was comin' down a old trailway an' heard somethin' that cracked just like you'd crack a whip or a .22 rifle—somethin' right below me just a little piece, like from here t'that bee gum. An' I think, 'What in th' world was'at?' I went kind'a slow, y'know, lookin' t'see what I could see. I thought somebody maybe shot a .22 rifle. Went just like a whip crack. I got pretty close t'where I thought it was. I seen that snake, an' I believe it was th' longest one here and above, and it was a'runnin, and right at where I heard that, an' it was black. If hit weren't a coachwhip, I don't know what it was. I believe that thing hit somethin' with its tail."

❖HARV REID: "I've seed them. They grow about five or six foot long. They look just like a black snake, and about half their tail is like a whup. It's platted int'a about four plats. You can see them plats in it. They say they'll whop th' dickens out of y'. Them thongs'll just wrap around yer leg two or three times and just come over'n'give you a good'un. They's an old fella'—this here old fat boy that died, I believe I heared him tell it—about a snake one time that got int'a fightin' one a'them. Said it split his hide all over. They *is* some a'them in here, but y'don't see many."

JOINT SNAKES

❖ HARV REID: "Yep. I've seed them too. They look like these here old king snakes—kind'a spotted—an' when y'hit one, it'll break up in pieces about as long as yer finger. Just like you had cut it up. And if y'leave it there 'til th' next mornin', it will be a snake again. That's a funny snake t'me. I've seed a lot of'em down here.

"That's th' funniest thing I ever did know—how they done that. But they'll grow back t'gether. They'll just fall all t'pieces like somethin' y'break, y'know. That way you'd think y'killed him. I don't know what they *would* do if you was t'move one a'them pieces."

❖ LON REID: "I never seen one only when I was a boy. I could see'em as I was out in th' field. Sometimes I would plow'em up. You could take a hick'ry limb and hit one a'them snakes and he'd break up in pieces. And folks told me, said they'd work around and get'em back t'gether; but don't seem like I can't hardly believe it. I don't think they could have done that. They might though. I don't know. They break inta pieces. I hit one one time and it just broke all up."

❖ HILLARD GREEN: "Well, y'take them there joint snakes now. Why, y'can hit one and it'll fly all t'pieces. Th' pieces of it's about six inches long.

"And you'll go on and leave him, and if you'll turn back and watch him, that head hit'll just take back'erds and hunt ever' piece, by grannys, and he'll go right back t'gether.

"They ain't poison, but anything'll hurt y'when it brings th' blood out of y'. *All* these snakes ain't poison, but now they'll hurt y'just th' same as anything else bitin' blood out of y'will."

HOOP SNAKES

❖ MANN NORTON: "They claim they've got a sting in th' end of their tail. And they just roll up like a hoop, and they just roll I've heered."

❖ JUDDY CARPENTER: "A hoop snake, they say, has a spike on their tail; and if they stave that spike in y', it'll kill y'. Tree or anything they stave that spike in dies. They look like these racer black snakes. They just roll up in a roll. And when they git after'y, they'll stave that spike in y'. I don't know, but it'll take one about fifteen minutes t'kill a tree I guess."

PLATE 257 "They cling by th' end of their tail just as hard as they can be."—Lon Reid

❖HILLARD GREEN: "I've seen'em. They look like a hoop. They'll just double up and they'll give theirselves a roll and go right towards y'! They've got spurs on their backs, and they hit you with them and it's just th' same as you bein' bit by a rattlesnake'r—anything.

"They're longer and slimmer than a rattlesnake, them hoop snakes is. They're spotted up like a rattlesnake, but they got spurs on their back and that stinger on their tail. If one happened t'hit a tree that way and sticks one in it, that tree'll die in just a few days."

❖LON REID: "They's just like hoop on a barrel just twisted over and rolled at'y'. Some folks calls'em a horn snake. They cling by th' end of their tail just as hard as they can be, and then they stick that tail in th' air and that's th' reason they roll. My daddy said one a'them old hoop snakes was a'rollin' after some man, and it was just nearly up with him. Said that fella' jumped behind a big honey locust, and said that snake just turned over and hit it with his tail, y'know. That's what they hit y'with—that horn. He said that big old locust tree was wilted before twelve o'clock. That could hit a man and kill him dead as a hammer.

"My brother said he killed one'r two up yonder where he lives. He said their tail was as hard as it could be all over th' end. They roll after y'."

BULL SNAKE

❖LAWTON BROOKS: They're five or six feet long and look like a yellow rattlesnake with black spots. They're about three inches in diameter in the thickest part. "They make a blowin' racket a y'. They just kind'a blow like a bull when they get mad."

SPREADING ADDER

❖HOYT THOMAS: "I've seen lots'a them. They's two kinds: a black'un and a yaller'un. You devil'em 'r'an'thing, and he'll just *spread out.*"

❖LESTER ADDIS: "They tell me they're a awful poisonous snake, but I never knowed'em t'bit me'r'an'thing. I *have* killed a few of'em around here. They got a blunt tail an'a fat head. Most all snakes that got a blunt tail is poisonous.

"Yeah, there's a yeller'un and a black colored'un. They look just alike all except th' different colorin'. They get per'ty good size— about th' size of a copperhead. They tell me they ain't no cure if they bit anything. They ain't no cure fer'em if they was t'bite y'r'an'thing."

BLACK SNAKES

❖MANN NORTON: "Black snake'll swaller a half growed rabbit. He must be made out'a rubber. Used t'put them in corn cribs. They'll really get shed'a rats now. Th'rats'll just *move out*.

"They can't climb down a tree. They can climb up, but when they get ready t'come down out of a tree, they just roll up and fall out. I've heered'em lots'a times, and thought it'uz a big wet limb fell out'a th'top of a tree."

❖HARLEY CARPENTER: "They's two kinds. One's a reg'lar old black snake, an' one's a racer. If y'tinker with'em, I've heered, they'll get on'y an' get around yer neck an' choke'y t'death.

"Daddy always said not t'kill'em. They eat rats. Sometimes they run at'y with their heads up. Daddy always said just step off t'one side when they get about right there an' they'll miss an' go on by an' give y'a chance t'get away."

❖ETHEL CORN: "I never had but one snake t'get in my house, an' hit was a black snake. Th'house was a log house, and th'doors was open. And just its keen tail was a'stickin' out. I thought it'uz a rat's tail, an' I reached up and went t'get it by th'tail to jerk it down, an' I see'd it'uz a black snake; an' I run out'a th'house an' hollered fer Kenneth, an' he comed t'th'house an'killed it."

RATTLESNAKES

❖BILL LAMB: "We peeled a sight'a tan bark in this country, an' ever' once in a while you'd run on a nice rattlesnake. Biggest'un I ever saw, I'uz'a cuttin' late one evenin' t'get a pile a'tan bark t'load up t'go out with, an' I don't know t'this day what kept me from seein' that rattlesnake when I went an' struck with m'axe. They'uz a little Spanish oak bush up about four foot high—leafy—it'uz in th' fall. An' hit'uz under that. Hit had a bed I bet that'uz a foot in diameter where it'ud lay under there. Biggest yeller rattlesnake I ever saw.

"An' I cut some briars right over th'top of it, an' boys, it just made fer me like I'd hit it. An' I jumped on a log an' it run at me. Then it'd turn an' start t'run off an' I'd jump off an' it'd turn back on me. I'uz cuttin' me a stick t'kill it with, an' Mel Lamb struck at it. T'tell you th'truth, I believe it had a string a'rattles three inches long. I never seed such a string a'rattles on one, ner never seed as big a snake before, or since, as it was.

"An' Mel struck at it wi'some kind of a old limb an' knocked its rattles clean off—ever' one a'them. An' I cut me a stick t'kill it with, an' hit just started t'strikin'. An' it looked t'me like hit could open hits mouth *that wide*—an' just as white inside as bleachin'. An' it never stopped strikin'.

"Boys, I reached out directly an' I settled 'im. An' I never found but nine a'them rattles, but I do honest believe that it had *at least* nine more. An' I believe y'could'a heard it sing fifty yards. They go scarey t'me.

"It'll give y'kind of a ticklish feelin' t'go t'a rattlesnake den. An' sometimes y'kill copperheads, pilots, an' rattlers t'gether. It'll make y'feel a little funny t'get inta'em thataway. I've been t'a den several times, but th' most rattlesnakes that ever I got was five in one place.

"That smell'll make y'sick. It'll make'y feel quare, y'know, smell-in'em when they get mad an'y'get t'killin'em. They just naturally got a poison smell. It'll make y'feel as quare. Some people, it makes 'em s'sick they can't hardly walk."

❖LON REID: "I went over yonder lookin' fer some bees—I had a bee course in there. I just felt like I was goin' t'run over a snake all th' way. I got way up there nearly t'where I had m'bee course, and I quit thinkin' about snakes. I went, I guess, about a hundred yards— never thought of a snake.

"I felt somethin' soft under my foot just like y'step on cotton or a quilt'r'somethin', y'know, and I heered somethin' make a little noise. I thought I stepped on a frog'r'somethin'. An' I stepped just as quick as I heered it and looked down, and I had my right foot layin' right smack across a big rattlesnake—that thing's head an' neck stickin' out from under my foot. I'd done caught th' weight on it though. I thought I'd stepped on somethin', y'know, that I wouldn't like t'kill.

"I stood there a second'r'two an' looked at that thing; and it was on th' wrong side fer me t'put my right foot down hard—I didn't want't'mash that snake. Not then. I had t'jump th' wrong foot, and uphill at that.

"I run about pert'near here t'that persimmon tree. I was afraid it was goin' t'go strikin' at me an' get that poison on me. I got a stick an' come back an' killed it. Big'un—and me a'standin' on it! I'm afraid a'snakes. I've come right'near gettin' bit sometimes."

SNAKEBITE REMEDIES

For anything as potent as a poisonous snake, there should be panaceas—and there are. Numerous ones.

PLATE 258 Kenny Runion showed us a "rattlesnack weed."
He says it's a cure-all for rattlesnack bites.

Bill Lamb says that when he was young and doctors were scarce, one remedy was to give the victim whiskey. Others say rattlesnake plantain will do the job.

Lester Addis claims a dog that has been bitten can be fed salty meat and that will kill the poison and reduce the swelling. He thinks the same remedy will also work for people:

"That dog was bit on th' jaw there somewhere. I took that piece of meat and I rubbed some extra salt on it, and he held it just about a minute in his mouth an' begin t'whine an'spit it out. And in just a few minutes you could see the swoll'ness goin' out of his jaw.

"If I was t'get bit right bad and had salt, I'd put me some salt on that place right where it bit me. And if I had a rag'r'somethin', I tie to it. Leave it on as long as y'want to as far as that goes.

"Me an' Earl Moore, one time his dog got snake bit—we'uz diggin' 'taters—an' he bit th' dog on th' nose. We took a piece a'fat meat'n'- salt'n'onion. I believe maybe we put some turpentine on it too. An' we beat that all up t'gether an' put it on that night. Th' next mornin' you couldn't tell that dog had been snake bit.

"It'll work for people too. Make a paste out of it an' dot it on there. Anything that'll cure a dog like that is good fer a person. You know that salt'll draw, salt will. If you got a risin' on y', get a piece a'fat meat with plenty a'salt on it. Ordinarily it'll draw it t'a head and kill that risin'."

One of the most persistent stories concerns a weed that is a sure cure for rattlesnake bite. It can be found in several ways. One is to tease a rattlesnake until he strikes repeatedly and works himself into such a frenzy that he accidentally bites himself. On that instant, he will head into the woods in search of the weed. Follow him, and he'll lead you to it.

Other versions of the same story abound:

❖HARLEY CARPENTER: "They was two fellas a'goin' along one time in th' woods, an' saw two snakes a'tangled up fightin'. They just stopped an' watched 'em. It was a big black snake and a rattlesnake. Th' black snake'd work all th' time t'get wrapped around an' get up next t'his neck'n'head, y'know. Rattlesnake, he'd keep bitin'im an' pushin'im back.

"An' said directly that black snake just quit an' wheeled an'run. Said, 'I reckon th' fight's over.' It wadn't though, fer here he come back, an' they hooked up fer a fight again. An' said directly th' rattlesnake pecked'im again, an' he fit just a little more with'im and took off in th'same direction he did in th'first.

PLATE 259 "They was two fellas a'goin' along one time in th' woods an' saw two snakes a'tangled up fightin' . . ."—Harley Carpenter

"So when he come back an' they went t'fightin', why, he bit'im again. And while they's doin' th' fightin', way I always heered it, one a'these men follered th' black snake. An' there was a kind'a a bunch a weeds a'standin' there, an' that black snake went out a lookin' about an' directly he see'd it an' made a run fer'it and grabbed off some'a it an'eat it, and back he went fer his fight.

"An' that man reached down there an' just pulled that up an' had it in his hand? An' th'next time that black snake went back fer his weed, he couldn't find it since th' man had pulled it up. He hunted an' hunted around there an' couldn't find any like it, an' directly he sort'a keeled over on his side, an' in a few minues he'uz dead.

"Never knowed what weed it was, but looks suspicious like it might work fer humans."

It might indeed, if a man could just find it. Meanwhile, until the cure-all is found, the serpents thrive and continue to give rise to some of the most fascinating tales in the Appalachians.

MOONSHINING AS A FINE ART

The manufacture of illicit whiskey in the mountains is not dead. Far from it. As long as the operation of a still remains so financially rewarding, it will never die. There will always be men ready to take their chances against the law for such an attractive profit, and willing to take their punishment when they are caught.

Moonshining as a fine art, however, effectively disappeared some time ago. There were several reasons. One was the age of aspirin and modern medicine. As home doctoring lost its stature, the demand for pure corn whiskey as an essential ingredient of many home remedies vanished along with those remedies. Increasing affluence was another reason. Young people, rather than follow in their parents' footsteps, decided that there were easier ways to make money; and they were right.

Third, and perhaps most influential of all, was the arrival, even in moonshining, of that peculiarly human disease known to most of us as greed. One fateful night, some force whispered in an unsuspecting moonshiner's ear, "Look. Add this gadget to your still and you'll double your production. Double your production, and you can double your profits."

Soon the small operators were being forced out of business, and moonshining, like most other manufacturing enterprises, was quickly taken over by a breed of men bent on making money—and lots of it. Loss of pride in the product, and loss of time taken with the product increased in direct proportion to the desire for production; and thus moonshining as a fine art was buried in a quiet little ceremony attended only by those mourners who had once been the proud artists, known far and wide across the hills for the excellence of their product. Too old to continue making it themselves, and with no one following behind them, they were reduced to reminiscing about "the good old days when the whiskey that was made was *really* whiskey, and no questions asked."

We got interested in the subject one day when, far back in the hills whose streams build the Little Tennessee, we found the remains of a small stone furnace and a wooden box and barrel. On describing the location to several people, we were amazed to discover that they all knew whose still it had been. They all affirmed that from that still had come some of the "finest home brew these mountains ever saw. Nobody makes it like that any more," they said.

Suddenly moonshining fell into the same category as faith healing, planting by the signs, and all the other vanishing customs that were a part of a rugged, self-sufficient culture that is now disappearing. Our job being to record these things before they die, we tackled moonshining too. In the six months that followed, we interviewed close to a hundred people. Sheriffs, federal men, lawyers, retired practitioners of the old art, haulers, distributors, and men who make it today for a living; all became subjects for our questioning. Many were extremely reluctant to talk, but as our information slowly increased we were able to use it as a lever—"Here's what we know so far. What can you add?"

Finally we gained their faith, and they opened up. We promised not to print or reveal the names of those who wished to remain anonymous. They knew in advance, however, that we intended to print the information we gathered—all except that which we were specificially asked not to reveal. And here it is.

IN THE BEGINNING

According to Horace Kephart in *Our Southern Highlanders* (Macmillan, 1914), the story really begins with the traditional hatred of Britons for excise taxes. As an example, he quotes the poet Burns' response to an impost levied by the town of Edinburgh.

> Thae curst horse-leeches o' the Excise
> Wha mak the whiskey stills their prize!
> Haud up thy han', Deil! ance, twice, thrice!
> There, sieze the blinkers!
> An' bake them up in brunstane pies
> For poor d—n'd drinkers.

Especially hated were those laws which struck at the national drink which families had made in their own small stills for hundreds of years. Kephart explains that one of the reasons for the hatred of the excise officers was the fact that they were empowered by law to enter private houses and search at their own discretion.

As the laws got harsher, so too the amount of rebellion and the amount of under-the-table cooperation between local officials and the moonshiners. Kephart quotes a historian of that time:

> Not infrequently the gauger could have laid his hands upon a dozen stills within as many hours; but he had cogent reasons for avoiding discoveries unless absolutely forced to make them. [This over two hundred years ago.]

A hatred of the excise collectors was especially pronounced in Ireland where tiny stills dotted rocky mountain coves in true moonshining tradition. Kephart quotes the same historian:

> The very name [gauger, or government official] invariably aroused the worst passions. To kill a gauger was considered anything but a crime; wherever it could be done with comparative safety, he was hunted to death.

Scotchmen (now known as Scotch-Irish) exported to the three northern counties of Ireland quickly learned from the Irish how to make and defend stills. When they fell out with the British government, great numbers of them emigrated to western Pennsylvania and into the Appalachian Mountains which they opened up for our civilization. They brought with them, of course, their hatred of excise and their knowledge of moonshining, in effect transplanting it to America by the mid 1700s. Many of the mountaineers today are direct descendants of this stock.

These Scotch-Irish frontiersmen would hardly be called dishonorable people. In fact, they were Washington's favorite troops as the First Regiment of Foot of the Continental Army. Trouble began after Independence, however, with Hamilton's first excise tax in 1791. Whiskey was one of the few sources of cash income the mountaineers had for buying such goods as sugar, calico, and gunpowder from the pack trains which came through periodically. Excise taxes wiped out most of the cash profit. Kephart quotes Albert Gallatin:

> We have no means of bringing the produce of our lands to sale either in grain or meal. We are therefore distillers through necessity, not choice, that we may comprehend the greatest value in the smallest size and weight.

The same argument persists even today—battles raged around it through the Whiskey Insurrection of 1794, and over government taxes levied during the Civil War, Prohibition, and so on right to this moment.

THE LAW vs. THE BLOCKADER

The reasons for the continuous feud implied in this heading should be obvious by now. The government is losing money that it feels rightfully belongs to it. This has always been the case. In the report from the Commissioner of Internal Revenue for 1877–78, the following appeared:

> The illicit manufacture of spirits has been carried on for a number of years, and I am satisfied that the annual loss to the Government from this source has been very nearly, if not quite, equal to the annual appropriation for the collection of the internal revenue tax throughout the whole country. In [the southern Appalachian states from West Virginia through Georgia and including Alabama] there are known to exist 5,000 copper stills.

It's different now? Clearly not, as seen in an article in the May 3, 1968 Atlanta *Constitution* on the interim report of the Governor's Crime Commission. In October, 1967, there were around 750 illicit stills in Georgia, operating at a mash capacity of over 750,000 gallons. This amounts to approximately $52 million in annual federal excise tax fraud, and almost $19 million in state fraud. The article quotes the Commission, placing the blame for Georgia's ranking as the leading producer of moonshine in the United States on "corrupt officials, a misinformed and sometimes uninterested public, and the climate created by Georgia's 129 dry counties."

Originally arrests had been made by government officials ("Feds" or "Revenuers"), but during Prohibition much of the enforcement was left up to the local sheriffs. This put many of them in a peculiar position, for the moonshiners they were being told to arrest were, in many cases, people they had known all their lives. As it turned out, however, most of the lawbreakers were reserving their hostility for the federal agents and the volunteers (called "Revenue Dogs") who helped them. They had nothing against their sheriff friends who, they understood, were simply doing their jobs. The sheriffs, for their part, understood the economic plight of the moonshiners. For many of these people, making moonshine was the only way they had at the time of feeding their families. As one told us, "I felt like I was making an honest dollar, and if it hadn't'a been for that stuff, we'd a had an empty table around here."

The situation resulted in a strange, friendly rivalry in most cases.

As one moonshiner said, "I never gave an officer trouble except catchin' me. After I'uz caught, I'uz his pickaninny."

The same man told us of a time when he was caught by a local official who was as friendly a man as he had ever met. He wasn't treated like a criminal or an animal, but treated with respect as another man making a living for a large family—which he was. After it was all over, the local official had made·a friend instead of an enemy, and the two are still fast friends today.

During the same period of time, there was another sheriff whom he often encountered on the streets of a little town in North Carolina. The sheriff would always come up to him, greet him, and ask him what he was up to down in Georgia. The other would usually reply, "Oh, not much goin' on down there." If, however, the sheriff had gotten a report about one of his stills, he would follow that reply with, "I hear you're farmin' in th' woods." The moonshiner would know that that was a warning for him to watch his step. Despite the warnings, the sheriff was able to catch him and cut down his stills on three separate occasions, but they remained fast friends.

We talked to several retired sheriffs (one of whom, Luther Rickman, was the first sheriff to raid a still in Rabun County), and they agreed completely. Most of the blockaders that they had encountered ran small operations, and the whiskey they made was in the best traditions of cleanliness. Besides, times were hard, and a man had to eat. Despite the fact that the sheriffs at that time were paid on the "fee system," and thus their entire salary depended on the number of arrests they made, they did not go out looking for stills. They made arrests only after reports had been turned in voluntarily by informers who, as we shall see later, usually had personal reasons for reporting the stills. They were never hired to do so.

Operating on the fee system, the local officials got $10 just for a still. If they were able to catch the operator also, they received between $40 and $60. Extra money was given them if they brought in witnesses who could help convict. For the blockader's car, they received approximately half the price the blockader had to pay to get it back which was usually the cash value of the car. And they were allowed to keep any money they could get from selling the copper out of which the still had been made.

Confiscated moonshine, beer, and the like were poured out. The sugar was often donated to an institution like a school or hospital.

The number of stills actually uncovered varied drastically from month to month. Some months, twenty or thirty would be caught and "cut down," but other months, none at all would be discovered.

Hardest of all was catching the men actually making a run. In almost all cases they had lookouts who were armed with bells, horns, or rifles, and who invariably sounded the alarm at the first sign of danger. By the time the sheriff could get to the still, the men would have all fled into the surrounding hills. We were told about one man who was paid a hundred dollars a week just as a sentry. Another still was guarded by the operator's wife who simply sat in her home with a walkie-talkie that connected her with her husband while he was working. The still, which sat against a cliff behind the house, could only be reached by one route, and that route passed directly in front of the house. The operator was never caught at work. On those occasions when the sheriffs did manage to catch the men red-handed, they usually resigned themselves to the fact that they had been caught by a better man, and wound up laughing about it. On one raid, a sheriff caught four men single-handedly. There was no struggle. They helped the official cut their still apart; and when the job was done, everyone sat down and had lunch together. When they had finished, the sheriff told the men to come down to the courthouse within the next few days and post bond, and then he left.

The same sheriff told us that only rarely did he bring a man in. He almost always told them to show up at their convenience, and they always did. To run would simply have shown their lack of honor and integrity, and they would have ultimately lost face with their community and their customers. They simply paid their fines like men, and went on about their business.

It was a rivalry that often led to friendships that are maintained today. One of the sheriffs, for example, spent two evenings introducing us to retired moonshiners, some of whom he had arrested himself. It was obvious that they bore no grudges, and we spent some of the most entertaining evenings listening to a blockader tell a sheriff about the times he got away, and how; and naturally, about the times when he was not so lucky.

Today federal agents have largely taken over again, and so the character of the struggle has changed. The agents actively stalk their quarry, sometimes even resorting to light planes in which they fly over the hills, always watching. In the opinion of some people, this is just as it should be. One said, "The operations are so much bigger now, and sloppier. If the Feds can't get'em, the Pure Food and Drugs ought to try. That stuff they're makin' now'll kill a man." And another said, "People used to take great pride in their work, but the pride has left and the dollar's come in, by th' way."

We was stillin' one day away up on a side of a hill away from everything, mindin' our own business, just gettin' ready t'make a run when my partner all of a sudden sees somethin' move in a pasture one hill over. Couldn't tell who he was. Too far away. I couldn't see him at all, stuck away behind a fence post like that. We went on workin', keepin' one eye out, and after we was through, and whatever that was over yonder had gone on, we went over to see. It was somebody there all right. I seed that checkedy sole print in th' soft ground and we moved her out that night. It was a revenuer all right. I know because I ran into him again later and he asked me about it. But know how I knew before that? Because of that boot print, and because he didn't come down and say hello. A friend of ours would have.

HIDING THE STILL

Since the days of excise, moonshiners have been forced to hide their stills. Here are some of the ways they have used.

1. Since cold running water is an absolute necessity, stills are often high up on the side of a mountain near the source of a stream. Water on the north side of a hill flowing west was preferred by many. Some count on the inaccessibility of the spot they chose for protection. Others, however:

build a log shed over the still and cover this with evergreen branches (*Plates 260, 261*);

bend living saplings over so they conceal the still. The branches continue growing and their leaves provide cover;

find a tree that has fallen over a ravine or gully and build the still under it, adding branches, if necessary, for additional coverage;

find a ravine, dig out its bottom, place the still in, and then set branches and saplings over the top like a roof. They should be arranged so that they blend in with the landscape;

find a cave and cover up the front of it;

find a large laurel thicket, crawl into the center of it, and cut out a room right in the middle of the thicket big enough for the still;

find a large spruce and put the still under its branches so it can't be seen from a plane.

2. The legend has grown that all one has to do to find a still is follow a likely looking branch up into a cove and then poke around until uncovering something suspicious. Moonshiners have countered by locating many stills in so-called "dry hollows." They find a cove

PLATE 260 This log framework was built in the woods to conceal a still. When finished, it was covered with branches.

PLATE 261 A huge still operated under this shed for over a year before it was discovered and cut down by federal officers.

that has no stream and pipe in the water they need from a higher, "wet" cove. Using all the hiding devices mentioned above, they:

buy two-inch piping, and run the pipe underground, around a ridge and into the dry hollow;

get plastic pipe and run it under leaves, or in a trench;

forget about the cove, and put the still right out on the top of a dry ridge, or in a laurel thicket, and pipe the water from a higher source.

3. Other moonshiners get far more elaborate and actually dig out an underground room big enough to stand in comfortably. Rows of beams are set in overhead, covered with dirt, and plant materials are actually planted overhead. A small trapdoor in the center of the roof, also covered with a growth, lifts up, exposing a ladder which goes down into the room. A vent pipe, cleverly concealed, carries off fumes. Some rooms are even wired for electricity.

4. Another way to avoid detection is by moving constantly. Some men follow logging jobs, figuring that the loggers will destroy all signs of their moonshining activities. In fact, loggers themselves often run stills in conjunction with their logging job.

5. Some men set up in a site the revenuers have just cut down believing that they won't be back for at least two months unless they get another report of activity there.

6. Others place their stills right in existing buildings that are not often visited, or would not normally be suspected—barns, silos, smokehouses, tool sheds, abandoned homes or buildings, even the basements of their own homes. Others run right in the center of town behind a false-fronted store or in a condemned building.

7. One man we know, believing that the revenuers will be looking for his still to be concealed, has it right out in the open, near the main highway, with only a few trees in front. He hasn't been caught yet.

8. Smoke, too, is a problem, but only at the beginning of the run. When the fire begins burning well, it gives off heat waves rather than smoke. Thus, often the fire is started just before dawn and is burning well enough by daylight to escape detection.

Others, however, worried about smoke, "burn their smoke." A worm or pipe which runs out the side of the furnace and back into the firebox recirculates the smoke and makes it invisible. We also have heard of a man who somehow piped his smoke so that it came up underwater—this supposedly dispersed it so effectively that it could not be seen. Others counted on the leaves and branches over their shelters to disperse the smoke.

Now any conceivable problem of smoke has been wiped out with the use of fuels such as butane or kerosene.

9. A dead giveaway as to the location of a still is a "sign" or trace of activity. Moonshiners constantly guard against this. An empty sugar bag, the lid from a fruit jar, a piece of copper—all can reveal their location.

An even bigger problem is that of trails. There are various ways they have dealt with it:

if the still is in the woods, always enter the woods from the road at a different point. Then, one hundred fifty yards up the hill, cross over to the main trail which begins as many yards or so off the road.

enter stills that are in a cove or hollow from the ridge above the still, instead of coming uphill from the front. One man who lives at the base of a high ridge said he could sit on his porch on a summer night and sometimes hear the voices of men, on the way to their still, shouting at the mules that were carrying in the supplies. If he looked carefully, he could see their lanterns winking high up on the ridge as they came in the back way to keep from being caught.

locate the still on a stream that runs into a lake, through brush, and far away from any road. Then always enter the still at night, by boat.

find a cut in the road the top of which is capped with a rock ledge, and is either level with or a little higher than a pickup truck bed. Load or unload from this rock to prevent leaving trails.

use fuel like butane gas to prevent leaving signs such as stumps of trees and wood chips and clipped off foliage.

Once a man was caught selling whiskey. He had painted some of the jars to look as though they contained buttermilk, but then he ran out of paint and had to use clear jars for the rest of his supply. When the revenuers caught him, they confiscated the clear jars; but so convincingly were the others painted that they did not even bother to open them. They simply left them behind, and the salesman was able to clear a profit, despite the loss of part of his wares.

FINDING THE HIDDEN STILL

Law officers have used many methods for finding hidden stills. Each time one became popular, the blockaders countered by hiding it in a different way. Here, however, are some of the methods used.

1. They are always alert for signs. A brick dropped in the middle of the woods is an obvious one. Why would it be there except for a furnace? Spilled meal or sugar on the side of a road is suspicious. A ladder left at the top of a high cut in the road is an obvious signal; probably it is used to load and unload supplies from the back of a pickup. Other signs include an empty sugar bag, a broken jar, a place in the woods where trees have been cut, a pile of charcoal, an empty cement bag, a broken shovel handle, a barrel stave, a burlap sack.

2. With an officer on either side of a backwoods dirt road—each two hundred yards away from the road, walking parallel to it—they search for a place where a trail begins.

3. With a boat, they search the edges of a lake. They look for signs of activity near a place where a branch empties into the lake. Such signs might be places where a boat has been pulled up on shore or slick trails made by dragging heavy feed bags.

4. They stake out a road and watch for signs of unusual activity in the early morning hours. They follow any cars heading up little-used roads. Or an officer might stake out a section of woods and listen for sounds such as a hammer against metal, the sound of a thump barrel, etc.

5. Usually areas where moonshine is being made have a distinctive smell. Law officers may detect that while walking through forest.

Many stills are found by people like hunters who spend much time in the woods and merely stumble across one by accident. Others are found by searching small branches that flow from hillsides through heavy growth.

The most prevalent means of finding stills, however, remains the informer. Often, they are people with a grudge or an axe to grind. One moonshiner characterized them as people, "who don't have enough of their own business to mind, and so they feel obligated to mind th' business of other people. Th' lowest man I know," he continued, "is one who wins your confidence, buys your liquor, and then turns you in. I believe there's a special place for people like that after they die."

Some informers hardly deserve such criticism. A mother whose young son comes in drunk and inadvertently tells her where he got the whiskey might well try to do something about it. A man who finds a blockader operating on his property without his permission has a right to ask the sheriff to remove him.

A more common motive, however, is jealousy. Sheriffs told us story after story in which a man whose still had just been cut down would turn in another out of spite. "They've cut mine. I'll fix it so they'll get some others too. If I can't be running, I don't want them running either."

Another ex-sheriff told us the following story. "While I was in office, a man who owned a still invited a neighbor to come in with him and make a run of apple brandy. When the run was finished, they ended up with thirty-nine gallons. The owner of the still took twenty, and gave his neighbor nineteen. The more the neighbor thought about it, the madder he got. What really irked him was that the owner of the still already had a buyer for his twenty gallons; he had none.

"They took their brandy and hid it in separate places. That night, the neighbor came to me and told me that he knew where twenty gallons of fresh brandy was hidden and wanted me to do something about it. So I got out of bed and went and poured the brandy out, like I'm supposed to do.

"Later I found out that when the buyer came to get his twenty gallons, the neighbor stopped him, told him that the sheriff had already found it and poured it out, and then sold him his nineteen. I found out all about it from the owner of the still who came in here as mad as any man I ever saw. I just did keep him from going and killing that neighbor."

Sometimes the stories take surreal twists. The same officer also told us this story, and swore that it really happened. "A man that lived around here while I was in office knew of an underground still that was a beautiful thing to look at. He wanted the rig himself, so one night he broke the lock on the trap door, got into the underground room, and took it. The next day he came to me saying he knew where a still was that I should cut down, and he'd even come with me to show me where it was. I was suspicious, but I went.

"When we got there, I saw right away that the lock on the door was broken, and when I got inside, I saw that the still was gone too. Well, I broke up what was left in there and then came back out and told the man that the still wasn't there. He really carried on when I said that, but I knew right away what was up. He had taken it, and wanted me to bust up the place so that the owner would think that *I* had gotten his still during my raid.

"I went back to the office, and not too long after that, the owner showed up and asked if I had gotten his still. When I told him I hadn't, he wanted to know who had stolen it. I knew all the time, but

I never said anything. I never once let anyone know who I had gotten information from. It just would have caused trouble.

"Finally the man who owned it asked me if I would just keep my eyes open for it. He didn't want it back necessarily—just wanted to know when it showed up out of curiosity. Then he told me how he had dropped it one day and broken a piece of the collar. Said he had put a "V"-shaped patch on the broken place, and that's how I'd know it was his.

"Well, I found out later that the man who had taken it in the first place had taken it home and put it in the loft of his barn. Two boys working for him loading hay found it up there, and *they* stole it from him.

"Several days later, there was a robbery in town, and that night I was in there looking around to see if I could pick up a clue or something. Just keeping my eyes open. While I was in there, these two boys came along. I got back out of the way out of sight, and these two sat down on some steps not far from me. I could hear everything they were saying. Turns out they were still laughing about this new still they had gotten and wondering where they could set it up and when they could get it running. You won't believe this, but they finally decided to set it up on a vacant piece of land that *I* owned—said I'd never look for it there in a hundred years. They'd make four or five runs and then they'd move it somewhere else.

"The next day I went up on the land where the boys had talked about setting it up—in some laurels up there—and sure enough, there it was, and there was the patch. I got it and took it into town to the office.

"When I saw the original owner again, I called him over. Said I had something to show him. Boys, his eyes popped right out of his head. That was it all right. I didn't tell him how I got it, but we had many a good laugh over that later on."

The fact that hogs love the corn mash that whiskey is made out of is legend. Often moonshiners were forced to put fences around their stills to keep hogs, who were kept on "open range" then, from falling into the mash boxes and drowning. Once a two hundred-pound sow fell into a mash box where she drowned. The men running the still found her body in there several days later, but went on and made whiskey from the same mash anyway. From then on, if whiskey was too strong, the man drinking it would say, "That must'a had a dead hog in it."

A GLOSSARY OF STILL PARTS AND TOOLS

Bale—wire or chain strapped across top of cap to keep it from blowing off during the cooking process.

Cap—the top third of the still. It is removable so that the still can be filled after a run.

Cap Arm—the copper pipe connecting the cap with the next section of the still; it conveys steam to this section.

Cape—the bulge in the main body of the still. It is the point of greatest circumference.

Collar—the connection for the cap and the body of the still.

Condenser—a two-walled, sealed pipe which is submerged in water. Steam forced into the top condenses and flows out the bottom.

Flake Stand—the container through which water is constantly flowing for final condensation of the steam. Holds the worm, condenser, or radiator, depending on which apparatus is being used.

Funnel—usually holds whatever material you are using to strain the whiskey. Whiskey passes through it and into the jug or jar.

Furnace—stone structure in which the still sits for heating.

Headache Stick—the long thump rod.

Heater Box (or pre-heater)—a device which heats the fresh beer which will be used in the next run (see diagrams on pp. 325–26).

Long Thump Rod—an open-ended copper pipe which conveys the steam into the bottom of the thump barrel where it is released.

Mash Stick—the stick used to break up the cap that forms over the mash and stir up the contents of the barrel. Sometimes it is made of a stick which has a crook in the end. Several holes are drilled in this crook, and pegs are inserted to form a comb-like device. It can also be a stick with several nails driven in the side.

Plug Stick—a hickory or white oak stick with a bundle of rags fastened to one end. The rags jam into the slop arm thus sealing the bottom of the still.

Proof Vial—a glass tube used to check the bead of the whiskey. A Bateman Drop bottle was the most popular as it held exactly one ounce, and was just the right shape. Others used now are bottles that rye flavoring comes in, or a government gauge.

Relay Arm—the pipe connection from the bottom of the relay barrel back into the still.

Relay Barrel or *Dry Barrel*—a fifty-gallon barrel with connections for the cap arm, relay arm, and a long thump rod. Catches "puke" from the still during boiling and conveys it back into the still.

Still—the container into which the beer is placed for boiling. Also called the *Evaporator, Boiler, Kettle,* or *Cooker*. The name can also refer to the entire operation from the evaporator through the flake stand.

Swab Stick or *Toothbrush*—a hickory stick half as thick as your arm and long enough to reach from the top to the bottom of the still. One end is beaten up well so that it frazzles and makes a fibrous swab. This is used to stir the beer in the still while waiting for it to come to a boil, thus preventing it from sticking to the sides of the still, or settling to the bottom and burning. If the latter happens, the whiskey will have a scorched taste.

Thump Barrel—also *Thumper* or *Thump-Post*—a barrel which holds fresh beer, and through which steam from the still bubbles thus doubling its strength. The strengthened steam moves from here into the *short thump rod* which carries it either into the heater box, or into the flake stand.

Worm—a copper tube, usually sixteen to twenty feet long which is coiled up so that it stands about two feet high and fits inside a barrel. Water flows around it for condensing the steam which passes into it from the still.

A GLOSSARY OF SOME OF THE EXPRESSIONS AND TERMS USED IN STILLING

Backings—also *singlings* and *low-wines*—what results after beer is run through a thumperless operation once. They have a good percentage of alcohol, but they won't hold a bead.

Beer—the fermented liquid made from corn meal bases which, when cooked in the still, produces the moonshine.

Blockaders—men who made moonshine. The name is a holdover from the days in our history when blockades were common, as were blockade runners. Also gave rise to the expression "blockade whiskey."

Blubber—the bubbles which result when moonshine in the proof vial is shaken violently.

Breaks at the worm—an expression used at the moment when the whiskey coming out of the flake stand turns less than 100 proof, and thus will no longer hold a bead.

Dead devils—tiny beads in the proof vial which indicate that the whiskey has been proofed sufficiently. Stop adding water or backings at the moment shaking the proof vial produces dead devils.

Dog heads—when the beer is almost ready to run, it will boil up of its own accord in huge, convulsive bubbles which follow each other one at a time.

Doubled and twisted—in the old stills, all the singlings were saved and then run through at the same time thus doubling their strength. Whiskey made in this fashion was called doubled and twisted.

Faints—dead beer; or backings that steam has been run through in a thumper to strengthen a run. These are drained and replaced before each new run.

Goose Eye—a good bead that holds a long time in the vial.

High Shots—untempered, unproofed whiskey. At times it is nearly as strong as 200 proof.

Malt—corn meal made from grinding sprouted corn kernels. It is added to the barrels of mash to make the beer.

Mash—corn meal made from grinding unsprouted corn kernels. It is put in the barrels, mixed with water, allowed to work until it is a suitable base for the addition of the malt.

Pot-tail—see *Slop*.

Proof—see *Temper*.

A Run—an expression meaning to run the contents of the still through the whole operation once. It gave rise to expressions like, "There's gonna be a runnin' tomorrow," "He'll make us a run," etc.

Singlings—see *Backings*.

Slop—that which is left in the still after the whiskey will no longer hold a bead at the end of the worm. It is too weak to produce and so it is dumped at once. Left in the still, it will burn. Some people use it for hog feed, others in mash.

Sour Mash—mash made with pot-tail.

Sweet Mash—mash that has been made with pure water. The first run through the still is made with sweet mash.

Split Brandy—a mixture that is half whiskey, half brandy. It is made by mixing mash that is one-quarter fruit content. Then proceed as usual with the beer-making, and running.

Temper—the process of adding water or backings to the whiskey to reduce its strength to about 100 proof.

Various names given moonshine include ruckus juice (pronounced "rookus"), conversation fluid, corn squeezin's, corn, white, white lightenin', cove juice, thump whiskey, headache whiskey, blockade whiskey, etc.

"Busthead" and "popskull" are names applied to whiskey which produces violent headaches due to various elements which have not been removed during the stilling process.

PLATE 262 Buck Carver kneels behind a one-gallon still he made for the *Foxfire* museum. The still is authentic in every detail from the flue of the furnace to the tin-locked copper joints in the cooker and condenser to the chestnut barrels Bill Lamb made for the model.

THE CONSTRUCTION OF THE STILL

First find the proper location for the operation. The next step is the construction of the furnace. The following pages include diagrams and photographs of two furnace styles which were extremely popular during the days of Prohibition. Only a few of them are seen today.

The fuel used was almost always a hard wood such as oak or hickory. Ten- and twelve-foot logs would be fed into the bottom of the furnace with their ends sticking out in front. The fire was started, and as the logs burned, they were slowly fed into the furnace. Since the furnace was made to burn wood, the firebox was spacious.

A bedrock platform above the firebox kept the bottom of the still from ever coming in direct contact with the fire. This prevented the contents of the still from burning or becoming scorched. All heating took place around the sides of the still in an area that was completely enclosed except for the flue. The sides of the furnace touched the still at only one point, and that was above the cape at the point where the sides of the furnace tapered in to seal flush against the top half of the still (*Plate 263*). This area had to be sealed tightly to prevent heat escaping from below.

The flue was most carefully constructed for maximum draw. One man told us of a furnace he had built in which the draft was so strong that it would "draw out a torch."

Natural stone was used, chinked with red clay. The first furnace illustrated is the "return" or "blockade" variety (*Plate 264*). The second is called the "groundhog" (*Plate 266*).

The construction of the actual still was an exacting process. Everything had to fit correctly or the still would leak. A retired practitioner described how the best moonshiners made their forty-five-gallon stills:

Three thin sheets of copper were purchased. The copper had to be absolutely smooth and of good quality. The sheets purchased were approximately thirty inches wide and five feet long. As money was at a premium, every part of the operation had to come out of these three sheets—still, cap, cap arm, slop arm, condenser walls and caps, washers—everything. Planning before cutting, therefore, was essential.

On two sheets of copper, the top and bottom halves of the still were drawn. This was accomplished with the use of a long string which was anchored at a point below the sheet being marked (*Plate 267*). A top arc was drawn so as to be tangent with the mid-

PLATE 263 A furnace made of rock and red clay. A fire has been started in the firebox, the cap has been sealed on with rye paste, and the operation is ready to go.

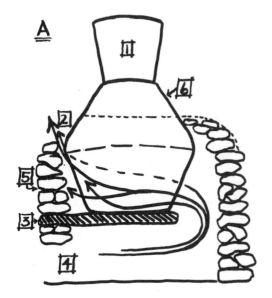

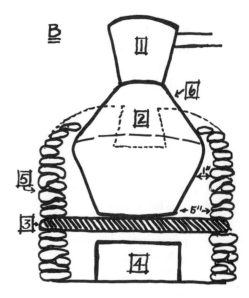

PLATE 264   In both of the above diagrams: (1) is the cap, (2) the flue at the front of the still through which hot air from the firebox escapes, (3) the bedrock platform built into the furnace wall on which the still rests. As is shown in *Diagram A*, the platform is not wide enough to extend all the way to the back of the furnace. A large space is left to allow passage of heat from the firebox around the sides of the still. (4) is the firebox. In earlier days, the ends of hardwood logs were used to start the fire, and as the ends burned away, the portions of the logs that extended outside the furnace were gradually fed in to provide constant heat. The arrows in *Diagram A* show the direction of the heat as it goes around both sides of the still and out the flue. (5) is the furnace wall. It was usually built of natural stone chinked with red clay which would harden through successive burnings. (6) is the still itself—usually made of copper.

PLATE 265   An abandoned furnace. Often the copper cooker (the "pot") was removed and hidden in a laurel thicket after each run to prevent its being stolen before the operator was ready to make another run.

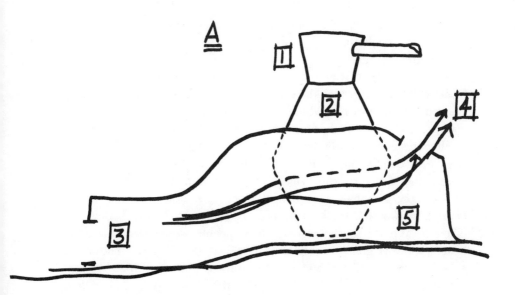

PLATE 266 *Diagram A* illustrates an interesting variation on furnace design which was once fairly popular. Called the "groundhog" or "hog" still, it was unique in that the still sat directly on the ground, and the furnace of mud, clay, and rocks was built up around it with the flue at the back. (1) is the cap, (2) the still, (3) the firebox. The heat was drawn to the flue (4) and circulated around the still in the space left between the furnace and the copper wall of the still. The arrows show the direction of heat. (5) is the back of the furnace—sometimes this was against a bank, and sometimes the furnace hole was dug directly into a bank. The surrounding earth, in the case of the latter design, was extremely effective insulation. When cleverly built, this furnace could also be much easier to hide than the stone furnace which sat right out in the open in most cases.

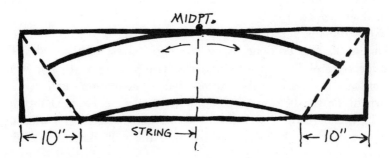

PLATE 267

point of the top edge of the sheet. The lower arc was drawn so as to intersect the bottom edge of the sheet at points ten inches from each bottom corner.

The third sheet was used for the bottom of the still, the arc from which the cap would be made, the cap head, and the slightly tapered rectangles from which the arms would be rolled. When this was finished, any blank areas on the sheets were used for drawing small items such as washers. Then everything was cut out. Holes were also, cut in the cap, and in the bottom half of the still to make room for the arms which would be attached later.

Next, the two halves of the still were assembled. If the copper being used was too thick to be pulled around by hand, then it was taken to a place in the woods where people would be unlikely to hear what was going on. A large tree was felled in the bottom of a hollow so that the sounds of the construction would go straight up in the air instead of out all over the countryside. The stump of the tree was rounded out to a smooth, concave surface, and the sheet of copper was placed on top. Next, with a wooden mallet made of dogwood that had been well-seasoned, the copper was beaten until the flat sheet curled around and the two ends touched. One edge was pounded more vigorously than the other so that the sheet would curl unevenly to make the taper. Then holes were punched along the ends of the now-tapered sheet, and brads were inserted to fasten the ends together tightly. The same was done to the other half. Often, to ensure that there would be no leakage at all, these joints would be tin locked.

Now holes were punched along the cape, and the two halves mated and bradded together. The cape edge of the bottom half was crimped slightly so as to fit inside the cape edge of the top half. The arc for the cap was curled in the same manner, and the ends joined as before.

Next the bottom of the still was fastened to the bottom half. (This could also be done before the two halves were mated.) The outside edge of the bottom piece was crimped up so that it would fit *outside* the wall of the bottom half. The bottom half was set down inside the bottom piece, and the two were fastened together.

The tapered slop arm was now rolled and fastened. Its wide end was crimped up. Then it was fed into the still, narrow end first, and out the hole provided for it earlier. The crimped-up wide end would catch inside the still wall. A washer made of copper slid the length of the arm and fitted snug at the wide end of the arm, but outside the still wall. Holes were punched through and the brads inserted, thus mounting the slop arm firmly to the bottom half of the still. (To taper arm, it was wrapped around tapered wooden pole.)

In like manner, the head of the cap was mounted, the cap arm, and so on until all the parts had been shaped and fastened in their proper places. Then all the joints were sealed with liquid metal so that they would not leak. The still was now ready to carry to the woods and mate with the furnace. The worm was made there by coiling the pipe around a stump, then slipping it off.

The following pages present a portfolio of diagrams which illustrate most of the still varieties we have found. They are arranged in roughly chronological order.

The very first illustration, for example (*Plate 268*), shows the simplest still of all, and the oldest of the ones we have seen. This is the variety which produced much of the best moonshine ever made. It was also the most time-consuming of all the operations, and yielded the smallest return for the time involved. All the beer was run through, a stillful at a time, and the results of each run ("singlings") saved at the other end. When all the beer had been run through once, the still was thoroughly cleaned, and then all the singlings placed into the still at one time. Then the stillful of singlings was run through. The result was the doublings, or good whiskey. It was also called "doubled and twisted" whiskey, the first because it was double strength, and the second, because it twisted slightly as it came out of the worm. Using this rig, a man could get about two gallons of whiskey per bushel of corn, or a final yield of about twelve gallons after proofing.

By way of contrast, there are operations running today which yield as much as three hundred gallons *per run*—a far cry from the old days.

The two previous stills show what happened as moonshiners got more and more impatient with the slowness of the first operation described. Perhaps the most revolutionary addition was the thump barrel. Steam bubbling up through the fresh beer in this barrel was automatically doubled thus removing forever the necessity of saving the singlings and running them through again to double their strength.

The still in Plate 278 illustrates effectively what happens as man's desire for quantity overtakes his desire for quality. The yield from this still is immense; the quality, questionable. A truck radiator serves as the condenser.

The dead man still in Plate 279 is a purely modern variety with

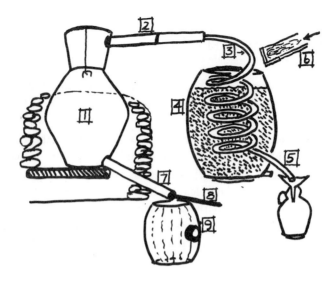

PLATE 268 Above: (1) the still (the furnace, bed-rock platform, firebox and still cap will be recognized from a previous diagram). (2) the cap arm. This copper pipe (often four inches in diameter, but sometimes tapered from six inches at the cap end to four or less at the other) conveys the steam from the still to the copper worm. (3) the worm. This pipe is about three-quarters of an inch to an inch in diameter, and is coiled tightly to get maximum length of pipe into minimum space. The steam condenses into liquid in the worm. Sometimes the worm is simply fixed in midair, and the steam cooled by a water jacket which surrounds the pipe and into which fresh, cold water is continually fed, but more often the worm is fixed inside a water tank of some sort—in this case a fifty gallon barrel (4) —through which cold water is constantly circulated. (5) the end of the worm. The alcohol which flows out here is usually strained through hickory coals to remove the fusel oils (barda grease)—thus the funnel above the jug in the diagram at the end of the worm. (6) the pipe, or trough from the cold water source—usually a mountain stream. (7) the slop arm. The spent beer is drained out this copper pipe (which passes directly through the furnace wall) after each run. (8) the plug stick. This is usually a hickory or oak limb with a wad of rags attached firmly to the end to keep the beer from draining out during a run. (9) the container for the slop (spent beer).

PLATE 269 Mickey Justice holds a section of a wooden water trough found at the site of one of the earliest and most famous stills in Rabun County. The trough carried fresh water from a spring far up the hill to the still's condenser.

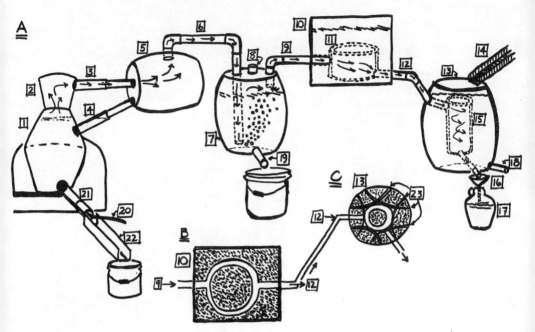

PLATE 270   Refined to the ultimate, this version—*Diagram A*—of the Blockade Still works as follows: The steam (arrows) from the beer boiling in the
still (1) moves into the cap (2), through the cap arm (3), and into the dry or
"relay" barrel (5). Beer which bubbles over or "pukes" into the relay barrel is
returned to the still via the relay arm (4). From this barrel (usually a fifty-
gallon one which is mounted so that it slants slightly back toward the still), the
steam moves into the long thump rod (6) which carries it into the bottom of
the fifty-gallon thump barrel (7) and releases it to bubble up through the fresh
beer, which was placed there earlier via inlet (8)—now closed to keep the
steam enclosed in the system. The beer in this barrel is drained after each run
and replaced with fresh beer before the next. Picked up again at the top by the
short thump rod (9), the steam moves into the heater box or "pre-heater" (10)
which is also filled with fresh beer. Here the steam is not set loose, however,
but is forced through a double-walled ring (11) that stands about nine inches
high, is thirty-four to forty inches in diameter, and mounted so that it stands
about a half inch off the floor of the heater box. The top and bottom of the
ring are sealed so that the steam cannot escape. Heat from the steam is transferred to this cool, fresh beer thus heating it to make it ready for the next run
when it will be transferred into the drained still via a wooden trough connecting the two (not shown here). The steam then moves via another connecting
rod (12) into the flake stand (13) and into the condenser (15)—in this case
another double-walled ring, higher and narrower than the previous one. The
steam is condensed in this ring by the cold water flowing into the flake stand
from (14) and exiting by outlet (18). As the steam is condensed into alcohol,
it flows through a strainer and funnel (16) into the container (17).

The still from which this diagram was drawn was a "fifty-gallon rig." The still and all three barrels each had a fifty-gallon capacity. The heater box was twenty-eight inches long, twenty-eight inches wide, and stood twenty-four inches high. The relay barrel and the heater box were both tilted slightly in the direction of the still-cooker for proper drainage.

Diagram B shows the heater box from the top, sliced in half. The dots represent beer; the steam is represented by arrows. *Diagram C* shows the flake stand from the top. In this case the condenser was held in place in the center of the barrel by twigs (23) which were cut green, then bent and wedged against its sides. The dots represent water.

At the end of each run, the plug stick (20) is pushed in, thus releasing the slop or "pot-tail" which flows through the tilted slop arm (21) and trough (22) into a bucket. The spent beer from the thump barrel (faints) is also drained and replaced. The plug stick is replaced, the cap removed, the still filled with hot beer from the heater box, the cap is replaced, the heater box is filled with fresh cold beer again, and the process is begun all over.

PLATES 271, 272 The still shown in Plate 271 is another of the highly refined Blockade variety. In this case, however, rather than being stretched out for convenience of illustration, the diagram's shapes match those of Plate 271 so that you can decipher the photograph itself.

It is basically the same as the previous operation, but in this case it is possible to see the trough which connects the heater box with the still. Part (8) is hinged to part (9), and when the operator is ready to move the beer, he takes the cap off the still, swings (8) down so that it is in line with its lower half, pulls the gate up via the gate handle (10), and lets the beer flow.

In the diagram, the log supports which hold up various parts of the operation and which can be seen in the photograph, are not shown as they would create too much confusion. Instead, they are indicated by dotted lines in those places where they pass in front of a portion of the still.

The flake stand, in this case, holds not the condenser which was used in the still on the previous pages, but a radiator from a Chevrolet truck. The radiator is just as effective a condenser but often not quite as healthy.

The numbers on the diagram refer to the following parts of the still shown:

1) the furnace
2) the still
3) the cap
4) the cap arm
5) the relay arm
6) the relay, or dry barrel
7) the long thump rod—its connection with (15) is hidden
8) top half of trough from heater
9) bottom half of trough

10) handle for heater box gate
11) heater box
12) copper connecting rod
13) flake stand—water filled
14) outlet from condensing unit
15) thumper, or thump barrel
16) bucket for slop, or "pot-tail"
17) slop trough
18) slop arm from still
19) handle of plug stick

PLATE 273   The beer in this cooker is being heated prior to sealing on the cap. The swab stick resting in the cooker is used to stir the beer while it is heating to keep it from sticking to the sides and burning. Both this and the next three photographs were all taken at the same operation.

PLATE 274   The thump barrel and heater box. The drain pipe, when lowered, carries warm, fresh beer from the heater box to the cooker, the top of which is visible in the foreground.

PLATE 275   The heater box from the other side, showing the connection between the heater box and the condenser which is mounted in the metal drum.

PLATE 276   The whole operation from the heater box, condenser end. The wooden barrels on the right are filled with fermenting mash. The furnace is hidden behind the heater box. The plastic gallon milk jar in the foreground is often used in place of glass jars for the finished product.

PLATE 277 This page reveals a heater box and a thump barrel in more detail. The barrel in the foreground of the photograph is the thumper. The pipe extending in the foreground is the long thump rod coming from the cap of the still. (This particular still did not have a dry or relay barrel). The large wooden box behind the thumper is the heater box. Arrow 1 points to the outlet which is blocked by the gate behind it. Arrow 2 points to the handle of this gate. Arrow 3 points to the wooden trough which is mounted into place when the operator is ready to transfer his preheated beer to the still for a new run. In the background, behind the thump barrel (bearing the number 4) can be seen the corner of the flake stand.

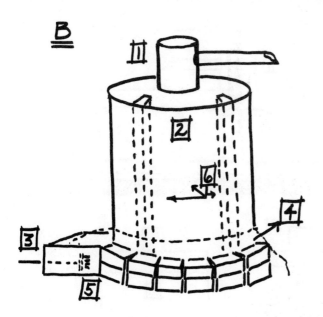

PLATE 278 (1) is the cap—usually a fifty-gallon barrel. (2) is a huge barrel
(the still) which sits right on the ground. It has, in this case, a capacity of
five hundred gallons. The sides are made of huge sheets of aluminum or copper,
and both the top and bottom are made of plywood. There are three 2 by 4
supports inside the walls of the still which help support its great size (6). (3)
is the firebox. The source of heat, in this case, is a huge gas burner mounted so
that the flames point toward the still. Heat is drawn in, around the lower walls
of the still, and out the flue (4). (5) is the furnace which in this case is a
double row of concrete blocks sealed over (dotted line) with clay, or some
other form of tight insulation. Space, of course, is left between the inside wall
of the blocks and the outside bottom wall of the still for the passage of heat.

The cap arm connects to a large thump barrel which connects directly with
the flake stand. There was no heater box in this particular model.

It is possible, by the way, to use a fifty-gallon barrel as the housing for the
gas jets (3). It would be turned on its side with its end toward the still, and
sealed to the concrete-block wall of the furnace with the insulating rocks, mud,
and concrete.

Those who use them say that the groundhog stills are much hotter than the
other varieties, and thus make better stills.

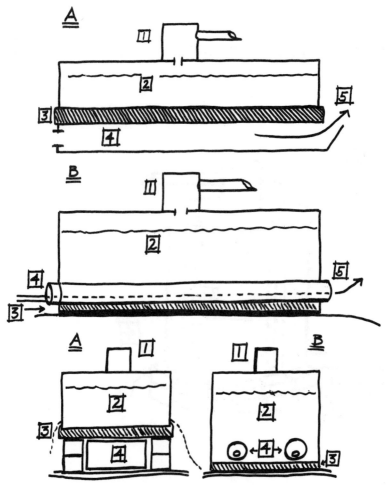

PLATE 279 These diagrams illustrate perhaps the simplest still of them all—
the "dead man" or "flat." In all cases (*Diagrams A* and *B*): (1) is the cap,
(2) the still itself—a rectangular box, (3) the bottom of the box (the diago-
nally shaded area), (4) the firebox or source of heat, and (5) the flue.

There are several differences between them, however, that make them interesting. In *A,* the cap is a twenty-five-gallon barrel, and in *B,* a fifty-gallon one.
The firebox in *A* is simply a channel cut into the earth. The still sits on the
ground directly over this channel. A hole is left at the back to serve as the flue.
In *B,* however, two 7 inch pipes sit *inside* the still box, surrounded by beer, with
their ends protruding out both ends of the box. A long gas line is fed into each
of these pipes, and its top surface is perforated in the manner of gas burners
on stoves. This design supplies heat directly to the beer thus making a faster
operation.

In *A,* the still stands two feet high, and six to eight feet long. A thin sheet
of copper lines the outside of the bottom, and rises up two to three inches all
around the sides. The rest of the box is made of wood. In *B,* the box is made
of two 4-foot-square wooden boxes. They are mounted side to side, and the
common wall is removed leaving a box four feet high, four feet wide, and eight
feet long. The bottom is lined with copper as before.

Diagram A at the bottom shows how concrete blocks could be used in lieu of
digging a trench in the ground. The dotted lines represent the insulation (mud,
rocks, cement, etc.).

a tremendous yield. The beer, rather than being made in separate boxes, *can* be made right in the still in this case. Twenty bags of sugar are used. One run can produce forty-five cases. There are six gallons in each case, so the total yield is 270 gallons. Early this year, the whiskey from this still was commanding $30 to $35 a case from the bootlegger's hauler. If the operator had had to haul it to the bootlegger, he would have added $10 more to the final price of each case.

The operation of a steamer still similar to the one in Plate 280 was described thus by one operator:

"It takes four men—a chief, a helper-pumper, and two haulers. We make our beer in six 4′ by 8′ boxes, and use two thousand pounds of sugar for every load. If we don't get twelve cases out of every box, something's wrong. And that's only seventy-two cases a day. That's not bad, but when I was running eight boxes I got ninety-six cases a day. And sometimes I could sell it for $60 a case. Not now. Price goes up and down—it depends.

"We use what we call 'mule feed' for malt, and we add beading oil to make it bead good. We use a radiator out of a Dodge truck in th' flake stand, cleaned out good, of course.

"I just want to move th' stuff out—get it to th' bootlegger quick as it's made. That's why I use haulers. I admit it's not good liquor. It'll give you a headache. But it won't hurt you. I've drunk it myself before."

Several things make a steamer still difficult. One is the amount of beer that must be on hand to begin with. From each 190 gallons in the Hodges Barrel, the yield will be approximately seven cases. Thus, in order to run off the ninety or more cases that can be run in a day, the main barrel has to be emptied and refilled about ten times. One man we talked to accomplished this with a pump and hose apparatus that he had rigged up. Contrast this with the old method of dipping the beer into the still with five gallon buckets and one can see how much things have changed. It still takes time, however, to prepare the beer. Thus a still like this one must lie unused for days at a time waiting for the beer to be ready to run.

Sugar presents another problem. Since anything over a hundred pounds must be signed for, sugar has to be bootlegged just like the whiskey.

In addition, the very size of the operation makes it more dangerous to run. Every effort is made to minimize the risk. One man, for example, told us that he never uses pegs in the outlet holes of his barrels. He has converted everything to valves. The reason: "Men

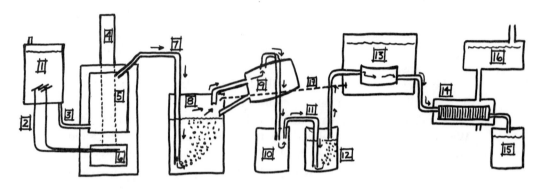

PLATE 280 The Steamer: (1) is a spare tank for pre-heating water. Pipes
(2) extend from the top of the furnace (6) into the bottom of the water tank,
and as they get hot, so does the water. (5) is the main water tank. The coke
burning furnace, which has a smoke stack (4), heats the water in (5) to the
boiling point, producing the necessary steam. When this tank is empty, it is refilled with the pre-heated water through a valved pipe (3), and the spare water
tank is refilled with cold water.

Steam from the main water tank, which is made of one and a third 50-gallon
metal drums welded together, moves directly into a long thump rod, and via it
into the bottom of a huge thump barrel (8) which is filled with 190 gallons of
fresh beer at the beginning of the run. The barrel is a wooden Hodges Barrel
with a 220 gallon capacity. From here the steam moves into a recharger or relay barrel of fifty-gallon capacity (9) which can return "puke" to (8); then it
goes into a dry barrel (10), and from there into another thump barrel (12)
through another long thump rod (11). This barrel holds fifty gallons of fresh
beer. From there the steam moves into a large heater box (13) which has the
same function as those we have already seen, returning pre-heated beer to (8)
through a valved line (17). The flake stand (14) is again, in this case, a large
truck radiator. (15) is the filtering or straining barrel which is the repository
for the final product. (16) is the water source for the flake stand. One inform-
ant told us that he could run ninety cases per day on a rig like this one.

who use pegs get in th' habit of hitting them three times whenever
they're putting them back in th' holes. They hit that peg soft th' first
time, a little harder th' next time, and on th' third time they really
whack it. You can hear those three licks on th' thumper peg for
miles."

PLATE 281

Once two men were fixing a leak in th' side of their still. One of th' men was inside th' still, crouched down, giving support from th' inside; th' other was outside with a hammer pounding away at th' patch he was adding. Suddenly th' man on th' outside saw th' law headed straight for him. Without a word to his partner inside th' still, he turned and fled into th' woods.

Th' federal man came up to th' still. Unaware that anyone was inside it, he took th' pick with which he demolished stills and gave it a terrible whack, piercing the side. "Now you've ruined it," th' man on th' inside screamed in anger.

HOW THE BEST OF THE BEST WAS MADE
as told by the men who made it

For this section, two men who are reputed to have made some of the best moonshine to come out of Georgia tell exactly how they did it. The process for making "pure corn" is the base of the discussion. Use of sugar in a run to increase the yield is also included, but in parentheses, as the addition of sugar would not allow the mixture to be labeled as pure corn whiskey. Use of a thump barrel is included for it does not diminish the quality of the product, and thump barrels were used during the old days.

Both of the men are now retired, and watch production today with increasing disdain. Here's how *they* did it, from beginning to end, using a fifty-gallon still and seven 50-gallon barrels:

1. Go to the woods and find a good place. Make a mudhole which contains plenty of good, thick red clay for use in the furnace. Also construct any water lines needed for the flake stand.

2. Choose the corn. Do not use a hybrid or yellow corn. Use a good, fresh, pure white corn like Holcomb Prolific which will produce about three quarts of whiskey per bushel. Inferior brands will only produce about two and a half quarts per bushel. Get nine and a half bushels.

3. Put at least a bushel and a half of corn (but not more than two) aside to sprout.

In *winter,* put this corn in a barrel or tub, add warm water, and leave it for twenty-four hours. Then drain it and move it to the sprouting tub. Cover it with pretty warm water, leave it for fifteen minutes, and drain the water off. Put the tub close to a stove, and turn the cold side to the stove at least once a day. Each day add warm water again, leave it for fifteen minutes, and drain it off again leaving the tub close to the stove. Also transfer the corn on the bottom of the tub to the top of the tub at least once a day to make sure it all gets the same amount of heat. You should have good malt in four or five days with shoots about two inches long, and good roots.

In *summer,* simply put the corn to be sprouted out in the sun in tow sacks. Sprinkle warm water over them once a day, and flip the sacks over. It is also possible to sprout the corn in sacks under either sawdust or mule manure—both hold heat well.

Be careful, however, not to let the corn get too hot or it will go slick. When it starts getting too hot, stir it up and give it air to cool it.

4. The day before the sprouted corn is ready, take the remaining eight bushels of corn to the miller to be ground up. Don't let him crush the corn or you'll have some heavy material left that will sink to the bottom of the still and burn. Make sure he grinds it all up fine.

Take this meal to the woods. The last three or four days should have been spent building the furnace and installing the still. It should be ready to work now. Build a fire under the still. Fill it nearly full with water, and stir in a half-bushel of corn meal. When it comes to a boil, let it bubble for thirty-five to forty minutes. Cook it well or it will puke too much when cooking later. When it has cooked sufficiently, bring one of the barrels over, put it under the slop arm of the still, push in the plug stick, and let the contents of the still fill the barrel. Add a gallon of yet uncooked meal and let the hot contents of the barrel cook it alone. Make sure it is stirred in well. Move the barrel aside, and repeat the whole process until all the meal is cooked, and all seven barrels are filled. Return home.

5. The next day, get the sprouted corn (malt) ground up at the mill and take it to the woods. Use a miller who knows you and will keep your activities secret. He will take no toll for grinding your malt. He'll take his toll out later when you are grinding straight corn again. You can also use a sausage mill.

In the woods, thin out the mash you made yesterday. This is done by standing the mash stick upright in each barrel. Add water and stir it in until the mash stick falls over against the side easily of its own weight. When all are thinned, add a gallon of malt to each barrel and stir it in. At the same time, add a double handful of raw rye to each barrel, sprinkling it around over the top. This helps to make the cap, helps the mixture begin working, and helps the final product hold a good bead. (If using sugar, add ten pounds to each barrel at the same time you add the malt.)

Cover the barrels. If they get rained into, your work is ruined. Return home.

6. The next day, the mixtures should be working. If one or two of them aren't, then mix them back and forth with those that are, using a dipper. You want them all to be working at the same time so that they'll all be ready to run at the same time. This liquid is now known as beer. Return home.

7. The next day, return to the site and stir up the mixture in each of the barrels to speed up their working. Home again.

8. About two days later, check again. At the same time, gather the wood you will need, bring in kegs, fruit jars, and whatever else you may need.

(On this fourth day, if you're using sugar, add a half gallon of malt to each barrel and thirty-five to forty pounds of sugar to each barrel. Stir in and let the mixture work for five more days.)

9. If you are not using sugar, then the whole mixture should be ready to run on the fifth day of its working. (With sugar, it takes about nine or ten days.) You can tell when it's ready to run by studying the cap that has formed over the beer. Sometimes this cap will be two inches thick. Sometimes it will only be a half inch thick, and sometimes it will just be suds and blubber, called a "blossom cap." All of these are fine.

When the cap is nearly gone, or only a few remnants are left scattered over the top, the mixture is ready to run. The alcohol has eaten the cap off the beer. Don't wait to run it at this point or the mixture will turn to vinegar, and the vinegar will eat the alcohol thus ruining your beer. It is better to run the whole thing a day early than a day late—you'll still get mild, good whiskey. Appearance of "dog heads" also indicates that it's ready to run.

[Note—one variation on the above process was also popular. Two bushels of mash were put in each fifty-gallon barrel, and cold water added. No cooking was used. This mixture would sour in three or four days and produce a crust. This would be broken up, stirred in, and the mixture left for another two or three days until it had soured again. *Then* a gallon and a half of malt was added to each barrel, and the mixture allowed to work another week. At this point, it was ready to run in the same manner as the other we have been describing.]

10. Now all connections on the still are sealed up with a stiff rye paste save for the cap and cap arm. The plug stick is inserted through the top of the still, handle first, and the handle pulled out through the slop arm until the ball of rags at the other end jams the opening.

Fill the still almost to the top (leave about three gallons off for expansion due to heat) with the beer. Put ten gallons of beer in the thump barrel.

Build up the fire underneath, and as the beer heats, stir it constantly with the swab stick to keep it from sticking to the bottom and sides of the still. Keep this up until it has come to a rolling boil and can thus keep itself stirred. Then paste on the cap and cap arm using the rye dough.

11. Chunk the fire easy, starting slowly, and gradually building it up in intensity. About fifteen minutes after the beer starts boiling in the still, the steam will hit the cold beer in the thump barrel and start it bubbling and thumping. On cold days, this thumping can be heard for several hundred yards through the woods.

When the thumping quiets, the beer is boiling smoothly in the still and doing fine.

Place a container under the end of the condenser. A funnel should be inserted in the container which is lined with a clean, fine white cloth on the bottom, a yarn cloth on top of that, and a double handful of washed hickory coals on top of that. The coals remove the "bardy grease" (it shows up as an oil slick on top of the whiskey if not drained off) which can make one very ill.

12. When the thumping stops, the whiskey starts. A gush or two of steam will precede it at the condenser end. This will be followed by a strong surge of liquid which quickly subsides to a trickle. On the second surge, "she's coming for good," as one man said.

Begin catching the alcohol on the second surge. (If it is being made with sugar, this first run will not hold a bead. Save it anyway.) Keep running the still as long as there is any taste of alcohol in the liquid being produced.

Then drain the thump barrel. Add the results of the first run— about ten gallons of backings. Then drain the still through the slop arm and fill it again with beer as before.

13. On the second run through, you'll have good whiskey because the steam has gone through the backings in the thumper. It will be double strength. Keep checking it with the proof vial, catching it as it comes out of the condenser, thumping it in the palm of your hand, and watching the bubbles. When it's dead, pull the container away. You should have two to three gallons of whiskey, the bead on which will be half under the liquid and half over it. (If you're running sugar whiskey, the results from the first run on will be whiskey, and the bead will be two-thirds under the surface and one-third over it.)

Catch the remainder of the second run in another container. These are the new backings for the third run.

Another way to tell whether or not the whiskey is still strong enough to catch in the container of good stuff is by taking some of the alcohol, dashing it on the hot still cap, and holding a match to the resulting steam. If it burns, keep it running.

14. From the second running, you should have two or three gallons of good whiskey and seven or eight gallons of backings.

Drain the faints out of the thumper and "let them hit the ground and run away." They are no good for anything. Add the new backings to the thumper.

Drain the still, fill it again with fresh beer, and run it the third time. This time, since there are fewer backings, you'll get less liquor, but more backings for the fourth run. On the fourth run, you'll get more liquor because you have more backings, but you'll also get fewer backings for the fifth run; and so on. The yield will vary up and down with each stillful.

Keep running until all the beer has been used up.

Without a thumper, all the backings would have been saved, and all run through the still together on the last run.

15. After about seven runs, the net result will be seven to ten gallons of pure corn (unsugared) whiskey, for an average of about a gallon to a gallon and a half per bushel of corn. (With sugar, the result should be about six gallons to the bushel.)

These are called the "high shots." They are about 200 proof and must be cut to be drinkable. To cut, either add about one-third backings from the last run, or water. Many prefer water. Add the liquid you are cutting the alcohol with until it holds a good steady bead in the proof vial. If the bead will hold steady after three good thumps in the palm of your hand, then it will stand any amount of jolting and bumping in shipment. From nine gallons of high shots, you should get about twelve gallons of fine whiskey.
Other hints:

1. If a wood fuel is being used, ash is the best of all. It gives a good, steady heat, and little smoke. Also good are hickory and mountain oak.

2. Always use copper. Beer doesn't stick to it so badly, and there is less chance of any kind of metal poisoning.

3. Never let the whiskey run too fast. Always keep it cold while it's running. If it is kept as cold as the water it is being condensed by, it will remain smooth and mild and not harsh to the taste. About sixty degrees is normal.

4. Use the best water available (many prefer streams running west off the north side of a hill). The water can make a difference of several gallons in the final yield.

5. Everything must be kept spotless. The copper inside the still should shine like gold. Barrels (or boxes) too must be kept clean. Smoke them out after each use with several handfuls of corn meal bran set afire.

6. Add three or four drops of rye flavoring to each gallon of whiskey to give it a yellow tint and a distinct rye flavor.

7. The place to make the whiskey is in the boxes. If it's not right there, no amount of boiling and cooking can save it.

HOW GOOD WHISKEY IS BEING RUINED

1. Stills are often made of sheet iron or valley tin instead of copper. These metals often burn the beer and give it a strange taste.

2. The beer is often run too early before it has a chance to sour properly.

3. The whiskey is sometimes condensed in a straight worm which does not let it slow down enough to cool off properly. This gives it a harsh, hot taste.

4. Often whiskey is scorched because it is not watched properly, not stirred while heating, or because the fire under the still is too hot.

5. If whiskey is not strained properly, it will contain elements that can make one violently ill.

6. Radiators used as condensers are extremely dangerous. They can never be cleaned out completely, and the end result is sometimes whiskey that can cause lead poisoning.

7. Potash is sometimes used to "fake" a high bead. This is the same material soap is made out of, and it can be poisonous.

8. Sometimes potash and ground up Irish potatoes are added to the malt to make it work off quicker and yield more.

9. Often vessels are left dirty, and produce "popskull" liquor.

10. Instead of pure corn malt, some use yeast.

11. Instead of pure corn meal, some use "wheat shorts" so it won't stick to the still.

12. Many cut the final product to 60–70 proof and add beading oil to fake quality and high proof.

13. It is rumored that some people set batteries down in the mash boxes to make it work more quickly; but another we talked to hinted that that might just have been a rumor put out by federal agents to hurt the sale of whiskey. We could get nothing concrete on this one way or another.

14. One of our contacts knows a man who uses a groundhog still which he fills two-thirds full of water which he then heats. Then he adds fifty pounds of wheat bran, four 100-pound sacks of sugar, and two cans of yeast. That's it. No souring—nothing. Apparently it makes "pretty" whiskey which holds a good bead, but has a funny "whang" flavor.

The biggest problem, of course, is as we have hinted several times before—the desire for quantity rather than quality. One retired moonshiner said, "When I was working for th' forest service and saw th' filth and th' nature of most of th' stills in th' woods today, th' prouder I was that I quit drinkin' th' stuff. I don't see how more people don't get killed."

Another claimed that he had often had people who make whiskey themselves come to him to buy the liquor *they* were going to drink. They were afraid to drink their own.

It apparently is not that difficult to get away with making bad whiskey, because most of it is sold through bootleggers who themselves don't know where it came from. In addition, much of it is shipped to the poorer districts of some of the bigger cities, and the people who buy it there have no means of finding out who made it. Thus the operator of the still is reasonably safe, rarely having to pay for his sloppiness.

He earns little respect among his neighbors, however. As one said, "A man ought to be put in a chain gang with a ball tied to him if he uses potash to make whiskey. 'Bout all you can call that is low-down meanness. He ain't makin' it t'drink himself, and he ain't makin' it fit for anyone else to drink neither."

HOW TO GET RID OF THE FINAL PRODUCT

In the early days of moonshining, it was a relatively easy matter to dispose of the whiskey. In the first place, there wasn't that much of it. Also, most of the neighbors knew who in the area was busy in that pursuit, and so they knew where to go when they needed to make a purchase. The moonshiner knew his neighbors, usually knew who could be trusted, and so everything worked out well. There were no big business overtones, no high pressure sales, just quiet, behind-the-scenes, low-key transactions during which no one asked unnecessary questions.

Things began to change, however, during Prohibition. One man we talked to could remember huge trailer trucks coming down off his mountain loaded with thousands of gallons of whiskey and headed north. The operation has remained the realm of the relatively big operators.

The great majority of the whiskey produced is distributed through bootleggers who buy it directly from the makers. They usually hire their own haulers so that they don't have to pay the owner of the still for moving it for them. The bootlegger usually gets it from his haulers, waters it down, puts it in jars, and then distributes it to his regular customers, making deliveries to regular customers on a regular schedule. Sometimes these customers are store owners who sell it again to *their* customers.

It is a tight, shadowy operation, sometimes run by men who are among the most highly respected citizens in the community. For these men, their double life also pays off in a handsome double income.

Sometimes bootleggers have ingenious ways of hiding their wares while waiting for them to be disposed of. One we heard of has a clothesline strung across a lake in his backyard. The line is circular, and runs on a pulley system. The bottom half of the line contains clips which are, in turn, hooked to the tops of fruit jars that are full of whiskey. These jars remain submerged under the lake all the time. As customers show up, the correct number of jars is pulled up and sold. Another operator, this one relatively small, kept the product he was selling in the sleeves of the clothing which hung in his closet.

The men who run the real risks, however, are the haulers, who have perfected hundreds of ways of moving whiskey. Some of these:

1. One man hauled only on Sundays. On these days, he would have eight cases concealed in the trunk, two under the hood, and his wife and little girl in the car with him. The car was "shocked up" so that no excess weight showed, and he rode around enough so that no one suspected that he was in a hurry to get anywhere. He was never caught.

2. Another filled the bed of his pickup truck two cases high, and then put a black plywood form on top so that at night it looked empty. The truck held twenty cases.

3. Others have big trucks with false beds in which they can fit a single layer of cases.

4. Some haul, even today, in dump trucks or cabbage trucks which have such high sides that they can't be seen into from the road. If they are afraid of getting caught, they sometimes stack all the cases of moonshine in the center of the bed and cover it completely top and sides with ears of corn.

5. Some remove the back seats from their cars and load them full from the front seat all the way through to the taillights. We heard about one man who even took out the front seat and rode sitting on a case, with several more beside him.

6. Still another method is to hire a "hot" lead car. The car containing the whiskey follows this lead car at a leisurely pace. When the lead car spots an officer, it takes off at a great rate of speed, obviously driving recklessly. The officer gives chase, and the driver in the car containing the whiskey proceeds unhindered to its destination.

7. Others steal several cars, repaint them, switch their motors, and have three license tags for each car—North Carolina, South Carolina, and Georgia. The tags have hooks, and are interchanged according to which state the hauler is working.

IN CONCLUSION

By any standards, moonshining has to be counted as one of the most fascinating mountain endeavors. Few occupations can lay claim to funnier stories—or sadder stories—than this.

Despite the glamour of it all, however, it remains one of the most difficult activities around. Officers are getting more concerned and more proficient daily and are pressing harder for more crippling penalties. In addition, the cash outlay required to get into business, the logistics of moving vast amounts of sugar and grain around, the difficulty of hiding the operation, the impossibility of protection against informers, the long hours required of hot, dirty work—it all adds up to a rather unattractive way to spend an afternoon. And as any moonshiner will tell you, there is no burn on earth like the burn one gets from coming in contact with boiling hot meal. It sticks to the skin and removes it surgically in one neat piece.

The sheer fact of its ceaseless and unrelenting difficulty perhaps adds to the glamour rather than detracts. This difficulty, however, coupled with the fact that there really *are* easier jobs to be had nowadays, may also be the most successful element in destroying the practice as it exists today. It at least did a textbook job of demolishing the craft as a fine art. Perhaps we have succeeded in preserving some particle of that art for history. We hope so.

FAITH HEALING

In the southern Appalachians today, there are still people who claim to be able to heal by faith. We have interviewed several of these people and tape recorded our conversations with them. The pages which follow contain large portions of these recorded interviews.

We must make it clear that we do not scoff at the information we are about to present. We are a little skeptical, true; but that is natural for several reasons. First, we have not actually seen any of these healers at work; we have only talked to them. Second, we are young, and we are the products of an age that has taught us to believe that things that cost money are better than things that do not.

The elderly healers with whom we talked are quiet, simple, strong and sure. They are people with a faith of such quality that the differences between them and us were abundantly clear. They have faith in themselves, and they have faith in their God, believing that it is through Him their words carry weight. They do not heal in tents before throngs. They do not cry out over radios. They do not accept money for their work. They work with neighbors and neighbors' children individually, when asked to help, and they respond as a gesture of friendship and concern.

The healers with whom we spoke are sought after primarily for their skills in three areas. The first of these is burns. Their theory is that when a person has been burned, the fire continues to flame inside the wound until it has been "blown out" or "drawn." If this is not done, they claim, the fire continues to burn into the flesh until it reaches the bone. This condition makes it infinitely more difficult for a doctor to cure the actual wound, and it makes it infinitely more painful for the wounded.

The second ill which they claim to be able to cure is any bleeding that is not of natural causes. They claim to be able to stop bleeding not only in humans, but even in animals such as horses and mules.

The third ailment they treat is a childhood disease which they call "Thrash" or "Thrush." Its symptoms are clear or yellow blisters which well up around a baby's lips and inside its mouth. These blisters are so painful that they can make it impossible for the child to nurse. If not cured, the healers claim that the blisters can infect the entire digestive tract and thus kill the infant.

Each of the healers said he could cure at least one of the above. Several said they could cure them all. Two others said they could even take off warts. Each of the healers had some personal variation in his actual method of treatment, but all admitted that an essential part of the treatment was a certain verse from the Old Testament. Each illness has its own appropriate verse, and the verse is never uttered out loud. If it is spoken by the healer and others hear it, the speaker supposedly loses his power to cure from that moment on.

Each healer also admitted that he could teach others the gift. Most of them said that they could teach only a certain number of people (usually two of the opposite sex not related to him by blood), but one healer claimed that belief was merely a fiction of his grandparents that was being preserved. He claimed to have taught many people with no ill effects to his own abilities.

But we are cheating you by not letting these people speak for themselves.

A WITNESS: LESTER NORTON

One of the first people we interviewed was not a healer himself, but he had known two people who were, and his stories of what they did whetted our appetites.

"Old Aunt Caroline Korn could certainly take fire out of you if you got burnt, and old Uncle Joe Teague could certainly stop blood when it'uz bleedin'. Once they'uz a logger cuttin' timber and cut his foot. He went to see Uncle Joe that evenin' and his shoe'uz just

PLATE 282   Lester Norton

about full'a blood, and he wanted him to stop it. And he said, 'How long'll it take ya't'go home?' and he said, 'About twenty minutes'; and he said, 'All right.' Well when he got t'th' house in about twenty minutes, that blood stopped and never did bleed n'more.

"And he'uz over at Sapphire at that little hotel there, and they said t'him, they said, 'They say you can stop blood.' He said, 'Yeah.'

" 'All right,' [they] said. 'We'll just let ya' try your luck on this beef.'

"He said, 'All right, but it'll ruin yer beef, man.'

" 'Aw shuck.'

"They killed it'n stuck it. It never bled a drop. Blood stayed right in th' flesh an' ruined it. Couldn't eat it. He shore could stop blood. It's in th' Bible. You can get that stoppin' blood out'a th' Bible. It's in th' Old Testament somewhereabouts. I've read it, but it's been s'long."

A HEALER: MRS. ANDY WEBB

Several days later, we were traveling in our jeep far off the main road. The dirt track took us across a divide on the flank of Pickens' Nose, and as we came down into a hollow we saw a ramshackle house on our left. Stopping to get acquainted with the family who lived there, we mentioned that we were looking for healers. As it turned out, the matriarch of the huge family that lived there was a healer herself, and she agreed to tell us what she could.

"I can blow fire out. I can stop blood. I can cure th' thrash. I do all that by th' help o'th' Lord. I don't do that by myself. If I ain't got th' Lord wi'me . . ."

She hesitated, so we asked her if she could teach someone. She said, "I can't blow fire or cure th' thrash or anything like that if I tell anybody. I don't know if I can teach anyone. I never did try."

There was a long silence, so we asked her how she found out she could do it. "By th' hand o'th' Lord," *came the reply.*

"How old were you?" *we asked.*

"I don't know how old I am now, an' I don't know how old I was."

A few more false starts followed. Gradually, however, sensing our genuine interest, she began to talk freely and naturally.

"My son, Jim, his child's nose commenced bleedin' one night at th' supper table, and they live away down yonder in Georgia. An' he said t'his brother, 'I'm a'gonna' take him t'Momma.'

"Well, when they come, they had him rolled up in a sheet and that blood—hit was just as bloody as it could be. Y'couldn't tell whether

PLATE 283 Mrs. Andy W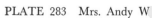

it'uz a sheet or what. And he just come in th' door and said, 'Here, Momma. I want ya' t'stop Lewis's nose from bleedin'.'

"I said, 'All right,' and he laid him down in m'lap and it'd just squirt. Ever' time his pulse'd beat, y'know, it'd squirt. And it wasn't long though 'til it stopped bleedin' and it's never bled another drop.

"To do it, you don't have ta' touch the person. I can just talk t'th' Lord and it's all right. And when y'blow fire, you blow on th' burned place an' say somethin'—it's out'a th' Bible, but I can't read a word of th' Bible—not a word. I can't read. And I can't write. It's just a gift from God. I just commenced at it."

Soon she was talking about thrash. "It's in a child's mouth and it can't eat, and if it's a'nursin' th' breast it gets all in th' breast and they can't stand fer 'em t'nurse. It just comes up in yaller blisters. Ther's three kinds of thrash. There's white thrash, and yaller thrash and black thrash. And th' yaller thrash's th' one that's s'hard t'cure. It just comes up in clear blisters, and they can't eat ner they can't drink. I can cure all three kinds.

"My goddaughter brung her two twin babies up hyear an'they had th' thrash and I doctored them and got them well and here she come back. It was in her breast, an' I doctored it and cured it.

"Doctors tell everybody goes to 'em with a baby with th' thrash

PLATE 284 Andy Webb

t'go hunt'em up a thrash doctor. A neighbor's child had th' thrash, and they hunted everwhar. They took it t'th' doctor out yonder t'Clayton, an' he said he couldn't do nothin' fer it. Says, 'If you know whar there's ary a thrash doctor, you better hunt it up and right now.' So they commenced huntin' and they come down hyear t'Mrs. Rogers, and she said she'd quit, so she told 'em t'come on up hyear. They fetched th' baby on up hyear an' I doctored it, an' I told 'em t'bring it back th' next day. It had th' thrash bad. So they brung hit an' *two more*—they'd took th' thrash. I doctored them and cured'em up. I had t'tell'em t'bring'em back, they had it s'bad."

When we asked her about drawing fire, she had another story for us. "My grandson burnt his arm on th' power saw—it'uz hot. And he burnt his arm and he come up hyear night before last night I believe it was, and I blowed th' fire out of it. He said it hurt awful bad. I told him t'come back if it didn't quit burnin', but he didn't come back. I reckon it's all right.

"I don't have t'be alone. I can be right in a crowd and do that. They don't hear me. They don't know what I say. I just talk t'th' Lord and that's all."

Soon her husband, Andy, joined in the conversation. "I tell y'what

I seed her do one time. We lived on Mud Creek up yonder. One of our neighbor's boy there had a big, black horse, and he'uz back over at a little place at work and throwed his mowin' blade down, and th' horse'uz a'pickin' around there and he happened t'run against it, and he cut his front leg plumb inta th' bone just like that [demonstrating]. And that horse had bled 'til he'uz s'weak he couldn't hardly walk. They'uz goin' t'try t'get a doctor up there t'see about him, and Zero told'em she could stop th' blood. And they stopped then with th' horse in th' road'n hollered and told her t'come up there. She told'em wan'no use, just t'stand still a few minutes. And they said in less'n five minutes that horse's leg was quit bleedin'.

"I've seed her doctor lots'a times. They was a fella' over here on th' creek. His wife, she got burnt s'bad. I don't know how she *did* get burnt myself. And they doctored and doctored and doctored and some woman told'em about her. She went t'see'er and she begun doctorin' her. Just a few days she could turn over in her bed and roll back. And she was burnt all down her back, plumb down to her hips. I don't know how she got it done. I believe th' boy *did* tell us, didn't he?"

Mrs. Webb said, "I believe that a candle blowed up. Some way r'nother thataway. I can't think back like I used t'."

We talked on about other things until it was past time to make our way back down the mountain. As we left, we thanked them, and Mrs. Webb answered, "All I've got's been a gift from God, and it's perfect. But when people get old like me an' him, younger people don't pay much attention to'em. They don't come to'em for advice like they should."

A HEALER: AUNT NORA GARLAND

Not long after our visit with the Webbs, we were told by a friend that one of the best healers in the area lived not five miles from where we were standing. We got her name, and four of us went to visit her one afternoon after school in her home just north of Clayton. She was a tall, thin, elderly woman, and she talked to us freely and with great conviction. "I can stop blood. I can draw out fire, and I can take off warts. I can't cure thrash. My brother does that, and I'm proud of it."

On teaching: "One person can tell one, y'see, and that other person that y'told can tell someone else. Sorta like these chain letters. My mother told me where t'find it at so I found it. And it's somethin' every doctor ought t'know. It's simple, and you don't have t'turn over far in Ezekiel to find that about bleedin'. You

PLATE 285   Aunt Nora Garland

don't have t'read any farther than th' sixteenth chapter. You memorize it by heart, but don't leave one little thing out. If you do, it won't stop."

She went on to talk about bleeding and how to stop it, and how important it was not to forget to say a single word of the Bible verse. "My brother one time—well, he was pretty good size; about half grown I guess—but my mother told him to go and cut some wood one afternoon. So he went, and she could stop blood. She's th' first'un I knew could. Anyway, he cut his heel string on this big broadaxe— you know what a broadaxe is—sharp on both sides. He cut his heel string slap in two. Just slap in two.

"Well, we thought it was goin' t'bleed him t'death, and my mother failed t'stop it. I can remember goin' after th' minister; and when he came, he failed t'stop it. I don't know whether they was scared or— listen; if y'leave one little thing out, it won't stop. One little error. I knew she'uz excited for she'd made many a dress, and she just grabbed that dress as she sat at th' sewin' machine, and wrapped it around his leg. Well, it was nine months he never walked a step in th' world, and we had t'teach him t'walk just like a little baby, y'know. And he was turned down in th' army on account of that foot. It was an awful lookin' thing. He's not crippled, but he was turned down in th' army."

Another time: "There'uz a lady—she'uz expectin' t'go t'th' hospital at any time. All th' time durin' that time, her nose had almost bled her t'death. So this man rid up inta our yard one night, and that's been twenty year ago, I guess. And he said, 'I want y't'go t'my house.' It'uz way down on Chechero. He said, 'My wife's nose is a'bleedin' her t'death.' Said, 'I don't believe she'd be alive 'til I get back.'

"I said, 'Oh yes she will.'

"He said, 'Would y'go?'

"I said, 'No.' It'uz after dark. I said, 'No use in me a'goin' down there. It'll be ok as soon as you get back.'

"So th' next day I seed him in town an' asked him about her. Said, 'It'uz stopped when I got back.'

"I don't have t'know their name. Don't have t'know a thing about them. You just think about'em and say th' verse three times. . . . I've been sent for t'Lakemont and different places t'come and stop th' blood, and I say, 'There's no use in me a'comin'.' I could do it in New York if they'uz t'call me."

Then we asked her what doctors thought about all this. "I don't

know, but Doctor Neville thought it was wonderful. I'll tell ya',
we'uz a'milkin' one night. We had about sixteen cows to milk, and
we'uz a'milkin' one Sunday night, and you can see th' scar there
[pointing to her forehead]. There's twenty-six stitches took up an'
down there, and a blood vessel bursted over here. A cow kicked me
in th' head. And Doctor Dover that was, he just didn't know a thing
in th' world t'do. And that blood'uz a'comin' up and spillin' back
down in my face after he got th' other places fixed up and m'head
sewed up, and he says, 'I just can't get that stopped t'save my life.'
And I never thought t'do it. I never thought th' first time it hurt s'bad.

"He said, 'Try *your* luck on it.'

"We tried, and it stopped right quick."

*When we asked her how fast the blood usually stopped, she snapped
her fingers and said,* "About that fast." When we asked her why she
thought it worked, she said, "Well, I don't know. I guess that's
th' Lord's work. Faith? I guess that has a lot t'do with it. I *believe*
that I can stop it." *Did she take money for her services?* "I don't
believe I could do it if I started chargin' money for it. It's from
th' heart. Doctor Neville wanted to know how t'stop blood. . . . He
offered me twenty-five dollars in money to tell how t'stop it, but I
wouldn't."

The conversation then turned to burns. "You know a burn—how it
hurts. Ther's fire in th' place where y'get burnt. You know that.
You blow your breath on that and th' fire's gone out." *Her method
for drawing the fire is to pass her hand over the burn three times,
blow her breath gently over it following the hand each time, and
repeat the verse silently each time. Thus, unlike stopping blood, she
must be present to draw fire.*

*As we were preparing to leave, we thanked her for being so
helpful and open. She answered,* "Well, it might be of some use to
you when I'm gone. I believe in th' healin' power because the Lord
has healed me. I know he has. That's the greatest thing they is is
th' healin' power of th' Savior."

A HEALER: CHARLEY TYLER

*A small silver trailer above Mountain City is the home of Charley
Tyler. On the afternoon we visited him, he was working in his yard,
but he was glad to put down his work to talk with us. Our conversation lasted far into the evening.*

"Thrash is a thing that just works in yr'mouth, you know. It'll go all the way through you. It'll kill y'an' a doctor can't do anything about it too much. You got t'have a different way a'doctorin' th' thing.

"It's caused from bein' not too clean—bein' dirty a lot. Lettin' th' kid go dirty too long. It's a germ and that's th' way it's caused. Kids handlin' things, and babies put their hands in their mouth and got th' thrash first thing you know. And then curin' it makes a different thing. It's hard t'cure, and a doctor can't cure it. They claim they ain't no such thing as thrash but they are. I been curin' it for forty years and I know. And I've had some terrible times a'curin' it.

"There's a yellow thrash, and they's what they call a red thrash. That red thrash is not too much trouble t'cure; hit'll cure pretty easy. Doctor *can* cure it. But that yaller thrash is a thing that's a blister. It blisters up in yaller blisters—look like it'd have pus or somethin' under it—inside his mouth. And hit'll bust their lips up and th' outside dries out. Down their throat. Their tongue'll be a solid blister on th' bottom side. Top side won't blister much; it'll just have a yaller coating on it. And you have to know how t'cure thrash t'cure it. It's different ways—oh, I'd say they's five hundred different ways a'curin' thrash. Everbody don't do it alike, y'know. What few that does it like I do is the ones I have taught t'do it, y'know. I can cure one in a half a minute, and y'don't have t'bring it back a second time."

We asked him what would happen if the child wasn't taken to a thrash doctor. "It'll kill it. That yaller thrash'll kill it, if it goes through it. It cooks all th' way through. They can't eat. I don't know whether th' thrash is all'at kills it or not, but part of it's starve t'death. They can't eat, y'know. Mouth's s'sore they can't swaller. They can't do nothin'; and th' thrash and without somethin' t'eat together, they'll die, y'know. And their throat'll get to where they can't breathe. It'll swell t'where it gets t'where they can't breathe hardly, y'know.

"Some of 'em cures it by th' faith they have. And they's some of 'em that does it with a few words out'a th' Bible 'at they use. And then some of 'em uses chemicals, y'know, like some kind a weed they use t'doctor with. Some takes 'em t'a barn. My way a'doctorin' though, if I met you out here in th' road, is you stand still and I'll get behind ya' an' doctor it that quick. If you're in a car, I'll just step behind th' car. If y'come t'my house, I'll just go through that door there an' just pull th' door to long enough t'doctor it. Just so I'm out'a your sight. An' I don't never say a word. I just do somethin'.

It don't work, they claim, if y'don't stay out'a sight, without you're teachin' somebody—that don't make any difference. But just like before th' crowd here, why they—I don't know. It might not be any difference, but they claim they are.

"I can teach all I want I guess. I guess I've taught five hundred. I've always taught women, and then th' women folks teaches th' men. A woman told me how. She was from over on Persimmon. That'uz back in my young days—see, I got a'lot a'people over'ere, and I used t'go there a lot and I picked up those things like that ever' time I got a chance.

"They's nothin' to it. They just ain't anythin' to it. They's nothin' t'remember about it. They's no verses of no kind, no words of no kind to remember. It's just th' action, and you remember how t'do what they tell ya'."

His method? "Well, y'use your hand. You get th' kid to cry or laugh and have it in your arms; and when it does, you set your hand over it thataway [cupping the fingers around the mouth] and then you breathe. Don't blow in th' child's mouth. You do like you was tryin' t'suck th' breath away from th' child. (*Plate 286*). You do that three times, and then that's th' motion. That's all y'got't go through with. That's it. Don't breathe in. Just pull it to ya'. Blow it away from him when y'blow your breath out. Blow it out of his face and then pull back t'it again. Do that three times and you'll never have t'do it but one time without they're awful bad. I've never doctored one in all th' years I've been at it but one that I had t'doctor actually twice t'get it stopped. I had one that th' first time I doctored it, why it was some better, but it wa'n't half well. It could eat a little. But I let'm miss one day, and then th' second day I doctored it again and then I never did doctor it any more. It got all right. Most of th' time I can doctor it and tomorrer that kid'll never know it's ever had th' thrash.

"It *can* get it again because it's a germ. It's caught from filth and dirt, y'know. Lot'a women don't keep children clean as they ought to. Now if they're nursin' on a bottle, they don't scald that bottle enough. They don't keep it clean. They let'em waller it around on th' floor and pick it up and th' nipple's been in th' dirt and everythin' else. Well they's germs in that stuff, and that's what y'catch a lotta things from, y'know. Th' doctor'll tell y'that—that you catch lots'a things that way. You can catch typhoid fever from filth and dirt, y'know. That's why when y'have a case of typhoid fever, they make y'keep everythin' clean. If you ain't able t'do it, they'll send somebody there that can."

PLATE 286 Charley Tyler demonstrates his method for curing thrash in a young child.

We asked him how many he had cured of thrash. "I dogged if I know. You take, well, close t'forty years I've did it. Sometimes a year or two that I don't cure one, and then sometimes you'll cure maybe forty or fifty in the run of a year. Course they don't have a certain time t'have it. It just when they catch it, y'know. I don't know. About a thousand of 'em, I guess. Course now if it'd been all alike like it is some years, why, it'd'a been ten thousand of 'em, but it don't work like that. They's several other folks 'at cures 'em too, you know, round over th' country; now more'n they used t'be, an' 'at's why I don't cure as many as I used to. There's more thrash now than there's ever been in years, and there's other folks that cures their friends and kindred and like that they've learnt. Now they's a few old women used t'wouldn't learn but three. They said that'uz all you's allowed t'learn, but I ain't never found that out 'cause I been learnin'em ever since I found that out.

"Now they's one man that can cure th' thrash—an' all he ever does is just walk up an' look at th' child and just blow his breath across his face, walk off an' leave it. Never says nothin'. But he's a person—reckon a woman can do th' same thing—that's never seen their father. If their father dies before they're born, an' they don't see their father, then they can cure th' thrash. Anywhere. Anytime. An' all they do just walk by it an' blow their breath across its face. Don't know why, but it is that way now. I know several fellers around here's never seen their father that can cure thrash. Some of 'em's hard t'get 'em at it—get 'em t'do it, y'know. Now they's a lot of boys growin' up this day an' time don't know it; they just don't know they can. Nobody's never told'em that they could cure a baby with th' thrash by just lookin' at it an' just blow breath through its face, y'know. And some of 'em's just bashful. Not that they don't want t'protect th' human bein' an' cure it or anything. It's just some of 'em's just bashful.

"And I've heard that th' seventh son or th' seventh daughter can cure thrash and draw fire too."

Soon the topic of conversation turned to burns. "Now that burnin', I wouldn't want t'push it too fur because it *does* come out'a th' Bible, y'know. It takes *good* faith with it."

Why did fire have to be drawn? "Well now, I'll tell y'why. When you're burnt, up here on top, and lot'a folks will when they're burnt—a hand or anything—they'll pour cold water on it, or stick their hand in cold water. Well, that drives 'at fire in further. It just keeps burnin' deeper and makes it worse to sore. An' if you c'n draw that fire out, you don't have no sore. It just peels off—no scar, no nothin'. It'll just peel off. But if you don't get that fire out'a there, they leave a scar. Ain't you see'd folks, face burnt where they's a slick place? I don't leave that. When I draw th' fire out, I leave that skin when it's well just like it was before it was burnt.

"It don't matter too much about th' time. It's accordin' t'what y'do. If you—like I tell y'if it's a bad burn that's burnt, it's cooked, and peeled it right off where th' clothes sticks to it—why, then y'have t'use somethin' t'keep that from stickin'; and y'can't tie a burn up 'cause if you go t'bandage up a burn, you just drive it to th' bone, 'at's all. They ain't no question about it. That's why it takes a doctor so long to cure up a burn—'cause you just drives it to th' bone, and then he got t'doctor from th' bone back out before he can do anythin' with it. That's why it takes so long.

"I can cure one in, oh, a third as quick as a doctor can because I just draw th' fire out of it and take common old baby powders— talcum powders they used t'call 'em—baby powders that they used t'put on a baby t'keep him from chalvin [chafing]; and simple as it can be, just cover that up because when I go to drawin' th' fire out, water'll come out'a that burn if it's a bad burn. Now just a little burn on your finger or on your hand or anythin' like that, if you don't make a blister hardly any water comes out of it. It'll just dry up. And you never *tie* it up.

"And I'll tell you somethin' else. You see that hand? You know, that hand don't look like a burned hand any more'n th' other one does it? But that hand'uz burnt from here to there. Ever' bit of it just rolled up and down there a wad a'cooked skin. I mean it just pulled off'n it just white as you please. Well, I caught a piece a'iron and it'uz red hot, an' a guy named Cusher below me—an' he'uz worse bald-headed than I am—and that piece a' iron started toward him, an' it'uz as big as your arm, about four feet long, an' all I had t'grab'uz that red hot end, an' I didn't have m'glove on. I just *had* pulled th' glove off and didn't put it back on an' then I needed it. And I just reached and got that thing and throwed it over my head an' th' skin an' meat all went with it—it red hot. An' I just run aroun' an' aroun'—just spun aroun' an' aroun'—helpin' t'build Fontana Dam up here—'til I got still. I'uz about half sick it hurt s'bad, y'know. Just for a minute. An' just as soon as I got still, I started doctorin' it right there. Turned around an' said t'th' welder, I said, 'Now listen. Now you keep your mouth shut. Now don't you tell nobody I got burnt.'

"He says, 'Why? You better go t'hospital.'

"I says, 'Doctor ain't goin' get aholt a'this 'cause I'll be back

here t'work in th' mornin'. If a doctor gets a'holt a'it, I'll be sick
an' suffer with it a'hurtin' all th' time'; and I said, 'It'll be all
right in th' mornin'.' I says, 'I've done doctored it.'

"I worked on 'til night. Put my glove on and worked on 'til
night. Back next mornin' t'work an' I dared him t'tell that. 'You tell
it, I'll stomp you in th' ground.' I says, 'I don't want t'get in
th' hospital.' An' I doctored that thing—put me a coat a'powders on
it that night an' just tied a thin gauze as thin a piece a cloth
as I could get aholt of pull over it just t'keep it from gettin' dirty.
I let that hand go. I kept th' back of it washed off a little—it got
awful dirty around that burn—and I wouldn't never let a drop'a
water touch it 'til it healed; cold water could give y'—catch a cold in
it, cause it t'inflame, cause it t'give y'trouble.

"Th' fire's in th' skin. That's why it's red around it. You c'n see
th' red. It's still burnin' in there. That's why it takes so long for a
doctor t'cure it up. If you don't get that fire out first, it takes a
long time to heal up. That fire's got t'automatically just work out,
grow out itself t'get out a'there before it'll ever heal up because
it's burnt in there, and it ain't comin' out if they ain't somethin'
done about it. Now they do make some kind a'medicines now
that helps t'draw that fire out, helps t'heal it. But it's not like as
quick as I c'n get it out because if you c'n get burnt an' I c'n know
it in five minute after you get burnt, ten minutes after you get burnt
you call th' fire in your hand. I'll get it out. It gone. It'll probably
pain y'a little bit. Naturally it'll be sore. But not enough t'amount
t'anything. But if it's a pretty bad burn and I go to draw th' fire out
of it, it hurts worse'n when it went in for a minute. Oh, you c'n just
sling that hand and say, 'Law, law, how that hurts,' and you'll
wonder what's a'makin' it hurt. You don't know that I'm doin' it.
But in maybe thirty minutes time it's quit hurtin' and you've forgot
all about it. All you got t'do is keep a few powders on it, and
th' powders makes a crust on it, y'see, that keeps cold from catchin'
in it. It just heals under that and never leaves a scar. They ain't a scar
nowhere."

*Mr. Tyler then proceeded to tell us a story about a dog food
factory that blew up and scalded several men.* "One man got burned
with steam. Boiler blowed up. Burnt *him* all over, *and* his buddy
that was at work with him. And his buddy was harder to do anythin'
with than he were because he'uz young. He kep' his mouth shut,
and his buddy'uz a old-like feller and he breathed that steam down
his throat and he'uz a burnt down inside. That's why we had such a
hard time gettin' th' fire out from on th' inside where a doctor can't

get to it. That's why I say lots a'times these things comes in better 'cause a doctor couldn't get t'that on th' inside a'that thing, and we could because we let our Maker do that. We don't doctor it. Other words, I mean, we don't cure it. We're used as th' vessel for th' Lord t'let us do th' work and He does th' curin'. Do ya' see what I mean? It ain't me that cures it. I just do th' work and put faith in God and God does th' work hisself. I mean, he does th' curin' of th' man. He does th' healin'. It's not me that does it. See what I mean?

"And there was a bunch a'us there curin' them two people. Soon as I doctor one, I doctor th' other; and stayed right there almost day and night for about four days gettin' that fire out a'all of'em. Only one place Carl had t'have a patch. He had t'have a patch on his back 'cause he'uz burnt through t'th' holler, and they had t'patch that t'get it t'grow up. It'uz a hole in there. We got th' fire out a'him, but then th' doctors had t'cut a piece a'skin off this thigh, I believe it was—little place there that hadn't been burnt—after we got him healed up."

We asked him how many fire doctors were there helping. "They was me and m'wife. And they'uz one, two, three old ladies from Lawrenceville, and two from Gainesville. There's five. And two's seven, and m'daughter'n'law's eight. There was eight of us there. Doctor, he just turned us loose. Some doctors won't do that, but he said, 'Listen,' he says, 'I've got more here than I can handle.' And he said, 'If you people c'n do any good, for God's sakes get at it.' And he says, 'And I'll do whatever I can do, an' if 'ere's anything 'at I'm a'gonna' do that's again' yall's way a'doin',' he says, 'say so, an' le'me do it like you want it done, but le's do somethin' fast.' Well all right. We get th' fire out. Then he could cure up th' places 'cause they cure up theyselves, but if somebody t'he'p it t'cure up, y'know, why they cure up faster. So he just went t'work and done what we told him, and didn't take us too long—two week's time—'til we had 'em both out a'th' hospital. Had 'em at home. Carl'uz about ready t'go t'work soon's he got t'where he could use one a'his hands. And th' old man lost one a'his hands. He's still got it, but it's drawed up right like there an' he can't use it 'cause he wouldn't do what th' doctor told him. If he'd a'done what th' doctor told him, he could use his hand just as good as Carl did his. Carl kep' his a'goin' all th' time, an' th' old man, he wouldn't 'cause it hurt some t'make it do, y'know. And it healed up an'those leaders'uz burnt, y'know, and drawed, an' he wouldn't keep it stretched out, an' he just wound up with one hand.

"They wa'dn't any two of us doin' it th'same way 'cep' m'daughter'n'law an' me 'n'm'wife. It'll work different ways. It's not all worked alike. Now they's a old lady down at town—I don't know but she said she used a verse in th'Bible. She didn't exactly spit on ya' but she'd go [demonstrating] an' blow her breath again' it, y'know. She'd draw it out, too. She'd get it out in a hurry, but she just did it differ'nt from what I did. An' I don't know whether she used th'same verse that I did or not. I can't tell y'that. All faith, of course, more'n anything else. You don't have t'be religious. You don't have t'be a preacher. An' you don't have t'be a big church member, just as long as you got that faith. Th'Lord'll he'p y'in any way that He can if y'got th'right kinda faith.

"How do y'do it? Well, you start off, 'Blessed was th'day an' holy was thou when our Savior, Lord Jesus Christ first come in t'th'world.' That's all I'm go'n'a tell y' because they ain't but about six more words to it. I just stan' there an' look at it." *He doesn't touch the burn.* "Oh, a lot'a times I will pick up a hand, like you'uz burnt, y'know, just pick up a hand and look at it; turn it around an' look at it. But that's not—I just say that t'myself. Nobody's hearin' me say it. Fact, I'll be talkin' t'him over there and a'drawin' th'fire out a'your hand on th'same time, and neither one a'y'don't know I'm doin' it. I usually say th'verse one time if it's a small burn; but if it's a bad burn, why, I like t'go see 'em. I can get th'fire out an' me not there, but then, quick as I can, I *will* go an' git thar t'see how it was. But I don't *have* t'be thar. You c'n be at your house 'n'get burnt; pick up th'phone an' call me if I had a phone so's I could answer y'. An' th'first thing I'll ask y', 'Have y'done anythin' to it?' An' if y've put anything on it, I'll tell y't'get it off as much as y'can. But I'm a fire doctor an' I don't wait for y't'get it off. All I'll ask y'then is, 'What's y'r name, which hand, which foot, which laig, or whatever that it is that's burnt, and that's all I have t'know. An' I actually don't have t'know which hand or which foot, really. I *do* like t'get th'name. I like t'have your name, an' then after y'tell me your name, I get th'rest of it. What I do is always ast which hand or which foot, what part a'your body's burnt, or so on 'n'so forth."

We then moved to stopping blood. "Stoppin' blood's just like drawin' out fire. It's th'same identical thing. You do it with th'same verse and th'same words and everthin' except where y'ask for th'fire t'be taken out, you ask for th'blood t'be stopped. That's th'only difference is th'blood an'th'fire you ask for. Rest of it's all th'same thing.

"You don't touch it. My wife, she'd been over t'town, an' she'uz comin' back; an' a feller'd had a wreck—went as fur as from here't'that bank, I guess he went fifty yards or further down and cut a tree down with th' car, an'he went through a bob wire fence an' through th' windshield a'that car, an' him cut all t'pieces. And they's totin' him up out a'th' woods when she come along back, an' she stopped, an' she said blood'uz a runnin' through that thing they's a totin' him on, y'know, that stretcher. And she didn't even know th' man ner who he was ner nothin'. She just flew in an' doctored him, an' she got th' bleedin' stopped, an' time they got t'th' hospital he wa'n't bleedin' a bit, an' he lived. They all said he'd *never* live while they's a'totin' him out a'there—that he'd done bled all the blood there were in him out. But he lived, an' still livin'. That's pretty good right there too, y'know. And she did that just in th' car, an' didn't even know th' man ner who he was, ner nothin'; an' he'uz drunk he didn't know where he'uz at when he wrecked. Pretty near killed him. Cut all to pieces. An' 'course he didn't know nothin' after he wrecked.

"Doctors don't like it. They just plain don't like it. They just plain tell you it's not so. You can't do it. But they're wrong. It *can* be done. An' y'can show a doctor that y'can do it and still he'll argue with y'that it's just not right. I'd tell one doctor, I'd say, 'Well, Doc, you like I am. I just don't believe you got sense enough t'know right from wrong.'

"Doc say, 'Aw, you go on, shet your mouth' [laughing].

"I'd stop blood on a mule. Doctorin' an old mule, y'know. Cut his foot on a slip pan. Two handles on it, y'know. Hold it in th' dirt an' th' mule'll pull it 'til it loaded. You've seed 'em, I guess.

"An' that slip pan hit a root an' somehow'n'nother hit turned over. Jerked it loose from th' man an' caught th'mule right just between that holler place back of his leg an' like t'cut that foot off. An' Lord, did it bleed.

"An' Doc Dover's down thar, an' they had th' mule's foot tied up, pulled up tied 'cause Doc's afraid it'd kick him—might would, I guess. And he's a'workin' with it, and look like th' more he worked, worse it'uz a bleedin'. It'uz just pourin' th' blood'uz all.

"I come along an' I just stopped an' looked at it, y'know. Never said nothin' t'nobody. I just stopped an' looked at it. An' said, 'Doc, it's bleedin' pretty bad, ain't it?'

"Said, 'Yeah.'

"I said, 'Well, I'll stop it from bleedin' on y' if you'll bind it up.'

" 'Get away from here, Charley,' he said. 'You don't know nothin' about it.'

"I said, 'Hit's all right. I done doctored it. It won't bleed n'more no how. It's quittin' as fast as it can.' And it was. It'uz just slowin' up 'cause I doctored it quick as I saw it. And in just a few minutes it just come t'a slow drip.

"An' Doc, he looked at me an' he quarreled. Th' old man Doc was always quarrelin' t'me about everthin'. An' he fussed at me lots about that after that. He said, 'You believe you actually stopped that blood?'

"I said, 'Well, *you* didn't.' I says, 'Who *did?*' An' he'd laugh about it, but he argued all th' time. Wan't nothin' to it."

He then went on to give us some advice about thrash and about teaching others that he had forgotten to give us before: "You have t'watch. I come pretty near pullin' th' breath out of a little kid one time. Little too hard, an' he just quivered. You have t'watch about a little one. You know, lettle beety ones is worse to have it really than bigger ones at one time of th' year, an' another time of th' year th' big'ns has it an' th' little'ns won't. Now I don't know why, without they's just more germs goin' about in th' fall a'th' year like, than they are in th' spring a' th' year."

About teaching: "I can't see a reason for limiting it. That's th' reason I never did stop at it. 'Course, now, I've taught all women. I wouldn't teach a man. I didn't undertake that 'cause they was s'much of that said by nearly everybody that knew anything about those things. A man teach a woman and a woman teach a man, an' I just never did try t'teach a man."

He continued, telling us that the way he taught a woman was to write the verse down on a little piece of paper so she could learn it by heart. "Then you take that thing an' burn it—get rid of it. 'Course anybody's t'find it, they wouldn't know what it meant nohow. I don't put on it what it's fer. I just write it down, an' if y'need it and haven't learned it by heart, carry it with y'an'just read it over an' it'll draw that fire out, or stop blood.

"Then y'wind up askin' th' Lord t'—just like anybody else when they sayin' a prayer an' closin' it—'In Jesus name, amen.' You know. At th' end a'it. It seems a little more natural, y'know, t'do that. That's about all it's good for."

By this time, it was nearly dark. Supper was waiting, and besides, there was yet another healer that we had to talk to before we could consider the article finished. So we turned off the tape recorder

PLATE 287   Harley and Mary Carpenter

and began the forty-five minute leave-taking that is so customary in the mountains. Back at school once more, we made our plans for visiting the last healer, and then separated until the next day.

HARLEY CARPENTER

No article would be complete without our favorite source of information in North Carolina, Harley Carpenter. Talented in many areas, and knowledgeable in most where the mountains are concerned, we knew that he would have at least one or two things to add to the information we had already amassed. He didn't let us down.

"I can't tell ya' [how to heal] because it's handed down from th' beginnin'. It's in th' Bible. If y'tell somebody, y'lose yer power— in other words, like a man doin' somethin' t'destroy his rights, y'know.

"In that now, I could learn two women, or three I think it is, and then one of 'em that I'd learnt could learn a man person. So about th' biggest point I get in that is t'add a little mystery t'th' party that don't believe, maybe we'll say, in fire drawin' [laughing].

"I learnt two, an' I studied about it after that. Never asked 'em yet if they've ever tried it t'see if it works. But I think th' one that learnt me said learn somebody not no kin to ya'. Well, these parties wasn't, but they'uz my brother's wives, see? But I've never asked them if they've tried it."

When we asked him about people who refused to believe in the faith healers (including some of our editors), his answer provided a perfect conclusion to the survey. "Seein', in a sense, is 'a great believin'. You can hear things, but if you've seen it, you've got more sense out of it. If it had'n a'been true, it wouldn'a been handed down through th' years."

Not long after the faith healing article appeared in *Foxfire,* two women healers came forth who were willing to reveal their method exactly if we promised not to use their names. We agreed, and this is what they told us:

To draw fire pass your hand over the exposed burn, open and palm down, in a direction away from you and away from the patient —as if pushing the fire away from both you and the victim's body. Do this slowly *three* times, at the same time blowing gently on the burn. The head remains fixed over the burn, but turns so that your breath follows your hand thus blowing the fire away from the victim's body. Simultaneously, and each of the three times you do the above, repeat the secret healing verse silently.

The verse must be memorized word for word, for one mistake will invalidate the cure. The verse, as written down for us by the healer, is:

> *Thair came an angel*
> *from the East bringing*
> *frost and fire. In frost out*
> *fire. In the name of*
> *the father the Son and*
> *of the Holy Goost*

When I questioned her willingness to give us the supposedly secret method, her reply was, "Well, it might be of some use to you when I'm gone. I believe in th' healin' power because th' Lord has healed me. I know He has. That's the greatest thing they is, is th' healin' power of th' Savior."

On May 20, 1968, another woman, a resident of Dillard, Georgia, was willing to give us her much-tested method for stopping blood:

The healer does not have to be present. She claims she has even stopped severe bleeding from cuts by talking over the telephone. To stop the bleeding, she simply *reads,* to herself silently, one time, the sixth verse of the sixteenth chapter of Ezekiel. She reads the verse for fear she will leave something out and thus invalidate the cure.

Essential to the attempt is the substitution of the victim's full name each time "you" or "thee" (depending on which version of the Bible the healer is using) occurs.

Thus if the victim were named John Doe, the verse would be read silently, to oneself, in this manner: *"And when I passed John Doe and saw John Doe weltering in John Doe's blood, I said to John Doe in John Doe's blood, Live. . . ."*

She claims that the cure works even on animals. She claims to have stopped the severe bleeding which resulted when the teat of one of her cows was sliced.

HILLARD GREEN

It's not often we get our jeep stuck. These red clay roads will do it though. If you're one of those who needs to see to believe, try driving to Hillard's after a good hard rain.

The "easiest" way to get there is to drive out Betty's Creek Road to the North Carolina line where the pavement ends. From there you go lurching and spinning miles up a dirt road to the top of the first mountain range, and then swing left onto a red clay track that snakes far out to the head of a jewel-like cove—a cove bounded on three and a half sides by national forest, mountains, and a silence that makes one realize with a rush how unnatural the sound of an automobile really is. Considering the road, it seems mad to visit there after a rain; but then again, that's a good time to find arrowheads, deer and bear sign, the mist that made the Smokies famous—and Hillard.

Did you ever have a hideout in the woods when you were a kid? A hideout big enough to stand up in? A structure elaborate enough to keep out rain and wind? Something that, on the evolutionary scale for buildings that stretches from cave to mansion, fell somewhere in between the lean-to and the cabin? Well, that's about where Hillard's place falls.

Essentially it's a room with a roof on it. The wooden floor is bare and unwaxed. There's no ceiling—it's open to the ridgepole except

PLATE 288

for places where planks ·have been laid on the joists to provide a storage area above. A wood stove, a battered sofa, an ancient double bed, a table covered with an oilcloth, and a stiff-backed chair are the basic furnishings. Throughout the room, however, one spots the little details that make it home: the sardine can nailed to the wall for a soap dish; the neat stack of wood beside the stove; the horizontal poplar pole on which a clean pair of overhauls and a dish towel hang; the axe, pile of onions, and canned tomatoes and cucumbers under the bed; the garden tools and walking sticks over beside the door; the kerosene lamp; the outside door pull made of a discarded thread spool, and the inside one made from the crook of a laurel bough; the bucket and dipper for cold water from the spring; the mop made of a pole with a burlap sack tied to the end—all these things label the house as Hillard's and make it his alone.

Hillard is almost eighty years old. In the rich soil of the cove, however, he still plants, cares for and harvests a giant garden that feeds not only himself, but also several members of his family and a string of friends. Anyone who has a freezer full of Hillard's beans is a rich man indeed.

The last time we visited him, he was busy peeling tomatoes he had just gathered and scalded. He waved us in, put a fresh plug of tobacco in his cheek, and went on with his work chuckling as we got our camera ready.

"People'll look at those pictures," he laughed, "and say, 'What is that crazy old man a'doin'? You tell'em I'm puttin' up 'maters for th' winter, that's what. People might laugh at such stuff as this, but I'll tell y', I'm not about t'let'em rot. And when you've got old, you're not a'goin't'lay down and die just because you're old. Feller's got t'have somethin' t'do. Well, this is one of th' things I do, and I'm proud I can. Let'em laugh. I'll be eatin' good this winter and laughin' back."

The peeling process over, he next sliced and cored them, put them on to cook, and began to heat the canning jars.

"Everyone ought t'learn how to do such as this. One a'these days, times might get back hard again, and then what will they do? Nobody not knowin' how t'do nothin'. Might have t'live off th' land again, one day. We never had nothin' fer th' winter only what we put up. What we put up was what we had. Goin't'be a lot of hungry people someday."

PLATE 289

PLATE 290

When the tomatoes were cooked to his taste, he carefully filled the warm jars one by one, adding a single spoonful of sugar to each just before tightly closing the lid.

"Lotsa people don't even know how t'cook any more. They just go t'th' store and get it fixed already. These girls nowadays go off t'school and learn about everything but what's really important. Get home and still can't even cook a meal. If your woman can't cook whenever you get married, let me know and I'll come cook fer y'!"

To the last jar, instead of adding sugar, he added a spoon of salt and then sealed it. "That's th' way I learn. Experiment and experiment. Try different ways. Never learned it by readin'—just by doin'. That's th' way we all learn, ain't it?"

On several different occasions, members of Foxfire's staff tape recorded Hillard as he talked. Excerpts from the tapes follow:

I was raised on Coweeta—twelve miles below Franklin down in
there. It used t'be I could take off here a'walkin' and walk in a day
down there twelve miles. I walked many a time before they ever
got that railroad through. Then I got t'ridin' on a train; and a few
years later they got th' bus. Got this here cement road.

It was awful back then. Everybody had t'work then. Everybody
worked on th' farm. There wasn't no factories or nothin' hardly.
About th' only plants there was around was over yonder at Sylva in
Jackson County.

It was about 1919 when they started gradin' th' highway. We
didn't even have a gravel road'r nothin' goin' through here t'Franklin
and across th' mountain t'Asheville. It wadn't nothin' but a mud hole
when it rained. In 1905 down there in Franklin they didn't have
no streets'r nothin'. Had planks laid out there t'walk on when it
was rainin' it was so muddy. They didn't have but about two or
three stores in th' whole town. If you could've seen what I seen back
then, 'n' look at it now, why it'd make you wonder how it was built so
fast.

I had t'work all th' time then; Lord, yeah. Take a man on th' farm—
he has to be goin' 'fore daylight 'til after dark. Keeps him a'goin'
just like these people up in th' chicken business, y'know.

When a feller had a little bit of free time, a feller usually went
huntin'—when he had time that way. He'd be out in th' woods. I used
t'always have t'go t'th' woods about once or twice a week anyway,
y'know, back when I was young that way. Had cattle, hogs, sheep—all
back in th' mountains. We had free range back then; no stock law.
Our *crops* were all fenced in. We'd go see about our stock, and salt
our cattle and sheep ever' week.

And they used t'have corn shuckins all th' time, y'know. You'd go
t'maybe a dozen different corn shuckins in one fall. Them old people,
y'know, they used to when they went gatherin' their corn have a big
old tin t'put it in so they could shuck it and throw it in th' crib.
Lots of times they'd set'em a gallon jug of good ol'corn liquor right
in th' middle of it down in there; then see who could shuck fastest—
get t'that jug in there first. Let me tell ya', it was liquor back in
them days. It wasn't just ol'potash stuff that'd make y'sick. What
they made—it was made right. If you had a gallon like they did back
then, you could make most any kind'a medicine you wanted to now.
All liquorish medicine we have is made with alcohol in it. But it ain't
good like it used t'be—I can tell you that!

My momma died whenever I'uz just eighteen months old. I'uz just
from one place t'another—pretty near like it is now most of th' time.

After I got up any size, I'uz in a camp cookin'r'somethin' thataway, y'know; or cuttin' old acid wood 'r'somethin' whenever they got that started up. I'uz about eight 'r nine year old when they started that first acid plant at Sylva. It was used for tannin'. My uncle hauled th' first load a'acid wood that ever went inta that plant at Sylva. First that was ever bought in Jackson County or anywhere around. He cut up a load a'ten-foot rails—cut 'em up in five-foot lengths y'know. Loaded'em on a wagon and took'em down there to'em.

All I got back when I'uz young was what I sold in th' fall. They'd come from Asheville over here and buy sheep and cattle and things like that. Always had a bunch a'sheep t'sell. I used t'keep about forty ewes all th' time. And a bunch a'cows and yearlings—yoke steers when I farmed all th' time for a living. I never could make a living without farming. With a family that way, you can't hardly make it.

If you've got your own hogs and sheep, and your cattle and your chickens and ever'thing, why you can have your own meat an'eggs, your own corn bread; and we always raised about a hunnerd bushels a'wheat. And we never went t'th' store for nothin', only just a little sugar and salt and sody and stuff like that. We'd get enough money out of what we sold that way. We'd sell our sheep—a bunch of 'em—and we'd get about seventy-five cents a head for sheep. When you got a dollar, it would go somewhere at th' store. You'd go t'th' store with a couple a'dollars and get more stuff than you could carry back home. You go t'th' store now and it costs about fifty dollars, looks like, to get as much stuff as we used t'get that way. I've seen my uncle buy coffee at three cents a pound.

This land here all belongs t'Dillard [his son]. I been here four years. I just stay up here. He wants me t'go down there and stay with him. A lot of'em want me t'stay with'em. I went over last week over Madison County. One a'my grandson's over there at my grand-daughter's. Boy, they wanted me t'stay over there s'bad. They said, "You just go back and fix up and come back and stay with us." I tole'em no, I couldn't hardly do that. They had a little family of their own and I might be in th' way.

I raise just about everything I eat here—what ain't give t'me. And I always plant by th' signs. I always want t'plant along after th' full moon—that's before th' new moon a while. I don't want t'plant anything on th' new moon at all. It all goes t'th' top. You can plant corn on th' new of th' moon that'a'way, and in May it'll just run a'way up yonder and be a small little ear stickin' right straight up th' stalk; and it'll be as high as this house almost. You can't reach it. You got t'pull it way over t'pull that little nubbin off.

We plant when th'signs'r down as low as possible, and git it on th'last quarter of th'moon. Why, it does a lot better. Or you gather it up anytime you want to that way after it's good and dry. After it gets growed, why you can just work on then. You don't have to gather by no signs'r'nothin'.

For most stuff, you have t'wait 'til it gets th'right time. If you ain't canning at th'right time, it'll not keep so good. It won't be as good. I go by th'Lord and th'signs—where th'signs go up and down, y'know. The signs of th'zodiac. You watch that Dog Star whenever it goes up—goes over in th'evening. They call it th'Evening Star at gatherin' time; Morning Star in th'spring. You know it's light as it comes up. If you don't watch the signs and git out here and git to plantin', you're in trouble. These beans here—if the signs happen to be in th'bowels, why them beans won't do much good. And if they did do any good, they'd make you sick when you eat'em. Th'Lord put th'signs here for us t'go by. It's all in th'Bible: th'signs of th'stars, moon, sun, and all. You've got t'follow all these signs if you do right. Don't you know the signs?

At this point, Hillard laughed for a few moments, paused, and then continued on about his solitary life.

I get my water right out of the spring out there. Good cold spring.

PLATE 292

PLATE 291

It's good water too. I like good water here in th' mountains. I like it a whole lot th' best now.

It's always nice and peaceful up here. I just took a notion I'd get out t'myself. Seem like ever'body never did appreciate what I'd do fer'em. You're better off to be like Elijah was. He was out to himself, but he still loved his brother. And they were parted, y'know; and th' wind carried him away unto th' mountain. Well, I reckon he was a good man. You know he fell from th' cliff; busted hisself up, and th' ravens come and fed him a certain length a'time. Nobody knowed where he went. But he was taken care of, and he was better off than he was down here in this wicked world.

People nowadays don't live right. It's just how long they're goin' live, and how soon they're goin' die. Just what they can get in their hands *now*. Always wantin'. They just reach an'take ever'thing they can seems like. Ain't got no mercy on no one else. If I didn't depend on Him, I wouldn't have anybody t'depend on. You can't depend on a neighbor these days. Ever'body is for themselves. Ever'body's looking out for money. They're not lookin' out for th' humans. We've got t'look out for ourselves. If we don't look out for ourselves, what are we goin't'do?

We had freedom back then. We was free. We went out anywhere and did kinda as we pleased. But now we can't do it. Money is th' root of all evil, and it rules th' world right now. Ever'thing goin' for money. They'll do anything. They'll kill, rob, steal, and ever'thing else all over th' world now. You hear tell of it anywhere y'go now.

It's fast time now, y'know. Ever'thing's flyin'. These automobiles runnin' to and from ever' corner of th' world. Well, ain't they goin' from ever' corner? You can't hardly travel fer'em. You can't walk along th' highways'r'nothin'. You ain't got no freedom'r'nothin'. You've got t'be in under some kind of control. If we didn't have no highway patrolmen, what would it be? Most folks sort'a dread'em, but some of 'em get so far along they don't dread'em. They just go along 'til they get killed. Look like they want t'kill themselves. And while they're killin' themselves, they want t'kill somebody else.

Parents keep lettin' kids go and don't control'em. *Their* parents hadn't been controlled in their time. They'll let their kids go on that way. Why sure kids are ungrateful. Why sure they are. That's th' way they was let go all th' time. There's just too much toys—too much playin'. They run together—too many of'em. They're too close. Th' town's full. Th' country's full. And gettin' inta trouble—one takin' off after another. And one'll take off after another just th' same as a dog will. And kids will do th' same thing. Yeah, I know parents are makin' it too easy.

Well now, our congressmen are a whole lot th' cause of it. They'll say, "Give a kid whatever it wants." "Give it just anything it wants." These men up in Washington say that over th' radio, television'r anything. "Give a kid what it wants," and you can't do that. They're goin't'learn that sure enough. They're goin't'learn it quick, that you've got t'control a kid th' right way and give it what you think it needs. It always wants things it don't need. Well anybody knows that. Well now, they can do without it and be a whole lot better off. They won't have their mind on these here *things*. They'll have their minds on somethin' else that'll be worth somethin' to'em someday.

Now you take old people. Why, don't th' Bible tell you honor your father and mother? Don't make no difference when they get old; why, don't do anything again'em. Young folks think they're far ahead of their old parents because they've got a little education from *man's* work—not from th' work of God, but from th' work of mankind. And we're livin' by his—man's—work instead of livin' by God's work, and that's where th' world's goin' be in th' end. They'll be no one saved, according to th' Bible. They'us but a few saved in th' flood, and there ain't goin' be but a few saved in th' end this time neither.

This here man's work will not save you if you listen to what they say, for they're not goin' try t'save your life. They want y't'make big money so they can get a little out of it. That's th' way these big men up here in Washington are: all want that war t'keep'em going an' keep on going. It's makin' them big money.

They raised our governor from ten thousand dollars a year to thirty thousand dollars a year just last year now. They're sittin' up there raisin' their big wages. We're livin' here a'doin'th' best we can. They can keep that war goin'. They're makin' bigger money all th' time. They're runnin' th' money out, y'know; goin' down, goin' down all th' time. It's goin't'finally go plum out 'til we don't have nothin' but stamps and coupons t'trade with here first thing y'know. Just about got it down here in Georgia *now*. Why, they're usin' these old coupons now t'trade with. You can go and buy them for half price or a little less—to t'th' store and get your stuff so's you can double up. See, th' government then pays them th' full price for that stuff fer them old coupons. And they're gettin' higher 'til that money got so sorry, and so much of it made, 'til it ain't worth nothin' nohow.

They've took our silver. They've took our gold. They've took th' silver certificates all in. And we ain't got a thing except our gover'mint on it. There's all we got t'back it up. It just left us, by granny, with a piece a'paper; an'if we lose our gover'mint, it's all dead anyhow just th' same as gover'mint bonds. We're all broke. If th' gover'mint go broke, we ain't got a thing in th' world.

Ever'thing here can just go at once if they happen t'keep on with this here war business 'til some nation comes over on'em. They can be bombed over here just th' same as we can haul'em over there. Goin' all th' time back'erds and for'erds with'em. They send stuff over there just like they did t'J-pan. They sent th' Japs lotsa stuff, and got a lot of it throwed back at'em. They have won at war a long time, but they ain't a'goin'always win. If they ever start another war with this here atomic bomb, it's goin' be a sad time. To get ready for th' bomb—th' main thing, they better get ready t'meet their God. That's th' main thing about it. For th' thing ain't goin't'go on this way no how. Times get worse an'worse all th' time. We can't hardly tell what's a'goin'happen. They may let man destroy hisself. They could do that with th' atomic bomb. They could destroy theirselves and not wait for th' Lord t'come down and destroy with Christ's second coming. And it might not be so many years away when He come.

They just got too much invention. You know, they say in th' Bible —it tells you that they'll be buildin' and rebuildin' all over th' old world and new just before th' end of time. This here buildin' got t'go on, and these inventions got t'go on before th' end of time. Only about thirty more year 'til two thousand years will be fulfilled, and they've been a destruction every time at th' end. You know th' flood come and Sodom and Gomorrah burned and all that. And how many were saved there? "But few," it said. "And Noah was a righteous man and for Noah's sake saved the whole family there though." He was th' only righteous man there was. Old Lot, he come out of old Sodom and Gomorrah. He was brought out by th' power of God, and th' rest of'em was all burnt up 'cept him and his two daughters. His wife turned inta a piller'a'salt fer lookin' back an' disobeying God. If we disobey, why we're just gone.

Well, now, ain't it th' fulfillment of th' Bible stuff comin'up this way? What has been will be again, it says. And what will be has been. It has been in generations back before this—this destruction. The last days is comin' all right. Th' two thousand years Christ said are about fulfilled, don't you think so? Th' way ever'thing's gettin' so fast. Ain't it a'movin up in a hurry? Ever'thing a'movin' up in a hurry all th' time—just a'gettin' faster and faster—building and rebuilding all

PLATE 293

ever'where, anywhere y'go. Boy, it gets worse all th' time too. Whole world.

Them astronauts that went up there? They got there on that planet where they thought there was water, and there wasn't a drop a'water t'be found on land there. It was all covered up in stones. They got some stones and brought'em back, but they didn't want people t'know what they was. I got this from a gover'mint man, now; and he said there wasn't anything there but *brimstone*. And don't your Bible tell you that this world will be burnt in th' end with brimstone and fire?

I believe them other two fellers, they won't none of'em go back 'cause they ain't got no business there. And them rocks they picked up there and brought back wasn't nothing but brimstone. The whole thing they said was just alike. Brimstone. The Lord made it. Created there. That's goin' be what's gonna destroy the world. You pick up the Bible and read it there. It says when Christ comes, the fire will already be kindled. And we don't know—that under there may be carbide. You know what it is, don't you? Well, when it hit water you know what it'll do. Take a feller that don't know what hit'll do and lay a piece in his hand and spit on it, and he'll soon find out, won't he?

The Bible says that brimstone will be what will destroy the world. You can't escape that fire in water or nowhere. It'll be unquenchable fire, it says. Might be carbide there with it. Now them places where they thought was water there, they said it was just as dry as it could be—but they didn't know what it was.

They never made it to the *moon* anyway. They took a picture over some desert. It was just all made-up stuff. Now that moon they had pictured up there was just a shadow on th' wall from a light they had a'settin' there. They could make a shadow that looked just like it on th' wall. I've seen it done. Now they can take a light and make most anything look real. But Lord'a mercy, they can't make it work out fer real though.

In Hillard's opinion, the astronauts went into space, but they never landed on the moon itself. Instead, they landed on a mystery planet called "Mars" that circles between the moon and earth. As he says:

Where'd they land at? Not the moon, but Mars. Well now ain't you got eyes to see it there when th' eclipse comes on th' moon? When th' eclipse comes on th' sun, what makes it? Ain't you read about th' Mars? There's a place above us, and when it comes over there fer enough, why it comes between us and th' moon there and makes an eclipse, and that's th' shadow of that extra earth up there. Why, you can see that with your naked eye if you'll just look! If it wadn't between us and th' moon—if it was on above th' moon—why it would never bring no shadow on th' moon. They's a place up there all right.

They went up there in a missile, y'know. Three of'em together. They sent'em up there and thought they'd send a man they could kind'a depend on. They won't let him talk though now. You've got t'find out from some gover'mint feller—have some friend in th' gover'mint business—t'find out. They won't let it be broadcast. They don't want t'let people know that they're that big'a fools—go right into what th' Bible tells'em not t'do. They don't want t'let'em know what was above, and what was t'come down in th' end.

For th' Bible says that th' world will be destroyed with fire an' brimstone. All man's work'll be burned up. All th' houses'n'everthing. These stones'll be melted and all run back t'gether.

And that moon you ain't supposed t'be on. That's th' second heaven, accordin' t'th' Bible. It ain't natural. T'ain't no place we ought t'be 'til we die. It's a spiritual place. Ain't no place fer human flesh and blood. Th' air is heavy there all th' time.

Th' last days is comin' all right. Within thirty year. He'll be down here judgin' th' livin' whenever th' end comes. Be judgin' th' people that's livin'. Don't have t'worry about them already dead.

You know, you could live t'see that day come—th' day that th' Lord comes. You could live t'see it.

Hillard is adamant about holding onto an independence he savors. The thing he likes best is the fact that there's "nobody t'ask you where you're goin', when you'll be back, or where you've been. I do just as I please. Tomorrow? Who knows? I might put up 'maters again."

PLATE 294

INDEX OF PEOPLE

THE KIDS:

Lynne Allen
Karen Anderson
Ellen Armstrong
Glenda Arrowood
Pat Arrowood
Perry Barrett
Bob Bradshaw
Joey Brockington
Benny Brown
Jan Brown
Judy Brown
Kathy Brown
Laurie Brunson
Emma Jean Buchanan
George Burch
Linda Burden
Andrea Burrell
Jimmy Carpenter
Brenda Carver
Joanne Carver
Dickie Chastain
Charles Childs
Becky Coldren
Kathy Coldren

Mike Cook
Barbara Crunkleton
Hubert Darnell
Loraine Darnell
Patti Darnell
Stanley Darnell
Susan Darnell
Henrietta Dillard
Bill Enloe
Jim Enloe
Linda Garland
Mary Garth
Paul Gillespie
Lynda Gray
Tommy Green
Gail Hamby
Charles Henslee
Sue Henslee
Elmer Hopper
Mike Ivey
Mickey Justice
Jean Kelly
Jerry Lanich
Lizzie Ledford

Mike Letson
Robbie Letson
Marti Lind
Gayle Long
Wayne Mason
Nelson Miller
Susan Mullis
David Myrick
Phil Neupert
Lois Nix
Ed Page
Richard Page
Ernie Payne
Paul Phillips
Brenda Rickman
Elizabeth Rickman
Bill Roland
Bill Selph
Greg Strickland
Mary Strickland
Jan Watts
Frenda Wilborn
David Wilson
Tommy Wilson

THE CONTACTS:

Lester Addis
Joe Arrowood
Jerry Ayres
Pope Bass
Dean Beasley
Hobe Beasley
Jack Beasley
Bill Blalock
Mr. and Mrs. Grover Bradley
Mr. and Mrs. Lawton Brooks
Dr. Harry Brown
Mr. and Mrs. Harry Brown, Sr.

Mary Brown
Jack Buchanan
Mr. and Mrs. Millard Buchanan
Mr. and Mrs. James T. Burden
Mrs. Clyde Burrell
Rom Burrell
Mr. and Mrs. Roosevelt Burrell
Elvin Cabe
Mary Cabe
Aunt Arie Carpenter
Avarilla Carpenter
Bob Carpenter

Evie Carpenter
Mr. and Mrs. Harley Carpenter
Juddy Carpenter
Lizzie Carpenter
Mr. and Mrs. "Valley John" Carpenter
William Carpenter
Mr. and Mrs. Buck Carver
Nate Chastain
Mr. and Mrs. Minyard Conner
Ray Connor
Mrs. O. Y. Cook, Sr.
Ethel Corn
Janson Cox
Taylor Crockett
Mr. and Mrs. Claude Darnell
Mrs. Fred Darnell
Mr. and Mrs. H. H. Darnell
Mrs. Ray Darnell
Ione Dickerson
Jane Dickerson
R. M. Dickerson
Barnard Dillard
Dave Dillingham
Mrs. Arthur Dills
Mrs. B. F. Douty
Kenneth Drake
Lizzie DuBose
Harriet Echols
Jim Edmonds
R. L. Edwards
Buck Eller
Mr. and Mrs. Turner Enloe
Dr. John Fowler
Aunt Nora Garland
Carrie Dillard Garrison
Serina Giles
Eva Gillespie
Mrs. Gilbert Gillespie
Hillard Green
Molly Green
Paul Grist
Carl Hamby
Mr. and Mrs. Milford Hamilton
Blanch Harkins

Mary Hine
Earl Holt
Mr. and Mrs. John Hopper
Mr. and Mrs. L. D. Hopper
Mrs. Selvin Hopper
Frank Humphries
Elcaney Jenkins
Daisy M. Justice
Mrs. Hershel Keener
Myrt Keener
Ada Kelly
Bea Kelly
Mrs. Thomas Kelly
Mary King
Bill Lamb
Myrtle Lamb
Kay Ledford
Lizzie Ledford
Oma Ledford
Harley McCall
Gay McClain
Joe McClain
U. G. McCoy
Wilbur Maney
Daniel Manous
James Marsengill
Bob Marshall
Pearl Martin
Myrtle Mason
Lanier Meaders
Mr. and Mrs. E. O. Mellinger
Lawrence Moffitt
Gatha Nichols
Mr. and Mrs. E. N. Nicholson
Algie Norton
Mr. and Mrs. Lester Norton
Mr. and Mrs. Mann Norton
Mr. and Mrs. Richard Norton
Mr. and Mrs. Tommy Lee Norton
Henry Page
Lamar Patterson
Mr. and Mrs. Bill Patton
Curley Pennington
Beulah Perry
Harriet Phillips

...ny Powell
Ellen Redden
Harv Reid
Lon Reid
Mr. and Mrs. Jesse Rickman
Mr. and Mrs. Luther Rickman
Kenny Runion
Mr. and Mrs. M. L. Scruggs
Julia Smith
Bill Stiles
Mr. and Mrs. Lake Stiles
Mrs. Floyd Strain
Thomas Stubbs
Calvin Talley
Harley Thomas
Hoyt Thomas
Roy Thompson
Bertha Thurmond
Charley Tyler
Grace Vinson

Joyce Vinson
Maggie Vinson
Ethel Waldroop
Grady Waldroop
Jake Waldroop
Joyce Waldroop
Les Waldroop
Martha Ann Waldroop
Mr. and Mrs. Marvin Watts
Mrs. Monteen Watts
Mr. and Mrs. Andy Webb
Bertha Watkins Webb
Zero Webb
Ethel White
Mrs. Delia Williams
Lum Williams
Edna Wilson
Grover Wilson
Zelhah Wilson
Mr. and Mrs. M. S. York
Will Zoellner